Gene,

Best wishes as
you trudge the
road of happy destiny.

Donna Bevan-Lee

Iron Legacy

Childhood Trauma and Adult Transformation

Donna Bevan-Lee

for Deb and James with love

ACKNOWLEDGEMENTS

Any book about surviving childhood trauma has to balance honesty with care for the feelings of other people involved. I know that candor matters in telling stories that will benefit readers who are struggling with the effects of trauma in their own lives. I know that, if I resort too often to silence or euphemism, I deny them an example of the fearless honesty I advocate. At the same time, my stories involve innocent people who might be distressed to see their names, or the names of people they love, in print. Moreover, my history occasionally involves other survivors, who deserve to tell their own stories in their own way--or not tell them at all.

Accordingly, in the narrative sections of this book, I have changed the names of all private persons except members of my immediate family. I have also altered identifying details if I thought a pseudonym wasn't enough of a disguise. On occasion, I created composite characters based on more than one real person. And I shaped my stories in other ways as well, all of which I explain in the book. If anyone depicted feels dismayed by my choices, I apologize. I genuinely did what I thought would be fairest to those involved and most helpful to readers.

I have many people to thank because many people contributed to this book, either directly or indirectly. First and foremost are my clients, who started asking for a book more than thirty years ago and never stopped. When some learned that I had finally begun writing, they redoubled their requests, never letting me forget that I had an appreciative audience waiting. Their enthusiasm kept me going when the writing got tough, as it always does, and for that they have my gratitude. In addition, I thank the hundreds who participated in Legacy Workshops over the years, some of whom were also clients and some of whom were strangers as the workshop began. Each one of them had something precious to teach me, and every page of this book reflects what I learned from them.

I also owe thanks to the founders of Codependents Anonymous, especially Ken and Mary Richardson. Since the mid-eighties, conversations with them have shaped my thinking about childhood trauma and recovery in ways too numerous to detail. I also want to thank the whole organization and its members. Over the years, they have offered a kind of continuing education that is not available in any college classroom, and I am inexpressibly grateful for it. In addition, observing the courage, insight, and resilience with which they confront the challenges in their lives continues to inspire me. I hope they recognize their influence in the pages of this book.

I wish I had time to name and thank all of the teachers who contributed to this book, starting with Dr. Rex Campbell, my philosophy professor at the University of Utah, who, quite literally, taught me to think. I feel the same way about colleagues who have written about childhood trauma or who have worked treating people affected by it. I will mention many and describe their contributions in the book, so for now let me simply say that their influence has been profound and that I owe them a debt of gratitude I cannot possibly discharge.

I do want to thank a few by name, however. The first is Pat Mellody, with whom I worked at The Meadows many years ago. Though he was not my first mentor, he was by far the most influential, and this book is a tribute to his wise guidance. The second is Pia Mellody, cherished friend, fellow traveler and pioneer author, whose *Facing* books have given hope and insight to three generations of survivors. The third is Rebecca Stoller, therapist extraordinaire and an oasis of collegiality in a competitive world. Fourth is Lorie Dwinelle, who, in addition to being a valued friend and colleague, wrote one of the best books on childhood trauma in recent years. So I thank her, not only for her support, but also for showing me how good a self-help book can be.

If clients, workshop participants, and colleagues supplied the fuel for the book, Gerry Zyfers supplied the spark. In a series of probing interviews, he pushed me to begin shaping my local insights into a coherent project. Giving generously of his time and formidable intelligence, he posed challenging questions that reverberate through every chapter. If there is one person without whom this book would not have happened, it's Gerry, and I thank him unreservedly.

Pat Terry gave invaluable feedback early on, when I needed to know whether I was on the right track. Incisive and exacting after many years in charge of hospitals and state health-care departments, she offered me the gift of knowing that my work had pleased someone with high standards. For that, as well as the gift of her long friendship, she has my unbounded gratitude.

Joan Sputh offered feedback at another critical stage, when the book was drafted but not yet in its final form. With her trademark mix of warmth and professionalism, she cheered the project on and gave me the push I needed to finish.

I would also like to thank my editor and co-writer Laura King. With her long experience of shaping scattered insights into coherent prose and her conviction that good writing can change the world, she made this book wiser and more lively than it otherwise would have been.

My siblings and my mother, despite having justifiable reservations about what the book might reveal, gave it their unfailing encouragement. All of them, in their different ways, told me, "I trust you," which was the most loving and supportive thing they could possibly have said. My personal debt to all of them would take another book to express, but I hope this one makes clear that I love them dearly and thank them from the bottom of my heart.

My aunt, Sharon Bevan, deserves a special thanks for her encouragement of this project. Since my teenage years, she has always been the wise adult who knew what mattered and what to do about it, so her endorsement means a lot to me.

In some ways, my father is the villain of this book and does not belong among my acknowledgements. I certainly do not thank him for the physical, sexual, and emotional violence he dispensed so freely during his lifetime, even if it did, eventually, produce the insights that inform this book. At the same time, he exercised some positive influence, not least by being gregarious and generous with his time, his interest, and his energy. That I am a person who talks easily with others, a person who goes out of her way to help her community, is due, in part, to his example, and I thank him for that.

If my father looms large in this book as an author of trauma, then my son looms equally large as an author of resilience. From the moment he arrived on earth, he was manifestly a precious child: kind, curious, loving, and generous. From the experience of raising a healthy, joyous child, I learned, at a very deep level, how to heal my own trauma and help other survivors heal. My gratitude for this gift is impossible to express, so I'll have to settle for a simple thank-you.

Last but as far from least as Antarctica is from Mount Kilimanjaro, my warmest thanks go to my wife, Deborah Nicholson, who believed in this book the moment it became a vague possibility and supported me throughout the process of making it real. In addition to her love and support, the example she sets every day--her courage, her honor, and her great compassion--are the best inspiration a writer could hope for. If I thanked her every day for a thousand years, I still could not convey my gratitude.

CONTENTS

INTRODUCTION

If I had to choose an emblem for my childhood, it would be a belt buckle—not just any buckle, but one my father won in a calf-roping competition. My dad was the ultimate American icon: a cowboy. When he could afford to, he raised cattle, and when he had to take other jobs to survive, he competed in small rodeos around Utah and Nevada, where he rode broncs and roped cattle for small prizes. For those unfamiliar with rodeo, a bronc was originally a wild horse, though most now are born in a barn, rather than captured. But they're bred to buck and jump and kick—and shocked into a terrified fury while they're in the chute—so they ride as wild as wild horses. As with bull riding, a cowboy has to stay on the bronc for eight seconds while the horse does everything possible to throw him off. Not surprisingly, bronc riding is risky, exacting a heavy toll of head, neck, and spinal injuries, along with ordinary broken bones. In fact, most observers agree that roughstock riding, whether bronc or bull, is the most dangerous professional sport in the United States.

Roping is another rodeo staple. My father roped calves and steers, the first by himself and the second as part of a team. In calf-roping, a rider twirling a rope chases a two- or three-month-old calf, throws the rope around its neck, jumps off his horse, grabs the calf by its belly or leg, flips it over onto its back, and ties three of its legs together in less time than it took you to read that sentence. In team roping, two riders twirling ropes chase a steer. The first rider ropes the steer's neck; the second circles around to rope its two back legs. The clock stops when the two riders face each other with their taut ropes fully controlling the steer. Both events involve a quick sequence of difficult skills for both the rider and the horse. My father was fast, precise, and as fine a horseman as I have ever known. He practiced constantly, both on the job and off. He didn't always win a buckle or a cash prize, but he won his share, as well as the adulation of the crowd, for he was handsome as well as skilled. He always had a bit more swagger when he brought home a new belt buckle.

While other sports' trophies sit on a shelf, rodeo trophies have a practical purpose: they keep a man's pants up. My father wore one every day of his life. A fastidious dresser with a sharp crease down the front of his jeans, he nonetheless insisted that his clothing be utilitarian: Wrangler or Lee jeans, single-pattern western shirts, cowboy boots, spurs, cowboy hat. Anything impractical or unnecessary was "for sissies." A bandana around the neck, for instance, was right only when airborne debris threatened to cause breathing problems—while haying or after a dust storm, say. If a man might need to cover his mouth and nose quickly, then he should wear a bandana tied loosely around his neck. Otherwise, bandanas were for sissies, along with shorts, sandals, two-toned shirts, Levi's jeans (because of the little red tag on the back pocket), and men's jewelry of any kind, even wedding rings. Rodeo belt buckles, though they might have more silver or filigree flowers than ten necklaces, were definitely not for sissies.

My father had more than a dozen buckles. One, for saddle bronc, was all pewter and showed a cowboy mid-ride, but the bronco appeared to be diving, rather than bucking, his legs flung out straight in front and behind, his body on a steep diagonal. Add a little water tank at the bottom, and he would look like one of those old diving horses in Atlantic City. Most of my dad's buckles were brass with just the name of the rodeo protruding from an ornately carved background. But the one he loved most, the one I remember best, was much more elaborate. It was not as deeply carved as the lettered buckles but featured three different metals and a lot of fine detail. It showed a copper cowboy roping a copper calf on an ornately carved silver medallion. The rider, his horse, and the calf were beautifully executed; you could see the calf straining to get away while the cowboy strained to catch it. The cowboy's rope, which was brass, stretched across the medallion and hung in mid-air, the loop right over the calf's head, ready to fall. The buckle captured the split-second before the rope clotheslined the calf and the cowboy jumped off his horse to flip it over and bind its legs. Frozen in that moment, the little calf ran as hard as its legs could carry it, unaware that there was no escaping the rope and the man wielding it. I didn't realize the fact until many years later, but looking at that belt buckle was like looking into a mirror.

There are two important facts in that last sentence. First, I was an abused child. Second, I didn't know it. Though my heart bled for the little calf on the rodeo buckle—and for all the calves I saw my father bring down in the roping arena—I never made the connection between us. That I did not make the connection becomes even more startling when I tell you that my father honed his skill with a rope on *me*, not playfully, the way a loving adult might pretend to munch on a child's foot, but with calculated detachment, his only focus being how well I could help him lower his time in the next rodeo.

"Run," he would shout. On two legs, I couldn't match the speed of a terrified calf or steer, but I was plenty fast, especially in a sprint, so I'd launch myself across the gravel in front of our trailer while my father stood about ten yards behind me twirling his rope. Sometimes he'd throw the rope from above so that the loop circled my torso. More often, he'd go low and trap one of my feet. He liked the difficulty of delivering the "heeler" rope, the angle and the timing necessary to snag the moving legs of a steer—or a child. He practiced a lot, so he was good at it. Though he missed some of the time, he usually connected, and, when he did, my momentum threw me forward onto the scattered gravel. When I was lucky, I landed on my hands and knees. When I wasn't lucky—or when my father pulled back hard on the rope—I landed on my face. Though not as fast as calf- or steer-roping, child-roping is plenty fast and unpredictable. I couldn't see what was coming from behind, so I really couldn't control how I fell or how hard I landed. The only thing I could control was whether I'd remove the rope from my foot or leg, stand up, and wait for my father to shout "Run!" again. I always did.

It has taken me many years to write that story. It may take you many years to write yours. All my stories began with overwhelming experience recollected in fragments like images projected onto a wall for a split-second. My father lunging toward me in daylight. My father creeping toward me in darkness. A belt lashing my back. A hand pushing me underwater. My mother cleaning grit from my bloody knees. My boy-uncle's high voice singing "doodle oodle oodle do." A rope around my neck. A peach dress, filthy and torn. Random slides from a terrible vacation: was it mine or someone else's, someone I barely knew? I couldn't always tell, though, every so often, one of those slides would punch me in the stomach so hard I couldn't breathe.

The stories began to take shape when I realized I needed to look deeply into my past in order to understand my present. Guided by therapists and friends, I worked to fill in gaps. I figured out chronologies and relationships of cause and effect. My random slides began to look more like old home movies with titles like "The Day I Dropped the Cucumber Slice" and "The Day I Stopped Crying Forever." I began telling those stories to other survivors of childhood abuse. Many survivors told me that the stories helped them, maybe even more than the concepts they were supposed to illustrate. That made sense to me. There are reasons why a culture's most essential, sacred knowledge takes the form of stories. Stories make ideas vital, engaging, and easy to remember. One reason is that vivid description is processed in the same parts of the brain as data from your own senses. In other words, more of your brain is engaged in processing a story than is engaged in processing an explanation. Because there's a kind of "seeing" and "hearing" involved, you don't just get truth; you get embodied truth. If I tell you stories, you understand the journey from trauma to healing in a deeper, more complex way than if I simply explain it to you. For that reason, I begin each section of this book with a story that illustrates a crisis or challenge in my history as a survivor of childhood trauma. Some stories are quite long and involved, more like chapters in a novel than like the brief illustrations in most self-help books. I'll say more about why in Chapter Five, which focuses on storytelling; for now, please trust that their ultimate purpose is to help you understand and tell your own story.

In addition to being vivid and memorable, stories register subtlety and contingency better than plain explanations; a writer can more gracefully show multiple perspectives or conflicting impulses operating at the same moment. For example, in the brief story I just told you, I tried to show both the perspective of the child and the perspective of the mature woman looking back at that child. In the longer stories to follow, that double perspective will be much more obvious. If I do my job, you will have a very clear sense of who I was at different ages and who I am now. If I do my job, you will care what happened to young Donna—and, I hope, will feel moments of recognition as features of her story align with features of your story, whether on the level of fact or on the level of feeling. You may even feel a bit sorry when the story ends and I shift into explanation mode.

But my reasons for emphasizing storytelling go further. One of those I'll get into very soon when I talk about how this book fits into the literature on childhood trauma and its effects. In a nutshell, it's that some of the best work on dealing with childhood trauma has come from people who relentlessly probed their own experience for concepts that could help other survivors. I've done that work myself, and it's time to share it. The other reason is that stories have tremendous potential to help, not just the people who hear or read them, but the people who tell them. This help goes beyond self-knowledge, although of course self-knowledge is crucial. The stories we tell can actively change us, help us in the hard work of becoming better versions of ourselves. In shaping our own narratives, we can make strategic decisions that will, in turn, shape us—not just the image we show the world or an aspirational ideal, but the self we inherited from the past and inhabit in the present, the self that will forge our future. I will show you, with my own stories, how I did that, and I will teach you how to do it with yours.

First I want to talk about what kind of book this is and how it fits into the vast genre it inhabits. The fact that I'm doing that already tells you that this is a book for thoughtful readers who want a project to be self-aware, at least once in a while. Psychology tends to be a very ahistorical discipline, assuming that people are all pretty much the same, whether it's 30,000 BCE and we're trying to throw Neanderthals out of the good caves or its 2018 and we're trying to throw Neanderthals out of Congress. Psychology shares with other ahistorical disciplines the assumption that the field has made steady progress toward greater and greater knowledge, so there's no point in dwelling upon (or even mentioning) the quarrels and missteps that produced some of the field's most distinctive features. I think both of those assumptions are wrong. Culture and individual psychology shape one another; there's no such thing as a transhistorical "mind" that we can study independently of its environment. There are continuities, yes, especially in physiology, where change happens more slowly, but no essential human psyche. And psychology has not made steady progress toward greater and greater knowledge; its history is marred by just as many prejudices, blind spots, and dangerous illusions as any other discipline's. With people's mental health at stake, these problems are not academic; they can cause great suffering. At the very least, they cause confusion among readers who need help and can't figure out why there are so many books saying so many conflicting things about a massive issue like childhood trauma.

So here's a quick history. Psychological trauma is not new, nor is reflection on it. As a Boston psychiatrist pointed out more than two decades ago, Homer's *Iliad* is a careful study of the trauma caused by war.[1] But scientists didn't focus on trauma until the late 19th century when new technology began to cause new kinds of injuries, both physical and psychic. The most notorious was "railway spine," a constellation of symptoms experienced by uninjured survivors and witnesses of train collisions, which were frequent and devastating. These symptoms included exhaustion, insomnia, nightmares, trembling, headaches, and an inability to concentrate. Not surprisingly, observers expressed strong opinions on the nature and existence of railway spine; possibilities ranged from deliberate fraud to a super-subtle back injury. Among those who took railway spine seriously, one physician, Herbert Page, proposed that the sudden terror of a crash could disturb the human nervous system enough to cause serious symptoms.[2] Within a few years, the field of trauma studies was thriving, and the 20th century supplied it with plenty of material to study, not least in the two world wars, which produced what clinicians called "shell shock," "battle fatigue," or "gross stress reaction."

Though some noticed after World War II that combat-related symptoms persisted well beyond the battlefield, it wasn't until the Vietnam War era that clinicians and researchers systematically observed the long-term effects of trauma. In 1980, after strenuous lobbying by mental health professionals, Post-Traumatic Stress Disorder (PTSD) was added to the third edition of the *Diagnostic and Statistical Manual of Mental Disorders* (DSM),[3] which governs what is and is not considered a disorder, as well as how it is treated. PTSD and associated mental states began to receive serious attention, especially after about 1990, giving rise to the new discipline of psychotraumatology, which investigates the neurobiological, biobehavioral, and physiological effects of trauma.

What about childhood trauma specifically? Where does that topic fit into this quick chronology? If we go back to the debate over railway spine, we encounter Jean-Martin Charcot, who argued that trauma caused the mental conditions formerly called "hysteria," which include acute anxiety, conversion disorder, somatization disorder, borderline and histrionic personality disorders, and some types of schizophrenia. It was one of his students who focused specifically on childhood trauma—and even more specifically on sexual trauma in early childhood. That student was Sigmund Freud, who in 1896 delivered a paper naming childhood sexual trauma as the cause of psychic distress in eighteen of his patients. Within two years, however, he had abandoned the so-called "seduction theory" in favor of a new theory: that what appeared to be memories of trauma were actually fantasies. After Freud's about-face—and scholars still debate why he reversed himself— psychology and psychiatry virtually abandoned the study of childhood trauma. Dissent was professionally risky, as an eminent psychoanalyst named Sandor Ferenczi learned when he used corroborating evidence of childhood abuse to challenge Freud. In response, Freud's biographer simply called Ferenczi crazy, and the label stuck.[4] The verdict was in: the alarming number of psychoanalytic patients who reported memories of childhood incest reflected the universality of a symbolic "drama," not the prevalence of actual abuse. For most of the 20th century, academic research shied away from the topic of childhood abuse and its adult consequences.

It was popular psychology that stepped into the breach. Clinicians involved in treating substance abuse—including their own—noticed patterns in the histories of addicts, patterns that included many forms of childhood trauma. They began investigating, discussing, and testing ways to address that trauma and deal with its effects on adult functioning. I say "they," but I mean "we," because I was one of those clinicians. As the result of our inquiries, a new term entered the therapeutic lexicon, and a new genre sprung up and took root. The term is "codependency," also known as "codependence," and in retrospect I wish we had tried harder to find a better word. I use "codependency" with my clients because I am right there to make sure they understand what I mean by the word, which is a problematic orientation in relationships, but I don't use it much in this book because of its imprecision. At the same time, the literature of codependency made great contributions to our understanding of childhood trauma at a time when academic psychology was ignoring the subject. So I'm not ready to throw the term out entirely.

The concept of codependency developed and spread wildly in the early to mid-1980s, with Claudia Black's *It Will Never Happen to Me* (1982), Janet Woititz's *Adult Children of Alcoholics* (1983), Robin Norwood's *Women Who Love Too Much* (1985), Melody Beattie's *Codependent No More* (1986), John Bradshaw's *Healing the Shame that Binds You* (1988), and Pia Mellody's *Facing Codependence* (1989) becoming classics in the field. With these books selling furiously and their authors ubiquitous across popular media, a backlash was inevitable. It began with Stanton Peele, who in 1989 attacked what he called the "diseasing" of ordinary problems, including codependency. Other specialists piled on, claiming that codependency and related diagnoses were cynical ploys to extract insurance payments and other revenues. They claimed the diagnosis operated via Barnum statements, or claims that seem specific but could really apply to almost everyone.[5] By 1991, the diagnosis of codependency was publicly called "dangerous" because it applied to so many people and promoted a "lopsided counsel of damage."[6] In other words, how could the millions and millions of people buying codependency books and watching Bradshaw on television and seeing therapists and participating in Codependents Anonymous or Adult Children of Alcoholics, how could *all those millions of people* be suffering from the effects of childhood trauma? To academic psychologists, psychiatrists, and mainstream medicine generally, the question answered itself: they couldn't. It must be a scam. Like children who think the world disappears when they close their eyes, they assumed that what they had failed to see simply didn't exist.

Within a decade, they were proven wrong by one of their own, a physician named Vincent Felitti. While my colleagues and I were wondering how to help the huge number of trauma survivors in our practices, he was wondering about some patients struggling with obesity. A specialist in preventive medicine, Doctor Felitti couldn't figure out why nearly half the participants in his weight-loss program had quit, most when they were losing weight. Quitting when they were failing he could understand, but half of his patients dropped out after substantial losses, which simply made no sense to him. To find out why, he studied their medical records and made his first startling discovery: the dropouts shared an unusual pattern. They were not chubby babies, and they did not gain weight gradually over time. Starting at birth, they maintained normal weights until a huge, sudden weight gain rendered them obese. More baffled than ever, Dr. Felitti interviewed the dropouts to gather more data, looking for links between obesity and other phenomena. In one interview, he jumbled his questions and inadvertently asked a woman what she weighed when she first became sexually active.

"Forty pounds," she replied.[7]

Sure, at first, that he had misunderstood her answer, Dr. Felitti soon discovered that her experience was not unique among his dropouts. Of the 286 dropouts he and his colleagues interviewed, most had been traumatized in childhood, had gained their weight in response, and had been unable to lose it, except temporarily.

Stunned by these results, Dr. Felitti presented his findings to a conference of obesity specialists in 1990. Their response was a mean-spirited echo of Freud: the dropouts had manufactured the abuse to explain their failure to lose weight. Nonetheless, the conference led Dr. Felitti to Dr.

Robert Anda, an epidemiologist at the Centers for Disease Control (CDC), and the two of them recruited 17,421 subjects for a survey of the relationship between childhood events and adult health called the Adverse Childhood Experience (ACE) Study. Recruits were members of Kaiser Permanente, so they were not a pure cross-section of the US population but a cross-section of employed and insured people. From 1995 to 1997, these people completed a detailed biopsychosocial (biomedical, psychological, and social) questionnaire plus ten yes/no questions about the most common forms of childhood trauma.[8] They also underwent a complete physical examination and extensive laboratory tests. This study was unlike any previous research in its consideration of many kinds of trauma, rather than a single stressor, and in its overall scope: number of subjects, breadth of health information, and duration of follow-up. The CDC continues to track the 17,421 subjects and collect data on their health and well-being.[9]

Initial results of the study stunned even the researchers. Dr. Anda told a reporter that when the data came in, he broke down: "I saw how much people had suffered, and I wept." Two-thirds of the respondents had at least one ACE, and one-fifth had three or more. Even more alarmingly, the more adverse experiences in childhood the greater the incidence of a huge range of adult problems, including addiction, depression, headaches, heart disease, pulmonary disease, cancer, academic difficulties, and absenteeism from work. One in six people had a worrisome score of four ACEs, and one in nine had five. Considering that the study subjects were employed and insured, these staggering numbers may even be low relative to the overall population.

This time around, Dr. Felitti's data were not dismissed as attempts to rationalize personal failure. He and Dr. Anda, along with colleagues at the CDC and major universities have published hundreds of papers on the ACE data in prestigious peer-reviewed journals. Yes, there are a few critics who claim that "self-reporting" yields imperfect data—though I'm not sure how else we could collect information on childhood trauma—but Felitti's and Anda's research has far more fans than critics. In the past two decades, it has begun to transform the fields of psychology, medicine, public health, social work, education, and criminal justice. Professionals in those fields now routinely speak of ACEs and adopt "trauma-informed" or "trauma-sensitive" policies, programs, and practices. Local leaders have developed radical new approaches to everything from school discipline to family court procedures to housing. As of 2017, there were forty trauma-related bills making their way through eighteen state legislatures, many concerned with better identifying and treating at-risk children in settings such as health care and education. My state, Washington, passed a bill in 2011 creating a public-private partnership to research the causes of ACEs in communities and to devise innovative solutions. Vermont passed a similar bill last year. Around the country, as basic information-gathering expands to include ACE-related questions, people researching a broad range of issues are discovering that childhood trauma plays a larger-than-anticipated role. As one neuroscientist phrases it, "Adverse childhood experiences are the most basic cause of health risk behaviors, morbidity, disability, mortality, and healthcare costs."[10]

Public awareness of these discoveries is another matter. When former Senator Heidi Heitcamp (D-ND) and Representative Danny K. Davis (D-IL) introduced the Trauma-Informed Care for Children and Families Act last spring, the silence was deafening. The media have shown some interest in individual trauma-informed projects and policies but not much in the ACE Study or what it revealed about the prevalence and the consequences of childhood trauma. There was a burst of media attention in 2012, including pieces in *The New York Times, Salon, The Huffington Post,* and *This American Life*. After that, national press coverage dwindled, and I don't see much evidence that the general public knows how widespread or serious childhood trauma is. They certainly aren't aware of some of the ACE Study's more surprising findings, such as data linking the most adverse outcomes to sustained emotional, rather than physical, abuse. I think that most Americans still believe that childhood trauma is relatively rare and that only the most severe corporeal forms, such as incest, do lasting damage. Perhaps the reality—that trauma is commonplace, myriad, and destructive—is just too disquieting to contemplate. Nonetheless, as a society we must address an issue that is, as one of the world's leading medical journals phrases it "a human rights violation and a global public health problem."[11]

After Dr. Felitti demonstrated conclusively that childhood trauma is both devastating and common, scholars finally got to work on the problem of childhood trauma and its adult consequences. Since the turn of the century, solid research has begun to emerge from academic departments. Unfortunately, this research hasn't offered much in the way of treatment. As a recent dissertation puts it, "The devastating effects of untreated adverse early childhood experiences have long lacked sufficient clinical attention.[12] In other words, it's more essential than ever to bridge the gap between academic psychology and the field observations of therapists who have been treating codependency. If we look in both places, rather than just one or the other, we find concrete steps that survivors can take to help themselves.

The literature of codependency has a lot to offer. One of its strengths is the deep reading of personal experience, which is something academic psychology has just started to do in the new genre of autoethnography, which looks very much like what I have done here, only with more footnotes. Autoethnography, which originated in anthropology is "an approach to research and writing that seeks to describe and systematically analyze personal experience in order to understand cultural experience."[13] Transplanted to psychology, it seeks to understand behavior rather than culture, but the method is the same: to gain large insights from a rigorous and searching examination of a single life. Some of the best codependency books have been doing that for years—Melody Beattie's work comes to mind—and I think it's no accident that a 2017 Ph.D. dissertation, an autoethnography by a survivor of both sexual and emotional abuse, is deeply indebted to classics of the codependency field written by my colleagues in the 1980s.[14]

At the same time, it's important to understand the limits of writing on codependency. Some writers do generalize too much, claiming flat-out that everybody is codependent. This claim weakens the link between childhood trauma and codependency—either that or it defines trauma so broadly that no child could possibly escape it, in which case we do a disservice to the tens of millions who suffered particular hardship and eliminate the incentive to identify help children who are suffering that hardship right now. If trauma is universal, then there's no point in developing programs to target sufferers and ameliorate their suffering. I'll admit that I occasionally see rhetorical value in overstating the extent of codependency—I have done it myself when I wanted clients to feel less alienated—but, on the whole, I think it does more harm than good.

Let me say a bit more about why so that you can read codependency literature more thoughtfully. Uncritically claiming that most, if not all, people are codependent does something that's subtle but dangerous: it privatizes a public problem. When a pattern describes an entire population, it's no longer a symptom of private trauma; it's a social problem. We may work privately to mitigate the effects on us—and I would absolutely recommend that we do—but a real solution will be a public solution. Everyone busily excavating their private trauma will get us only so far if part of the problem is traumatic systems, which it would have to be if everyone were traumatized. Even where codependency is not universalized, the literature does tend to ignore its social dimensions. For example, right now we're seeing a rise in toxic perfectionism, a problem I will discuss later in this book. That kind of perfectionism can originate in private trauma, of course, but a culture-wide spike probably owes more to factors such as the increasingly competitive "gig economy" or the pressure to curate a flawless social media profile. Shopping addiction is another such problem, where relentless marketing and pro-consumption ideology keeps many people on the edge of compulsion regardless of their personal histories.

Why does it matter? If both social and individual problems cause dysfunction or pain, why do we need to distinguish them? I've already mentioned one reason: that to solve problems, we have to understand their causes. But, even before we solve them, we have to understand where a problem originates so that we can deal with the emotions it generates. In Chapter Twelve, we will learn about carried feelings, which originate outside of us but which we experience as our own, often in extreme and disruptive ways, such as sudden rage or overwhelming shame. We can carry such emotions for other people, but we can also carry them for groups, communities, institutions, and whole cultures. When we discuss carried feelings, we'll learn about descendants of Nazi war criminals who carry the guilt, not just of their individual family members, but of the whole regime. That's an extreme example, but the phenomenon is not uncommon, and it's valuable to understand where your pain originates so that you can restore it to its rightful owners.

Another problem with the literature of codependency is the flip side of its greatest virtue. "Our angels are our demons," says a friend of mine, and indeed it's often true that the same trait can be both a strength and a weakness. In this case, the deep probing of personal experience that is such a virtue of codependency literature can lead writers to over-generalize from their own lives. Robin Norwood famously said either you recognize yourself as a "woman who loves too much," or you're in denial. That's the fallacy of the false dilemma, which reduces a complex range of options to a single pair of opposites ("You're with me, or you're against me," or "America: love it or leave it"). It's important to read critically, to realize that no book has all the answers you need, and to be wary when an author tries to foreclose disagreement by suggesting that it's likely a "symptom" of something undesirable.

Reading critically also involves being alert to oversimplification and the overuse of taxonomic systems. We human beings *love* classification, whether it's by astrological sign, somatype or position in a dysfunctional family: hero, scapegoat, lost child, or mascot. I'm a mesomorphic Saggittarian hero; what are you? There's a reason magazines such as *Cosmopolitan* regularly feature articles titled "What's your animal love style?" We take the quiz to learn whether we're a "cuddle bunny" or a "curious monkey" or a "protective mama bear" or a "lone wolf," and sometimes the answer offers food for thought. Schemes can conceal as much as they reveal, however. Lots of people either fall through the cracks because their experience doesn't fit any category, or they over-identify with one category when, in fact, they fit more than one. The minute I decide I'm really a mesomorphic Saggittarian hero, I begin to minimize my endomorphic tendencies, my long history as a scapegoat, and my Aquarius moon. Taxonomies and models are common in codependency literature; we should absolutely use them to think about ourselves but avoid adapting our unique experience to someone else's paradigm. With those cautions, we can glean a lot from codependency literature.

If we discover that childhood trauma is negatively influencing our adult lives, what do we do about it? Will remembering what happened to us and understanding how that experience continues to affect us actually help? As someone who has been a therapist for more than forty years, I'm convinced that self-knowledge has immeasurable value, both in itself and as the foundation of positive change. But the kind of understanding that really helps is not easy to achieve. It requires the courage to face painful truths and the commitment to keep going when the process becomes uncomfortable—and it *will* become uncomfortable. Some people fantasize that the process of personal growth will feel natural, like "coming home" to an authentic self. Yes, there are moments like that, as well as moments of pleasure in discovery and mastery. But much of the process feels quite *un*natural: awkward, forced, artificial, less like coming home than like colonizing Mars.

For those of us with histories of trauma, what's "home" is the dysfunction we grew up with and the coping strategies we evolved to deal with that dysfunction. Consciously or unconsciously, we gravitate toward situations that replicate those familiar patterns, and we often bail out of situations that challenge them. Many of those bail-out strategies are unconscious. We're working on an exercise from this book, making notes about a childhood incident, when boredom overtakes us. The incident we're reflecting upon suddenly seems trivial, a waste of time. Important tasks clamor for our attention, and we're suddenly struck by how self-indulgent it is to ponder things that happened such a long time ago. We look out the window at a neighbor painting his fence, and we think *that's* how a responsible adult behaves, and, before we know it, we're up a ladder replacing a window screen without even suspecting why our attention was hijacked. And boredom is just one, relatively benign, way our minds steer us away from uncomfortable topics and the feelings they arouse. When investigating our histories, we may also feel much stronger aversions, including intense fear and shame, along with uncomfortable physical sensations. Also commonplace are cravings for the distraction (or oblivion) of drugs, alcohol, gambling, compulsive sex, and other addictive behaviors. When doing the work of described in this book, it can be a challenge to remain focused long enough to discover exactly what happened to us and how it's influencing our lives.

Moreover, as valuable as self-knowledge is, it's rarely enough to heal the effects of childhood trauma. As we'll discuss in Chapter Three, trauma affects the developing brain, and its influence is both conscious and unconscious. Because understanding happens at a conscious level, we have impulses, reflexes, reactions, thoughts, feelings, sensations, and perceptions that understanding leaves untouched. For that reason, one of the best books on trauma in recent years, Bessel van der Kolk's *The Body Keeps the Score,* champions movement-based approaches, from yoga to psychomotor therapy, along with more traditional talk therapy. I too recommend a mixture of cognitive and somatic techniques, some traditional, some newly prominent, some my own innovation. I designed these techniques to work together as a comprehensive program, but they can readily be used piecemeal, alone or with other therapies. In every case, I supply instructions, work sheets, and supporting materials, such as audio recordings. But before I go into specifics, let me make a few general points about healing.

In researching trauma and its effects, scholars have begun to devote systematic attention to differences among survivors with similar histories. Such studies are simplest after an isolated catastrophe such as a plane crash, where survivors of roughly the same event[15] can be compared; nonetheless, the past twenty-five years have seen a number of longitudinal studies dealing with complex trauma, or trauma that is repetitive and prolonged, including childhood trauma. The quality that allows people to survive trauma and mitigate its effects is resilience, which is technically the ability to recover from or adjust to deformation caused by stress. Though resilience may seem like a personality trait we either have or don't have; it's more deeply understood as something we *do*. Developing resilience involves:

       1. taking back control over how we view our experience.
       2. finding meaning in those experiences.
       3. exercising our creativity.
       4. developing mindfulness.
       5. seeking support.
       6. working to reinvent ourselves.
       7. cultivating humor, optimism, or both.[16]

Some of these methods may seem a bit beside the point: how does creativity relate to childhood trauma? Because resilience is a relatively new focus of research, the mechanisms of influence are not always clear, though theories abound. Dr. Brené Brown, for example, believes that acts of creation, from ceramics to songwriting, help us move insights from our heads into our hearts and into our daily lives.[17] Writer and trauma survivor Jen Cross goes further, claiming that creativity has transformative power because it is fundamental to who survivors are.

> Creativity is us. We who are survivors of intimate violence are always creating, given our ability to adapt to horrifying, unendurable situations. . .. Trauma and creativity are inextricably linked, and, I believe, creativity can pull us through the after-effects of what was done to us, and what we did to survive.[18]

What matters is that the link between creativity and resilience has been repeatedly demonstrated, so it's a valuable tool regardless of why it's effective. My own experience has taught me that creativity is not something to put aside while we do the serious work of recovery; it's an essential part of that work.

Everything else on the list is essential too, so each section of the book will emphasize several of the activities and attitudes that cultivate resilience. Though all of them inform and reinforce one another, we'll highlight several at a time to better understand their role in healing from childhood trauma.

       Part I: taking back control of how we view our experience.
       Part II finding meaning in our experiences, being creative.

Part III: mindfulness.

Part IV: seeking support.

Part V: taking back control, being creative, working to reinvent ourselves.

Part VI: all of the above plus cultivating humor and optimism.

As you can infer from this brief summary, many of these categories overlap. For example, mindfulness fosters equanimity and compassion, which in turn foster a quiet but profound kind of optimism: a sense that things really are all right, just as they are. To me, that's far more effective than a cheery affirmation taped to the bathroom mirror or a resolution to use positive words and phrases, which ignore the complex sources of negative thinking and the heroic role it may have played in a survivor's life.

In combination, all of the material in this book seeks to guide survivors of childhood trauma toward resilience, both by demonstrating how I developed it and by explaining how other survivors can. If you recognize your own experience in these pages, I believe that this information can help you feel better and function better than you do now. I won't promise deliverance from your past in ten lessons or seven steps; nor will I ever imply that dealing with childhood trauma is easy or simple or straightforward. It's anything but. If I sometimes sound like a cheerleader, it's because I want to encourage you along this difficult path that we're both navigating. I'm not descending a mountain holding a pair of stone tablets; I'm climbing with you, and I have some knowledge and some kit to share. If they help, I'm thrilled, and if they don't, I fervently hope you find some that do. In fact, one reason this book includes notes and bibliography is to give you a sense of what information is out there and how it might serve you.

In that spirit, I'm going to end this introduction with the best description of resilience that I have read. It's in a dissertation that cites a conference paper, so it's on the obscure side, yet it perfectly expresses my motives for writing this book. Building on the idea that resilience is more verb than noun, the author defines resilience as "a phased process damaged persons must move through to reach eventual thriving and transcendence . . . a kind of mastery, where the capacity to face, address, integrate, and transform one's worst fears and darkest moments can, going forward, lead to new strength and empowerment."[19] If that sounds optimistic, the reason is that I have watched hundreds of people realize the benefit of this "phased process," including myself. I hope you'll find it too.

Part I

Causes and Effects of Childhood Trauma

CHAPTER ONE: A Tale of Two Dresses

I mentioned in the introduction that I was an abused child but did not know it. To explain how that is possible, I'm going to tell a story about two beautiful dresses I wore as a small child, one peach-colored and one white. Both were made for me with love by my maternal grandmother, and both represented the ways my family and my community shaped and misshaped my early life. The community was Tooele, Utah, where my mother's family had lived since Brigham Young led his followers to nearby Salt Lake City. A little south of the Great Salt Lake, Tooele, pronounced "Too-willah," was both typical and atypical of mid-century American towns. On the surface, it looked as wholesome and familiar as a peanut-butter-and-jelly sandwich on white bread, a town based on family farms and ranches with a lively business district and leaders who diligently looked after local interests. Kids in Tooele were a lot like kids in Arkansas or Pennsylvania: we went to public schools, built forts in the woods, watched "The Flintstones" on television, danced to Beatles records, and cruised up and down Main Street after school. In one crucial way, however, we were different—most of us, anyway—because we belonged to a church with a far-greater reach than the mainstream churches, temples, and synagogues most Americans know: the Church of Jesus Christ of Latter-day Saints, which most people call the Mormon Church. In Tooele, our diligent community leaders weren't just civil authorities; they were bishops, elders, high priests, and stake presidents; through them the church controlled pretty much everything in the whole county, from the distribution of irrigation water to the running of the schools to the punishment of lawbreakers. People still debate whether Utah is a theocracy; all I can say is that, growing up, I never saw a place where church authority ended and secular authority began. And that authority reached deep into our daily lives.

On Sundays, we attended church in the morning, drove home for a family lunch, then returned to church in the afternoon. Before school we sometimes had religious instruction, especially as we got older, and after school, more instruction via church-sponsored activities such as the Young Women's Mutual Improvement Association (MIA), where we learned how to become good Mormon wives. Some of those after-school activities were fun, especially when the MIA Maids teamed up with the Boy Scouts for square dancing, but even dancing helped create the impression that the church was all-encompassing. It monitored us constantly, checking our attendance and conduct, watching our spending to make sure we paid our full tithes, formally interrogating us about our lives—and even our private thoughts—then publicly declaring whether we had passed muster. If you've never experienced this level of surveillance, it's hard to imagine.

My family's position in Tooele rose and fell. My mother's aristocratic pedigree gave us considerable baseline status: Bevans had been Mormon pioneers, and the first of them had served with the Mormon Battalion, the only US military unit ever based on religion. My mother's father, owner of the largest farm in town, had served two terms as mayor and a lot longer as high priest, so the luster of the family name remained bright. My father, however, did not come from a long line of distinguished Mormon settlers; he came from a short line of religiously vague Indian agents and may have been part Goshute on his mother's side. His family had lived in a tent in western Utah during the Depression and eked out a meager living afterward. He and my mother met when his family moved to Tooele to look for work, which he found on my grandfather's farm.

But it wasn't his lack of a Mormon pedigree that caused my father's status in the community to go up and down; it was his volatile temper. Though at times the most amiable of men, he took offense easily and expressed his ire with his fists. He was regularly "disfellowshipped" by church disciplinary councils, which meant that, for a time, he'd be barred from certain forms of public worship, such as receiving the sacrament, leading prayers, and teaching. Then he'd be reinstated and rise again, not as high as my high-priest grandfather but high enough, occasionally serving as one of the bishop's advisers. Nonetheless, he possessed the one quality that the Mormon Church values above all others, one that confers holy office, demands respect, and guarantees absolute power over all who do not possess it. He was male.

When I was seven years old, my family moved to a ranch thirty miles south of Tooele. The Mack and Hack Ranch wasn't ours, but at least it gave my father a chance to do the work he loved, rather than toiling in a mine or driving a truck or climbing utility poles. Though no one spoke the wish out loud, we all hoped that ranch work would settle him down a bit, make him less volatile. And, for a little while, it did—or seemed to. More likely, it wasn't the ranching that sweetened his temper but the attention of the young girls in town. Still only twenty-six, my cowboy father was an attractive man with many admirers, including two high school juniors who rode my bus.

"He's so handsome!" giggled Sue, a pretty blonde.

"I swear, if he weren't married . . .." mused her best friend Amy, shaking her head.

"I don't care about that. He don't *act* married, anyway," Sue replied. At seven, I had no conscious notion what they were talking about; I just felt the presence of something ugly and forbidden, though uneasily familiar. I was grateful when the bus driver put a stop to the suggestive taunts.

Spring in northern Utah is spectacular. Hills turn green; wildflowers bloom; the pale core of the Milky Way spills across the night sky. Though the cold is gone, the air stays brilliantly clear, and the highest peaks keep their caps of snow. New England can claim title to fall, but for spring give me the Rocky Mountain west, especially after a winter like 1958, which had produced a string of heavy snowfalls. Now it was April 6, Easter Sunday, and I was wearing a beautiful new dress the color of the peach blossoms in my grandparents' orchard. The dress was very special to me, not just because my grandmother had made it, but because I rarely got new clothes of any kind. Most of what I wore were hand-me-downs from older cousins—and sometimes hand-me-ups because I was always small for my age and often had to wear the clothes of younger children. A new dress was an occasion just below Christmas in importance.

The peach dress was full-skirted with matching embroidered trim on the collar, sleeves, and hem. With it I wore black patent leather shoes, buffed until they gleamed, and white socks with lace at the cuffs. My mother had curled my blonde hair into fat ringlets, like Karen's on *The Mickey Mouse Club,* and added a tortoiseshell barrette on each side. We didn't have a full-length mirror in the trailer, but I could tell from the one over the sink that I looked pretty. Shunning a coat or sweater, I walked proudly into church, stopping occasionally to swivel so that everybody could get a good look at my new dress. Even though there was a lot of Easter finery on display, I was confident that my outfit ranked high in the crowd's estimation. With my younger sisters behind me wearing plainer versions of my dress, I felt like a princess leading her entourage.

After lunch at home, my mother gathered the children for an Easter portrait. She didn't have to ask me twice! Seating us one at a time on a stile propped against a white poplar tree, she made sure we couldn't fall off or soil our clothes on the weathered rungs of the stile. I sat on the top rung, Kriss, next in age, just below me. She had naturally curly hair that was fun to play with, so I fluffed it under the pretense of sisterly grooming. At the bottom sat Sharon and David, the two younger children, David twitching with impatience to be done with the photograph and Sharon twitching with something far more serious. After a recent bout of strep, she had developed Sydenham's Chorea, a rare neurological disorder that causes constant involuntary movement. Her shoulders bounced up and down as she swayed back and forth, while her knees jiggled and her arms moved aimlessly around. Had you seen her, you would know why the disease was once called Saint

Vitus's Dance. After my mother had straightened David's bow tie and made sure Sharon's movements would not unseat her, she backed up and raised her Instamatic to snap the picture, nearly backing into my father who had arrived to supervise.

"Hold still!" he shouted in our direction. Immediately, I quit playing with Kriss's hair, and David quit fidgeting, but Sharon continued to bounce, jiggle, and sway.

"Sharon, control yourself," said my father, but Sharon continued to move. "Right now!" he added.

"Trying," said Sharon in a tiny voice. Her hands began a rhythmic squeezing motion.

"Hold still so your mother can take *one* picture," he insisted. "Just one picture. Then you can fidget to your heart's content."

I heard sniffles from Sharon's direction and saw her head begin to bob.

"She can't help it, Daddy," I said softly. "The doctor said so." My father shot me a quick look, eyes narrowed in warning.

"She's not really trying," he replied. "Come on, Sharon, on the count of three. One . . . two . . ."

"Push on her shoulders," I whispered to Kriss. My father looked at me again, a dark flush rising in his face. Then he looked sternly at Kriss, who remained motionless, her hands clasped tightly together.

"Three!" my father bellowed, at which my mother dutifully snapped the photo."

"You're wasting film, Maurine," my father told her. Sharon's just going to be a blur. That beautiful dress her grandmother made for her: just a big blur." With every part of her body in motion, my little sister burst into loud, anguished sobs.

"She's *sick*, Daddy," I cried. As soon as the words were out, I wanted them back, fear and self-disgust erupting in my belly. I had done it again: talked back to my father. What kind of child does that? I stared at the ground, not willing to see what I knew was happening on my father's face: the dark red flush, the working of his jaw, the slitted eyes.

"Cheese!" sang my mother, snapping another photo. As I heard the click, I saw my father charging from the right like an angry bull. As quickly as I could, I scooted left, leaped off the stile, and started running for the house. I got about five yards before I felt a blow between my shoulder blades that dropped me flat onto my stomach. I felt my dress rip as I pushed up onto my hands and knees, but I crawled as fast as I could until a hard kick to the backside laid me down flat again.

"Stay down, you sonofabitch," my father roared. But I got up again and tried to run on wobbly legs. Grabbing my left shoulder, he shoved me down again, then stood over me, one boot on either side of my waist. I couldn't see him above me, but I heard the faint clinks that meant he was taking off his belt. Seconds later, I felt its leather around my neck as he used it to lift me off the ground. Choking, I scrambled to get my feet under me so I could breathe, but he held me so high that I couldn't. My vision was starting to go black when he dropped me again and pulled the belt free. This time, I just lay there gasping while he lashed my back and my legs with the thick leather belt. Finally, after many lashes, I heard a voice from far away. It was my mother.

"Clel, that's enough," she said matter-of-factly. "I think Donna has learned her lesson."

When I could breathe again, I went into the trailer and took off my new peach dress, placing the torn, filthy garment carefully in the laundry bag. As I was removing my socks, which were also dirty, my mother came in and moistened a washcloth to scrub off the dirt on my legs and arms. The rough cloth hurt, though I could tell she was trying to be gentle—as gentle as a cleanliness fanatic could be when confronted by a dirty child. I was crying, though less from pain than from misery.

"If you weren't such a bad girl, Donna," my mother said as she sponged off my face, "your father wouldn't have to punish you."

I didn't ask what I had done that was so bad; I knew. I realized that defying my father was a grave offense—and that it was only one of many I committed every day. I asked for bread between meals like a little pig. I chomped when I ate. When my milk glass was full, I leaned over and slurped from it or I spilled as I picked it up to drink, making a mess and wasting precious milk. I slammed the car door and dawdled in front of store windows. I responded slowly to orders, rushed through chores, and sometimes said "uh-huh" rather than "yes, sir." I was thoroughly bad, and every day I became more convinced that I was bad by nature, rather than a good girl who sometimes did bad things, like other girls. I had already begun to suspect that I was simply incapable of real goodness, though I tried very hard to do all the things good girls were supposed to do. I took care of my siblings. I cleaned my room and finished my homework before going out to play. I obeyed my parents—or *tried* to obey my parents—but I always seemed to fall short in some crucial way that I didn't perceive until too late. Then would come punishment, its brutality testifying to the enormity of my offense because, I realized, pure evil can't be corrected with words.

As she led me to the closet to pick out a dress for the afternoon services, my mother brought up another familiar theme.

"Your father loves you very much, Donna," she said as she helped me into last year's Easter dress, now too short and too tight. Remembering the beautiful peach dress I had worn that morning, I began sobbing again. "He loves you, so he punishes you when you're a bad girl, just like Heavenly Father does." As she spoke about my father's love, I suddenly realized something profound, something that changed my world forever.

"If that's love," I sniffed, I don't want it." My words shocked me, but they also rang true. As I said them, my crying stopped, and I felt something inside me harden. Somehow I knew that I would never cry over a beating again.

I slunk back into church that afternoon, my coat buttoned over the old dress and one of my mother's silk scarves hiding the welts on my neck. As I had hundreds of times before, I sang the hymn "I Am a Child of God" with the other children in Primary, a Mormon Sunday school. Normally singing comforts me, but this time I heard an ominous significance in the hymn's lyrics, which promise blessings to children who obey the will of God. The song begins:

> I am a child of God,
> And he has sent me here,
> Has given me an earthly home
> With parents kind and dear.

Singing the familiar words, I suddenly wondered: if God gives his children "parents kind and dear," then is it possible I'm not a child of God? And if I'm not a child of God, whose child am I? The questions would torment me until another special day—with another special dress—resolved them once and for all.

That special day was my baptism, a solemn and deeply meaningful event for Mormons. Though adult converts may be baptized at any time, the sacrament is normally given to children shortly after they turn eight—unless their parents are the same sex, of course, in which case they have to wait ten years and jump through a lot of extra hoops.[20] Mormons consider eight the age of accountability, when children become old enough to know right from wrong and to take responsibility for their sins. So in January of my ninth year, along with three other children, I donned my second new dress in nine months, white to signify the purity baptism would confer upon my soul. The dress was simpler than my peach dress, with a gathered natural waist, puffed sleeves, and a large Peter Pan collar, and I helped to make it, insofar as an eight-year-old lefthanded child is ever much help with a sewing project. I chose the fabric, a soft cotton, and I chose among the small number of patterns approved by the church for baptismal attire. I assisted in the construction by fetching pins or measuring tape and swapping regular scissors for pinking shears when they were needed. When the labor grew tedious, I entertained with a song, including, at my grandmother's request, "I Am a Child of God." She laughed and sang along, overjoyed about the baptism of her first grandchild.

"It's one of the most important days of your life, Donna," she told me many times. My mother and other relatives echoed the sentiment.

"All of your sins will be washed away, and you will feel like a completely new person," said one of my aunts.

"Pure and innocent," added my grandmother. "Pure and innocent." Words can hardly express how much I longed to have my sins washed away. My sinfulness lay so heavily upon my heart that I could hardly breathe sometimes, and the thought that, in just a matter of days, it would be lifted from me filled me with wild excitement. But right underneath was fear: how long could I keep my soul pure? Once I was baptized, my sins would count against me forever; there would be no second baptism to wash new sins away. And, given my track record, how could I avoid committing new sins? Wouldn't I blunder into them just as readily after baptism as before? So, as the big day approached, I felt both joyous anticipation and quiet dread. My great hope, so fervent that it vibrated in my chest, was that the experience of purity would change me in some mysterious way. Perhaps, if I tried really hard not to damage it, it could get a foothold in my soul and make me a good girl. For weeks before the big day, I walked around with all of my fingers crossed.

I woke early on the day of my baptism, less from excitement than from nerves—and the pink foam curlers covering my head, which were like sleeping on a pile of doll parts. While I waited for the rest of the family to wake up, I sat on the end of my bed and stared out at the field behind our trailer, surveying the ragged patchwork of old snow, scrub and bare earth in the growing grey light. In a few hours, I would take on the responsibility of preserving my soul's purity, which, for me, would be like keeping white gloves clean while making mud pies. I was hungry, but I was required to fast before baptism, so I'd get no food until mid-afternoon. And hunger on this holy day was not a good sign; it meant the little pig in me might end up running the show. At that thought, I began to cry. I needed a reason to postpone the baptism until I could get my badness under slightly better control.

No excuse moved my mother, who bustled about feeding my siblings and packing my accessories: black patent leather shoes, new white stockings and new white underwear. After a quick feel of my forehead, she pronounced my fever imaginary and my tummyache a hunger pang.

"Get your mind off of your stomach," she said sternly, herding the children into the car as my father emerged from the barn in his best cowboy hat. "Blessings are earned."

"*I* want blessings!" cried my brother David as we pulled onto the highway. "*I* want to be baptized!" My sisters also clamored for baptism as I stared through the car window at the distant mountains, suspended between hope and dread.

After dropping my siblings in the care of an aunt, my parents, grandparents, and I arrived at the Tooele stake house. A stake is the Mormon equivalent of a diocese, so it's larger and more important than a ward or congregation though still not very big by mainstream Christian standards. In the basement of the stake house was a windowless room set aside for baptism, which for Mormons involves full immersion. The baptistery wasn't large, perhaps thirty by thirty feet, and along each wall were metal folding chairs on which sat the immediate families of the children being baptized, about forty relatives in all. In the center was the baptismal font, a raised basin of white stone, perfectly round, resting on the backs of twelve stone oxen. A stone staircase wrapped around one side with a platform at the top. From the platform, three steps descended steeply into about three feet of clear water. At eight feet across, the basin was wide enough for even the tallest adult to be submerged with no stray finger or toe poking out of the water. I knew from my preparations for the sacrament that every part of me had to be completely under water.

After changing my clothes, I waited with the other baptizands in a small antechamber, standing because I didn't want to wrinkle my new dress, even though I knew it would soon be sopping wet. My mother had arranged my hair into a long pageboy with poodle-frizz bangs, a style I expected the water to improve—if it could penetrate the many layers of hair spray she had applied. After a prayer led by the gangly boy supervising us, called a Teacher though only fifteen, the other children sat down while I wandered around the room. I felt lightheaded at the thought that I would soon be completely sinless but terrified at the prospect of losing that bliss. How soon would I sin again? Would I drop a green bean on my grandmother's tablecloth after an hour? Would I slam the car door after half an hour? Would I drip too much on the baptistery floor after just a few minutes of purity?

"Don't worry," said the Teacher, who had walked up behind me and laid a paternal hand on my shoulder. "You're only underwater for a second. Close your mouth; breathe out through your nose, and you'll be fine!"

As the ceremony began, he led his four charges into the baptistery, where we sat in a meek row while the bishop prayed for us and reminded us of the responsibilities we would be taking on. As he spoke, I suddenly had a brilliant idea. If I made sure to keep a toe out of the water, then the baptism wouldn't be legitimate, and I could do it again when I had a better grasp of how to avoid sin. A tsunami of relief swept over me. Why hadn't I thought of it before? I scarcely had time to work out my strategy before I heard the bishop call "Donna Jean Lee." My fraudulent baptism was underway.

With fresh confidence, I walked to the font and climbed the stone steps to the platform. Standing in the water was my father, bareheaded and dressed in white: white shirt, white pants, and white socks. Like most Mormon men, he was a priesthood-holder and so empowered to administer the sacraments that Mormons call ordinances. The three steps into the water were very steep, especially for a child, so my father offered both his hands to help me down. Then he turned me so that I was perpendicular to him, held my right wrist with his left hand and put my left hand on his left wrist. After a moment, he raised his right hand as though taking an oath.

"Donna Jean Lee," he said in a solemn voice, "having been commissioned of Jesus Christ, I baptize you in the name of the Father, the Son, and the Holy Ghost. Amen." Putting his right hand in the center of my back, he began to lower me into the water. As he did, I straightened both my legs and popped a toe to the surface, hoping he wouldn't see it. He did because suddenly the hand under my back was gone, and the hand holding my wrist was pushing me down into the water. I barely had time to panic before I was standing upright again between my father's hands with my legs under me. I had lost control of my body and been submerged, so I was baptized, whether I wanted to be or not. I braced myself for the promised bliss.

Nothing happened, nothing at all. The annihilation of sin, the feeling of exultation, the soul-searing purity I had expected, longed for, and feared to lose never arrived. As my father helped me out of the font, I discovered something worse than having God's forgiveness and then losing it: not having it at all. I was not a child of God, nor had I ever been, nor could I ever be. I was something else, something wretched and loathsome and shameful, something that deserved all of the punishment a wrathful god and his mortal deputies could dish out. I stood stiff and miserable as my grandmother rubbed me down with a beach towel. My misery deepened as I watched my fellow baptizands go through the ritual, each child emerging from the water the same way: sputtering at first then broadly smiling. Radiant as they climbed out of the font, they broadcast their joy with every gesture, laughing and hugging the family members who converged on them. They exulted in the happiness they deserved, while I reaped the bitterness of my own evil.

The rest of that day was a teary blur. I didn't cry when I was beaten any more, but this spiritual blow was more than I could bear, and I wept on and off for hours. Though famished from fasting, I barely touched the succulent fried chicken that my grandmother had prepared or Aunt Marion's flaky apple pie. No one noticed my lack of appetite, however; they were all too elated about the baptism of the first Bevan grandchild. Over and over, different relatives asked me versions of the same question.

"Do you feel different?" I did feel different, but not in a way I could bear to explain.

"I'm cold," I said instead. It was true: I had not stopped shivering since I climbed out of the font and into my grandmother's beach towel.

"The water was chilly," said my father, "but I was in it a lot longer than you were, and I'm not whining."

"Your great-great-grandfather was baptized in the Colorado River," said my grandfather. "Now *that's* cold."

"You just need some hot food," said my grandmother. "Eat your potatoes." I tried, but I just couldn't eat; nor could I stop crying for longer than a few minutes. Finally, people did begin to notice.

"Knock it off," growled my father under his breath, "or I'll knock it off for you." Even as a wretched eight-year-old, I wasn't sure how a blow would "knock off" my crying, but then my father's threats often made little sense, as you might expect from a man who called his daughter "sonofabitch."

"Grandma Bevan has gone to a lot of trouble for you," hissed my mother. "The least you could do is smile."

"It's okay, honey, said my grandmother. "You're just overwhelmed is all. Baptism is a big step. Why don't you go lie down for a little while? A nap will set you right." Though I wasn't particularly tired, I jumped at the chance to get away from the party. My nine-year-old uncle (and best friend) Jimmy offered his bedroom, so I headed upstairs for some time alone.

I guess I was tired after all, because I woke to a dark room, which meant I had slept for a couple of hours. I could hear the party still going on, but it sounded far away, like it was next door rather than downstairs. I could hear distant voices singing "A Bushel and a Peck" an upbeat number from the musical *Guys and Dolls*. Much nearer by, I heard soft footsteps then felt a heavy weight depress my mattress.

"Jimmy?" I croaked, still half-asleep. But it couldn't be Jimmy, because I could hear his voice downstairs. "A Bushel and a Peck" was one of his favorite songs, one we had sung together since nursery school. As I listened to his loud soprano, the person on my bed shifted closer to me and whispered into my ear.

"Shhh. Go back to sleep." A large hand slid under the covers, found me, and began stroking my body. The hand was cold, callused, and familiar.

"Daddy?"

"No talking," came the hushed response. "Do you want your grandmother to come in here and find out what a bad girl you are?"

CHAPTER TWO: Causes of Childhood Trauma

In my first story, I tried to make clear how a child, even an intelligent child, can be both severely abused and completely unaware of that abuse. With extreme physical abuse, like mine, the idea that it may be hard to recognize seems absurd; surely a child knows when she is savagely beaten. Not necessarily. She may dissociate, though that did not happen in my case, except when I was very young. It's much more common to feel a beating and know it's happening but understand it as something else. Context is everything to a child. If physical violence is commonplace in the home, it may seem unremarkable, just the way things happen. To children, "normal" is whatever they grew up with, no matter how far from community norms it may be. The context that shapes the meaning of a beating also includes how the family defines it. It can be defined as justice, for example, the righteous correction of a child's wrong. It can be defined as love. The famous line "This hurts me more than it hurts you" defines a beating as both of those, a sacrifice made by a compassionate adult for the moral education of a child.

It's almost impossible to overstate the degree to which children's perceptions, thoughts, feelings, and behavior are governed by their caregivers' perceptions, thoughts, feelings, and behavior. Right and wrong, good and bad, normal and abnormal: all the criteria by which children make sense of the world—and they are constantly trying to make sense of the world—derive from their caregivers. Until they encounter credible alternative perspectives, such as school or television, they have an insoluble epistemological problem: they can't assess their experience because the means of assessment have already been deformed by that experience. Even after new perspectives become available—when observing friends' families, for example—these may be filtered through the deformed cognitive apparatus—and when I say "deformed," I'm referring partly to actual changes in the developing brain that can be seen and measured through functional Magnetic Resonance Imaging (fMRI). Abused children don't encounter a healthy family and suddenly think, "I deserve a family like that one!" Instead they fit the healthy family into the deformed world view that their caregivers have transmitted over the years. During my childhood, I observed plenty of loving parents and happy children, but I never thought of them as representing an alternative that might be open to me. Instead I assumed that loving parents were only for the children who deserved them. They were a kind of reproach: "See what kind of family you might have enjoyed if only you weren't so horrible!"

There was also, in my case, an institutional constraint on my ability to understand what was happening to me: the Mormon Church. My early life represented a toxic synergy between the abuse perpetrated by my father and secondary abuse perpetrated by the church. In some ways, they mirrored one another; in other ways, they were different but perversely complementary. It was important for me to understand that the intentions of the Mormons who guided me were irrelevant to the harm that was done. For example, I am absolutely certain that no one tried to hurt me by saying, "When you're baptized, you'll feel completely different, pure and holy." Either they believed it because they had enjoyed that feeling themselves, or they didn't quite believe it but hoped I could be induced to have that experience. Placebo effect is a powerful thing, especially for a child; tell kids often enough that baptism is bliss, and a lot of them will feel the glow, as my fellow baptizands surely did. If they don't, perhaps the solemnity of the occasion or their young, active imaginations will supply the deficit. In short, there's little inherent harm in the Mormon ritual of baptism or the beliefs surrounding it.[21] The harm lies at the confluence of this belief and my parents' insistence that I was beaten because I was bad. When I failed to experience the glow of purity, I logically assumed that I must be fundamentally unclean, not deserving of God's love and forgiveness. I didn't pull that idea out of thin air; I extrapolated it from what I had been taught in Primary (Mormon Sunday School) and around the dinner table. In other words, I experienced trauma that was produced, however unintentionally, by a ritual and a set of ideas. I suffered institutional abuse, as well as individual abuse, and the two sources multiplied each other's effects. I would have to deal with both.

There are other institutions that, alone or in synergy with individual abusers, may be sources or multipliers of childhood trauma. The military is one, with its emphasis on war, discipline, and rank, as well as its policy of constantly moving personnel (and their families) all over the world. Agencies such as the FBI, CIA, DEA, ICE, and state or local law-enforcement can cause related problems for the children of their employees, as can NGOs, even the most worthy. Other sources of institutional trauma include schools, camps, organized activities such as scouting, hospitals, treatment facilities, and, of course, churches of all kinds. In general, with churches, the more all-encompassing the religion, the more difficulties, which is why children brought up in separatist cults[22] face particular challenges. It's always hard for children to achieve enough critical distance to gain perspective on their lives, but children who have never even encountered other points of view have a cognitive handicap that is challenging to overcome, though many do. I consider the Mormonism of my youth about halfway between a cult and a mainstream religion. I don't want to suggest, however, that children raised at the heart of mainstream religions are not subject to institutional trauma. Any strict moral code can intersect with caregiver pathology in harmful ways. In addition, recent decades have furnished so many examples of priests and ministers violating the trust of children and their families that clerical abuse has begun to seem commonplace.

Recognizing abuse also requires understanding who is responsible for it, another difficult task for a child. What makes this task so tricky is simply the way children think. Babies are born profoundly self-centered; they gradually discover through observation and experience that everything in the universe is *not* part of themselves. This self-centeredness diminishes very slowly, persisting well into adolescence. At the same time, children are typically raised with rewards and punishments, taught that good conduct leads to rewards and bad conduct leads to punishments. So it's no surprise that they believe that their behavior causes things to happen. Even events clearly unrelated to a child's conduct, such as a car accident or a divorce, may prompt children to examine their own behavior for contributory offenses (or negligence). We're all self-centered magical thinkers as children; that's normal, so good caregivers help children learn what they're actually responsible for and what's beyond their control.

Abusers, on the other hand, exploit a child's strong sense of agency, often by actively reinforcing it ("You brought this on yourself!"). Even when not reinforced, however, this sense of responsibility tends to conceal abuse, both from the outside world and from the child herself. When children believe that their own behavior causes their suffering, they are much less likely to resist, acknowledge or report abuse. They believe that exposing the abuse is exposing the terrible child who caused it, so they keep quiet, not just to protect their abusers (though that can be a factor), but to protect themselves. Recognizing abuse requires a child to understand both the *what* of it and the *who* of it, a challenging (and sometimes life-long) assignment.

My clients regularly remind me just how challenging it is. As part of the Legacy workshop, participants must visualize themselves as children, create a detailed mental image from memory or from a recollected photograph. When asked to picture their younger selves, some balk at the instruction.

"Yeah, I remember that kid," is a typical response. "I don't want to do this. That kid was a bad kid." Their reluctance intensifies as the exercise continues, and they're instructed to imagine the child sitting on their lap. When I see such hesitation, I ask about the feelings that motivate it. Often the response is clear and blunt.

"I don't like him. I don't like that kid."

"I don't like her. I don't want her on my lap."

Even older clients who know, intellectually, that they were not responsible for their abuse, may still blame themselves unconsciously. Asked to use imagination, rather than reason, some discover impulses and attitudes that surprise them, one of the many reasons I value therapeutic performance and storytelling so highly. That these can reveal a residue of self-blame, even after years of adult reflection (and therapy) suggests just how deep the problem lies.

When an institution such as a church supports a child's natural tendency to assume blame, a toxic synergy is likely. Religions with a penitential emphasis can distort shame so that it no longer inspires the child to correct a problem, as it should, but instead becomes a permanent feature of personality. By "penitential," I mean religions that focus on sin and that value feelings of guilt and shame about sins committed (or, in some cases, just contemplated). Theologically, sin is the reason for salvation, so it couldn't be more central to Christianity, though denominations differ in how they conceptualize and describe sin. But I'm more interested in feelings than theology. In most Christian denominations, feelings of guilt, shame, remorse, regret, and unworthiness are very important, a necessary precursor to forgiveness and an essential element in spiritual growth. Responsible religious education clarifies the proper place of these painful feelings in spiritual life and balances them with love and acceptance. Irresponsible religious education cultivates guilt and shame but makes them impossible to transcend and ties their antidotes, such as the experience of God's love, to impossible standards of conduct or achievement. Some even insist that punishment *is* God's love. In either case, persistent existential guilt obscures the real authorship of the child's suffering and vastly compounds the abuse.

If context can obscure something as straightforward as a beating, then its concealment of more subtle—or more hidden—forms of abuse may be impossible to overstate. For that reason, it's essential that trauma survivors understand the vast number of forms abuse can take. As I've mentioned, one criticism of codependency paradigms is that they define abuse so broadly that everyone becomes a victim, and I've already admitted that it sometimes seems that way. The cynical implication is that therapists and writers of codependency literature seek to pathologize normal human experience in order to create an endless market for their self-help books, workshops, and fifty-minute hours. But that's not our motive at all. In many years of working as a therapist, some of them well before I ever heard the term "codependency," I've seen no need to drum up business. There have always been, and always will be, plenty of suffering people that need help. No, the reason for a comprehensive summary of the myriad forms of abuse is the invisibility we were just talking about: the way youthful perception and familial or institutional context can so thoroughly obscure abuse that victims become largely unaware of it. In other words, what's at stake is not seeing normalcy as abuse; it's seeing abuse as normalcy. I'd rather live with the accusation of casting my diagnostic net too widely than fail to help someone who was clearly suffering the effects of trauma but whose experience was atypical.

Some of the best examples are cases of childhood neglect. "Leslie" had been abandoned over and over by unfaithful partners but recounted her history of betrayal as though she were reading a weather report. Detached from her own emotions, as well as her partners', she tried to compensate by indulging their desires even when they conflicted with her core values. The men left her anyway, always for another woman, and at fifty-seven, she found herself alone and terrified. I was not surprised to discover that her childhood was marked by emotional deprivation. Her parents, both alcoholic, abandoned her in different ways. Her father, who had been a helicopter pilot in Vietnam and shared the problems of many veterans, went to prison when she was ten and never returned. When he left, Leslie had to take care of her depressed, hard-drinking mother and her brand new baby brother. Ten-year-old Leslie had no choice but to become the only adult in the family; her survival and the survival of her family demanded it. Immature and barely nurtured herself, she carried her crushing burdens by cutting off her feelings so thoroughly that they never returned. No one ever hit Leslie, but she was traumatized.

In the back of this book is a series of lists that identify types of abuse in five general (and overlapping) categories: physical, sexual, emotional, spiritual, and intellectual. These lists are suggestive, rather than exhaustive; they seek to inspire readers to think beyond media stereotypes of abuse and consider their own experience. As far as possible, reflections should adopt the child's perspective, rather than the adult's or some kind of hypothetical "reasonable person." We are excavating feelings, not making a legal argument. For that reason, we must also ignore the question of intent. What abusers meant to do, whether their motives were cruel, kind, or indifferent, is irrelevant at this stage. What matters is what happened and what effects it had on the child. One last consideration to set aside is how prevalent a practice is in a culture. When I was growing up, spanking was commonplace; now child-rearing experts condemn anything beyond a single swat on a clothed bottom. The shift is interesting culturally but has little bearing upon whether regular spanking frightened or humiliated the child who endured it. And it is that child's experience we are trying to recover.

Physical abuse covers more than just beating and mingles with other forms, such as emotional abuse. A caregiver might ritually delay punishment, for example, as in the familiar line "Wait 'til your father gets home," forcing the child to endure it many times in his or her imagination until the waiting becomes as terrible as the punishment. Other ritual elements reinforce the self-blame to which children are prone. "Bring me the hairbrush," says a caregiver, forcing the powerless child to become an agent of his or her own harm. In general, ritual elements enhance terror through repetition. During less active phases of punishment, dread magnifies anxiety so that the whole experience becomes worse than the sum of its parts, the physical and emotional dimensions creating a painful feedback loop. Here we see why the intention of the abuser matters so little when assessing abuse. Perhaps the caregiver meant to imbue punishment with formal ritual; perhaps the caregiver was merely lazy and unimaginative. The difference may deeply affect current feelings about the caregiver, but it has almost no effect upon how the abuse was experienced.

Sometimes abuse appears not to be physical but is. Driving drunk with a child in the car is an example in which physical harm seems more potential than actual. With an accident, there's physical damage; without one, there's none, it seems. But that's not necessarily true. Children very often know when a caregiver is driving impaired; they see, hear, and smell the signs. Moreover, especially in the last thirty years, children have learned in school and on television about the dangers of drunk driving. They may become very frightened by the possibility of crashing, hitting a pedestrian, or being arrested—likely outcomes of drunk driving, they have been taught. These days, they may even know that most children killed in drunk driving accidents are actually passengers of the drunk driver, a fact widely publicized in recent media campaigns. Aware of their caregiver's impairment but powerless to do anything about it, they experience stress, frequently if the caregiver regularly abuses alcohol. Protracted stress is bad for any human being, but for children it causes permanent damage to their developing brains. High levels of the stress hormone cortisol shrink the hippocampus, a part of the brain involved with memory and emotion, predisposing them to learning problems and mental illness. That's physical, as well as emotional, abuse.

Tickling is another practice often regarded as harmless. Though some human beings, both adults and children, enjoy it, many more find it distressing, so many that tickling served as a form of torture and punishment from the courts of Han Dynasty China to the Flossenbürg concentration camp. The laughter that tickling generates is mainly a nervous system reflex, rather than delight, and part of the satisfaction of tickling, whether to please or to torture, is the helplessness of the person being tickled. Tickling is not abuse *per se* but readily crosses the line into abuse. Again, the perspective of the child is important: was ticking pleasant and fun, or was it unpleasant and humiliating? Was there give and take, or was the child always the one tickled? If some examples of physical abuse seem relatively benign, remember that children cannot defend themselves. Most of the activities listed are harmful, even against the law, when perpetrated by one adult against another. Children, who need more protection, lack the legal and strategic remedies available to adults.

Sexual abuse can be overt or covert, can range from the grotesque horror of being raped as a baby to the more subtle practice of spousification, or being treated like a husband or wife. Rule number one in adult-child interactions is that adults must keep their sexuality contained—and I include in "sexuality" romantic feelings of any kind. Children begin to feel a need for privacy very early, usually toward the end of toilet training. When they start to close the bathroom door, that is a signal to the adults in their lives to cover up, not just to set appropriate boundaries in the home but also to keep their children safe outside of it. This principle is not negotiable in our world today, even for committed nudists or naturists. Children accustomed to seeing their parents' genitals, especially young children, may not think it unduly strange to see a stranger's genitals and so fail to recognize and respond to a sexual assault. As children mature, caregivers must police their own sexuality just as assiduously. They may think, as their teens become sexual with peers, that these children can now handle sexual comments or looks, but they are wrong. Teenagers do sometimes want to be regarded sexually by adults—by, say, twenty-one-year-olds—but normally not by their caregivers.

When children do enjoy a caregiver's sexual attention, it's usually a sign of something wrong, even if there is no overt sexual abuse. Caregivers who treat children as spouses, talking with them about grown-up problems and experiences, including sexual problems and experiences, engage in emotional incest. The children may feel special, but they suffer sooner or later. Children should be talking about such things with their friends and building relationships with their peer group, but they may not if talking with the parent meets their needs for social time, attention, and energy.

In identifying sexual abuse, these principles help sort through potentially tangled feelings. A child is just as liable to assume responsibility for sexual abuse as for physical abuse—or miss it entirely because it's such a familiar feature of life. Complicating matters is that, where physical abuse is usually unpleasant, sexual abuse can involve some pleasure, even when it is fundamentally unwelcome. Depending upon the age of the child, sometimes the body will respond in ways outside the child's control, which can deepen guilt and confusion, encourage the abuser, and perpetuate the abuse. The child's heart can respond as well, especially at an age when romantic feelings are naturally beginning to stir.

In some cases, abuse may be inferred from behavior, though care is needed not to jump to conclusions. It can be tempting to propose that an interest in child pornography indicates some kind of sexual abuse in childhood, but there's little evidence of such a link. In fact, an interest in child pornography is more likely the result of a cultural phenomenon: the explosion of internet pornography since the late 1990s. Online pornography is now so explicit, so varied, so specialized, and so available that once-popular skin-mags such as *Playboy* now seem quaint. Most women can resist the allure, but men have a harder time, especially men under thirty-five whose brains are most altered by viewing pornography. And men who use a lot of it become desensitized very rapidly, needing more and more extreme images to become aroused. This "kink spiral," to use Naomi Wolf's term, has brought child pornography closer to the mainstream, as viewers who do not consider themselves pedophiles have begun to consume it just for the novelty.

Where abuse *can* be inferred is in an alarming new trend: children, some younger than ten, have begun posting sexual images and videos of themselves online. When children objectify themselves this way, they have almost certainly learned to do so, either through direct sexual abuse or by viewing images of other sexualized children. The huge explosion of child pornography in recent years makes it ever more likely that children will encounter such images on the internet, and for some it will seem to legitimize their exploitation. At any rate, exposing children to *any* images of porn is abuse. It's not sex education; in fact, there's growing evidence that it impedes normal sexual development and compromises adult sexual intimacy.

Perhaps the most familiar form of emotional abuse is verbal abuse. In some cases verbal abuse borders on physical abuse, as young children's ears can be hurt by loud voices in close proximity. Regular shouting frightens and debases children, though it is usually less the volume than the content that does most damage. Habitual insults, commands, judgments, and other forms of aggressive speech are little better. The word "sarcasm" derives from the Greek "*sarkasmos*," which means, literally, "to strip off the flesh," and sarcasm is a common way to hurt, bully, and reinforce power asymmetries when delivered by a parent to a child. Because children unconsciously copy their caregivers' speech patterns, a predilection for sarcasm as an adult can sometimes indicate this kind of emotional abuse. It's worth noting, however, that some sarcasm is playful and affectionate, so it's not verbal abuse *per se*. The teenager who says "Nice one, Dad" when his father's empty cup misses the trash can may simply be learning to use irony, rather than imitating aggression.

Insisting on perfection is emotional abuse because human beings are, by nature, errant. Children must be able to make mistakes yet still know that they are loved and valued. Misrepresenting or exaggerating the consequences of a mistake can also be abusive, not just because it magnifies children's tendency to assume inordinate responsibility, but because it keeps them from learning to differentiate risks and make sound choices. If every mistake is a disaster, then they cannot appreciate the difference between misjudging the slipperiness of a soapy dish and misjudging the wisdom of cooking meth in the garage. Children raised with the notion that they must be perfect to be valued become adults with deeply embedded perfectionism, adults who have difficulty accepting their own humanity and that of other people. Relentless perfectionism, the inability to accept "good enough" in any endeavor, no matter how trivial, is usually an indicator of this kind of abuse.

Another form of emotional abuse is abandonment. Abandonment does not necessarily mean physically leaving a child, though divorce and death are common forms of abandonment. Just as it's possible to engineer a separation so that children still feel safe and loved, so is it possible to remain physically present yet desert them. Some of the ways caregivers abandon children are work, drugs (including alcohol), social or recreational commitments, and process addictions such as gambling. Caregivers can even be absent while interacting with children if they always have one eye on a cell phone or a basketball game. In such a case, the child feels like a distraction from what the caregiver would prefer to be doing and so feels guilty as well as abandoned.

One of the most severe forms of emotional abuse is social: impeding or sabotaging children's interpersonal development. Ways to do this include failing to impart basic social skills, creating such chaos in the home that friends cannot come over, forbidding friendships outside the family (or like-minded group), or imposing odd dress or grooming standards. Member of fringe religions, for example, often isolate children from their peer groups, handicapping them for adult socialization and magnifying the likelihood that they will be bullied as children. And bullying has terrible consequences for children and the adults they become. From Columbine to Virginia Tech, most perpetrators of mass school shootings turn out to be victims of bullying. Less well-known is the connection between bullying and pedophilia. Contrary to popular opinion, most pedophiles were *not* victims of sexual abuse as children. They were, however, victims of bullying. A child—let's say a boy, as most true pedophiles are men—grows up in a cult that rejects the clothing, values, and behavior of the larger community. In school, his unusual appearance and manners make him a target of bullies, so that, when he starts developing sexual feelings, he dares not express them with his peer group because they are too dangerous. Younger children, though, look up to him just because he's older, so they are safe. Eventually, he may turn there for sexual gratification.

I once had a patient who perfectly illustrated this paradigm. Rick, a man of twenty, came to me for counseling after he found himself on the threshold of abusing a child. Over many therapeutic sessions, he described growing up in Kansas City, Kansas. A shy white kid at a predominantly black school, he already faced a daunting social challenge, but his parents compounded it by shaving his head and forcing him to wear an ad hoc uniform that included a white dress shirt and a bow tie. They belonged to a cult that dictated strict dress codes for males and females, so Rick had no other option. Not surprisingly, he was beaten, sexually abused, and tormented during his school days. He had no friends at school, and few people in the cult had children, so he was profoundly lonely. After school, he joined the Air Force where the institutional camaraderie made him feel less alone, though he had no real friends. He simply did not know how to make them. Once he became a fighter pilot, he worked largely alone, which made his social isolation intolerable. One day, the day he first called my office, he found himself driving around a playground looking for a child like he had been: different and alone. Horrified even to contemplate exploiting a lonely child, he threw himself into therapy, where he grappled successfully with the legacy of his upbringing. His parents were not bad people. They honestly believed they were following a righteous path and giving their son the best possible start in life. But they hurt Rick, and, in order to heal, he had to understand their actions as abuse.

In spiritual abuse, other forms of abuse may be grafted onto a religious paradigm, giving exploitation the force of God's will or other unassailable authority. Some beliefs, including those most common in our culture, are easily deformed to justify domination. Protestantism, for example, traditionally sees the large structures of the universe replicated in small structures, such as the family, where the father's authority mirrors God's and must be obeyed. Understood correctly, this pattern requires the father to mirror more of God's attributes than just authority, but a little light cherry-picking produces doctrine that seems to throw the combined weight of God, the church, and eternity behind domestic tyranny. Some denominations give heads of household even more spiritual authority. In the Mormon Church, men don't mirror God's power and authority; they actually possess it. In other words, the power that sends you to your room without dinner is the same power that created heaven and earth.

Other denominations restrict spiritual power to priests, which makes possible a different kind of spiritual abuse. In the Catholic Church, only priests can perform the sacraments necessary for salvation. Regardless of their character, they alone have the ability to expunge your sins and ensure that you end up in heaven, rather than hell. Already overawed by adults, children can barely comprehend the magnitude of such power, before which even their mighty parents bow. Children can't conceptualize the difference between the office of priesthood (where the power actually lies) and the person of the priest; in fact, most adults don't grasp that distinction either. So a child may understand pretty well that a certain kind of touching is wrong yet believe that it's somehow consecrated by the fact that a priest initiates it. Abuse by such a spiritual authority is regarded as so damaging that, until recently, some rehabs treated priests and ministers for free.

Most of what I've just described explains how religion facilitates abuse of various kinds, including sexual abuse. Spiritual abuse is the accompanying deformation of religious or spiritual ideas. For example, children led to believe that God wills them to be beaten or raped are likely to understand God as cruel, arbitrary, and possessed of a special antipathy toward them. Even if they consciously reject religious belief, the ghost of this figure may continue to influence their understanding of the world and their place in it. Over the years, I've met a lot of atheists who discern a kind of orchestrated punishment in the patterns of their lives, as though a Calvinist nightmare-god were at work behind the scenes, arranging failure and suffering especially for them. If they also retain the conviction at some level that they deserve the suffering, then that banished god still has tremendous power. Even survivors able to mentally separate God's will (vast and mysterious) from Dad's will (selfish and destructive), can struggle with any belief in a just or benevolent universe. They wonder, quite legitimately, why they suffered when so many around them did not, a question that may ultimately lead them to quite a profound understanding of life but that is difficult to contemplate in the absence of intellectual and emotional maturity, which are often retarded by abuse and its consequences.

Another form of spiritual abuse results from the religious zealotry of caregivers. The nature of such abuse will vary with different belief systems, but there are some common elements. One we have already mentioned: that zealots tend to align their wishes with the will of a greater power, regardless of how well those wishes conform to the belief system. Another is that they tend to indoctrinate, rather than educate, children, punishing independent ideas or even normal curiosity. I'll say more about that when I talk about intellectual abuse. A related problem is that some zealots regard the world outside their community of like-minded believers as depraved and dangerous, so they deliberately withhold information about that world and skills vital to survival in it. A current staple of reality television is "Amish: Out of Order," a show about young people who have left that notoriously insular faith. These adults are like children, badly educated and unable to handle modern life. Sitting in rural trailers watching television all day, they appear stuck with an impossible choice: failure outside the faith or unhappiness inside. I know how they feel; when I left home, I knew frighteningly little about how to cope with the world.

Spiritual abuse shades into intellectual abuse when a caregiver's actions damage a child's ability to understand and function in the world. We've already noted the naïveté that insular communities can produce, but abuse can happen any time caregivers neglect training in basic reasoning skills. As with basic social skills, some capacities are difficult to acquire after childhood has passed, so intellectual abuse can be very long-lasting. Our public school system exists to ensure that children receive a basic education, but there are many ways a caregiver can sabotage that goal. One way is to take a child out of school without providing a responsible substitute. Though homeschooling can be superior to public education, it is not monitored at all in half the US states and monitored very lightly in the rest. Parents and guardians are free to teach whatever they like, no matter how extreme or impoverished the curriculum. An alarming development in homeschooling is the popularity of extreme physical punishment, such as that advocated by Michael and Debi Pearl, whose authoritarian educational philosophy has been implicated in the murder of several children in recent years, including one girl beaten to death for mispronouncing a word. The Pearls and their followers (possibly as many as half a million) use corporal punishment to break the will of a child and inculcate obedience, which is clear physical and emotional abuse, of course. But it's also intellectual abuse because it trains children to associate learning with punishment and pain. That kind of training goes very deep.

A public school education can be undermined when caregivers belittle teachers, mock schoolwork, or create a home environment too chaotic to support learning. Children who are hungry or sleep-deprived may be physically incapable of paying attention and fall behind; sustained conflict and domestic crises can have similar effects. Alternatively, children may do well in school but see their accomplishments disdained or derided by caregivers who define success in other ways. Somewhere in the middle are the mixed signals of caregivers who prize educational attainment yet saddle children with excessive chores, paid work, child care, or other responsibilities. Also intellectually damaging is intolerance of mistakes. Caregivers who insist on intellectual perfection produce children who forgo opportunities to learn because they fear looking dumb. Though they may excel academically, they avoid unfamiliar subjects, don't ask real questions, and prefer performing for the teacher to joining in discussions. And this pattern can persist for a lifetime, snuffing out intellectual creativity and joy in learning.

Thought control is another form of intellectual abuse. Whether a whole philosophy or an opinion on the fly, telling children what to think diminishes their curiosity, their resourcefulness, and their development of higher-level cognitive skills. To solve problems, children must learn to gather information, think through one or more issues, make decisions or assessments, and communicate their findings. These skills are not easy to develop, so children must rely on caregivers for help and encouragement. Unfortunately, some caregivers find it more convenient just to tell children what to think or what to do. They may even refuse the tiny grace of demonstrating their reasoning, killing further discussion with "Because I said so." When it comes to helping children communicate, caregiver egos can cause serious problems. If caregivers always have to be the smartest in the room, contradict every statement, turn every conversation into a debate, and, worst of all, invent data to fill gaps in their knowledge, children become discouraged or inhibited. Even if they do well in school, they may secretly suspect they are stupid as, no matter how much they learn about a subject, it is never enough.

This discussion of childhood trauma has focused mainly on abuse. The reason is that complex trauma, trauma that recurs over time, typically involves habitual actions by caregivers, which we call abuse. Abuse may be completely unwitting or even well-intentioned, as I've pointed out. It doesn't matter. To do this work, we have to set aside the motives of caregivers and focus on the lived experience of children. There are, however, some kinds of trauma that are hard to talk about in terms of abuse, even unintentional abuse. One is medical trauma. Children who suffer illnesses or injuries that require long-term invasive treatment, such as repeated surgeries, can experience profound physical and emotional trauma. Even with the most supportive caregivers, they experience fear, pain, and, perhaps worst of all, powerlessness. Because they are relatively small and dependent, children always experience some feelings of powerless compared to adults and older children. They envy grown-ups who can play with chainsaws, eat cotton candy for breakfast, and stay up as late as they want on school nights. For children who are seriously ill, though, that transient sense of powerlessness is persistent and greatly magnified. Sick kids cannot say "no" to undressing in front of strangers, being fed into huge, terrifying machines, being poked and prodded and cut open. They must eat strange food, whether they're hungry or not, and take drugs that make them feel weird. Unpleasant as all these experiences are physically, it's the loss of control that can do the most psychological damage, telling the child at a very deep level, "what you want doesn't matter." That can be a tremendous blow, especially to older children who have gained some control over what happens to them and now watch it slipping away.

Another form of trauma that's hard to talk about as abuse is poverty, or economic trauma. With one-fifth of American children classified as poor and another fifth living in low-income households, poverty is probably the largest source of childhood trauma in the US. Some of its harms are done by exacerbating the problems of caregivers. Struggling to survive is extremely stressful, as are the many burdens poverty trails behind it, from ill health to unsafe living conditions. Complicating matters is the myth that anyone who works hard enough can climb out of poverty. Because the media energetically propound this myth while real wages and social mobility decline, people who are struggling often feel great shame, believing themselves at fault because they can't bootstrap their way out of poverty. This shame, added to the persistent fear of financial catastrophe, increases the likelihood of caregiver abuse or neglect. So does substance abuse, which is also more prevalent at lower income levels. Nonetheless, to say that poverty is a risk factor for abuse and neglect is not to say that poverty causes abuse and neglect. I want to state emphatically that most poor children are *not* abused by their caregivers. Unfortunately, poverty itself is often traumatic for children in ways scholars are just beginning to appreciate. Recent work on eviction, for example, shows that it produces a classic trauma response for up to two years. If it's repeated or if housing insecurity becomes a perennial problem, the result is complex trauma. In other words, it's not essential that we be able to point to an abuser, even an institutional one, to recognize abuse.

CHAPTER THREE: Effects of Childhood Trauma

The effects of childhood trauma are physical as well as psychological. Recent advances in neuroscience have begun to explain how childhood trauma damages the physical brain. One of the biggest problems is that abuse of all kinds interferes with the brain as it's developing. Different parts of the brain mature at different times, so a child's age will affect the specific vulnerabilities of a given system. The limbic system, evolutionarily primitive, matures early, peaking in adolescence. These structures (the amygdala, hippocampus, and hypothalamus) handle emotions related to survival, such as fear, anger, pleasure, and sexual desire. They are also involved in memory formation, controlling which memories are stored and where—and so determining the emotional intensity of a memory. In other words, from an early age, we feel strong, primitive emotions and are capable of laying down memories of great emotional magnitude. The cerebellum, involved in autonomic regulation, motor function, emotion, affection, and co-processing of mental tasks, grows rapidly after birth and matures in adolescence, explaining why teenagers can excel in activities requiring coordination, such as gymnastics, video games, and dance, and why they develop such strong bonds of affection with friends and romantic partners.

From an early age, a child's "fight or flight" system operates really well. When danger threatens, the amygdala sounds the alarm and activates the body's stress response, releasing hormones that ready the body for drastic action. The amygdala is hyper-efficient; it doesn't wait for the conscious mind to decide whether that coiled brown thing you're about to step on is a rattlesnake or a dead vine. The amygdala operates on the principle that you'll live longer if you think "Snake!" and it doesn't much care if the over-reaction embarrasses you. This stress response is not diminished by false alarms, which is why the vine still scares you, just for a second, even if all the coiled brown things you've ever nearly stepped on have turned out not to be snakes. You can feel how well the system works in the jolt of alarm that hits before your conscious brain has the time to process that the coiled thing isn't moving and doesn't have a head or rattles.

Childhood trauma overworks this alarm system, which can cause physical, emotional, and even cognitive problems. Think of it this way: a twenty-first century child witnessing domestic violence has much the same physiological response as a Neolithic child encountering a dire wolf. The hormone cortisol raises her blood pressure and blood sugar while suppressing her immune system. It turns fatty acid into energy, preparing her muscles for action. Another hormone produces glucose for more energy. Her heart rate increases, as does her breathing rate. Her muscles tense, preparing for violent action. She stops digesting her dinner, and she may wet herself. Her body shuts down some processes and ramps up others to give her the best possible shot at getting away from the dire wolf or crushing its skull with a rock. The modern child doesn't have anyone to fight or anywhere to flee, but he has the response anyway. He has it over and over, and if the violence in his household is habitual, he may suffer chronic arousal of a system that evolved to cope with emergencies.

The twenty-first-century child's chronic arousal can have serious consequences. He will over-produce stress hormones and under-produce calming neurotransmitters such as serotonin. Habitual overproduction of adrenaline may exhaust his adrenal glands. Even if he's removed from the stressful environment, he may become hypervigilant, responding to minor stimuli with disproportionate fear or aggression. If afraid, he may have difficulty calming himself; if angry, he may have difficulty controlling himself.

The parts of the brain that do the controlling mature much more slowly. These are the cortex, which houses the brain's "executive function," and the corpus callosum, which connects the left and right hemispheres as well as the parts of the brain already mentioned. Not mature until well into the third decade of life, these are the parts of the brain involved in rational decision-making, planning, and complex cognition. In other words, during childhood, the parts of the brain that can truly understand—and deal with—abuse just aren't on line yet, though the parts of the brain that feel it and suffer from it are. In healthy families, parents help with rational decision-making, planning, and complex cognition until children's brains develop sufficiently to perform those functions. In abusive families, that supplementation may be unavailable—or only intermittently available. Worse, the children's own brains may never reach full maturity because abuse interferes with development of these "higher functions." Neuroimaging studies have, in fact, found differences in the amount of grey matter in cortical areas associated with cognitive control. Consequences may include impaired self-regulation, which can lead to addiction, impulsivity, anxiety, aggression, self-destructive behavior, and learned helplessness. Also compromised are memory, attention, and the processing of emotions.

Fortunately, modern neuroscience has good news too. The concept of "neuroplasticity," the brain's ability to adapt and heal, has overturned the old conventional wisdom that, once the brain had fully developed, all it could do was deteriorate. Scientists now know that meditation, exercise, new experiences, and learning change the structure and functioning of the brain. They can see and measure these changes. Just by reading this book thoughtfully, you're already changing your brain in positive ways by learning. If you do the contemplative exercises to be found in this book, you'll change your brain by meditating. If you try therapy or a support group or any of the techniques suggested in this book, you'll change your brain by presenting it with new experiences. Add a regular exercise you enjoy, and you will initiate synergistic changes that neuroimaging can see and measure. In other words, these techniques will not only change how you feel and act, but also alter the fabric of your brain. But before we go on to talk about healing, we have to think more deeply about injury from a psychological perspective. Only if we better understand the problem can we understand how and why particular solutions work—and become truly committed to making room for them in our lives.

Childhood trauma has many kinds of effects on adult functioning: physical and emotional, acute and chronic, dramatic and subtle. Many of them result, not from the trauma itself, but from the child's accommodation to the trauma. These adaptations can be deliberate or automatic and include everything from numbing to preternatural emotional radar. There's always a logic, however. A child who is being sexually assaulted may develop a shield of fat as an effort to spoil the body that is "inviting" unwanted attention. Whether conscious or unconscious, dramatic weight gain is a creative strategy that makes sense from the child's limited perspective. Unfortunately, it's a strategy that ultimately hurts the child, forging an association between fat and safety that is difficult to overcome, even long after the abuse has ended. And fat is just one of the many strategies of adaptation, evasion, and concealment that persist into adulthood. The perceptions, reactions, and coping mechanisms of a traumatized child—even the child's physiological responses—almost always outlast the crisis that produced them, and it is often these that lead us back into our difficult histories.

Childhood trauma has been conclusively linked to a shocking number of diseases and social problems. In addition to substance abuse and suicide, survivors have an increased risk of developing problems as diverse as cancer and chronic truancy. At the same time, there is no one-to-one correspondence; people whose childhoods were trauma-free also develop cancer and play hooky. What's significant are patterns, especially patterns with a logical relationship to trauma. Substance abuse is a good example. There are many ways to develop a problem with drugs, including alcohol. Some people consume them socially for many years then gradually increase their consumption until one day they notice that it has affected their health, job performance, and/or relationships. Some people find almost immediately that drugs alleviate a serious problem, such as acute anxiety, social phobia, or depression. They may notice negative consequences right away yet continue to drink or use because, on balance, the benefits outweigh the costs—even though, to an onlooker, the costs seem far greater. There's a tee shirt that reads, "I don't have a drinking problem; I have a drinking solution to a life problem." The shirt is joking, but it gets at a real truth. We've just seen that chronic abuse in childhood overstimulates the fight-or-flight response, producing a persistent hypervigilance that is extremely uncomfortable. Give chronically agitated people a soothing chemical, whether alcohol or heroin, and many of them will think, "Yes, this is what I've been missing!" and quickly integrate it into their lives. They don't need much to get from "yes" to full-on addiction; a genetic vulnerability, fetal exposure, or persistent stress will do the trick. In other words, the link between childhood trauma and substance abuse makes perfect sense if you think about drugs as self-medication, rather than rebellion or hedonism, as a clumsy solution to a preexisting problem. I think I can say without risking overstatement that any teenager who feels "fixed" by drugs, including alcohol, almost certainly has a history of childhood trauma, as does any adult whose drug use began that way.

Another place where the effects of trauma are particularly visible is in relationships. One reason for the term "codependent" is that the effects of childhood trauma were first observed as an unhealthy dependence upon someone with an unhealthy dependence, such as alcohol addiction. But trauma has a much broader range of effects on survivors' ability to develop, sustain, and conclude relationships, and these can lie at opposite ends of the behavioral spectrum. Sexual abuse by a caregiver, for example, can produce hypersexuality, sexual anorexia, both in turn, or a range of problems that lie between those extremes. In Part Three, I will describe the way my father's abuse misshaped my sexuality so that I was compelled by other people's desires and unaware of my own.

Among the relationship problems of trauma survivors, dependency issues are common. Because children are born completely dependent and develop very slowly toward healthy interdependence, trauma that disrupts this development causes specific kinds of difficulties. When children do not get their dependency needs met, they may respond by steeling themselves not to have any needs. Particularly visible when caregivers become dependent themselves, whether through illness, addiction, or their own unmet dependency needs, premature independence may be praised as "strength" or "maturity" and may in fact be essential to the family's survival. But it comes at a cost. Children who suppress their own dependency needs, especially long term, may lose the ability to perceive any needs at all. As adults, they may remain genuinely unaware of needs they have the capacity to meet, from hunger to higher-level needs such as love and belonging. Such people often have extremely high pain thresholds and can remain unaware of medical problems until they are beyond effective treatment. Socially, they can be profoundly lonely but not know it. Though they long for it at some level, they may regard healthy interdependence as weakness, a vulnerability that threatens their autonomy.

At the other extreme are adults who retain their unmet dependency needs and struggle to get them met via unhealthy relationships with caregiver substitutes. Some fear being alone so much that they stay in bad relationships or engineer "exit affairs" so they can jump from one relationship to the next. Some lose themselves in each new love, becoming so enmeshed with a partner that they hardly know where they end and their partner begins. To keep the partner around, some change everything about themselves—their appearance, their interests, even their manner of speaking. They may derive their opinions, their self-esteem, their transient moods, even their purpose in life from their partner. Not surprisingly, the partners in these duos also have serious dependency issues that likely trace back to childhood trauma. They may demand dependence to feel powerful and compensate for their own unmet dependency needs. They may not demand it; they may be completely unaware that they are drawn to dependent partners, frequently asking their friends "Why does everyone I date always turn out to be so *needy*?" Intimate patterns like these are key indicators of problems that may be related to childhood trauma. When we keep ending up in the same kinds of relationships—the same kinds of *unhealthy* relationships—at a certain point we have to stop blaming our bad luck and start considering other factors.

Dependency issues also manifest apart from romantic relationships. I've already mentioned the problem of not perceiving needs; it's also a problem to feel needs but be unable to express them. When children are shamed for having needs, as sometimes happens in abusive families, they may become adults who put everyone else's needs before their own. These are people with normal pain thresholds but who also delay medical treatment until they are very sick—or someone drags them to a doctor. Like those who don't feel their pain, they suffer preventable medical consequences, including death. Socially, they are loath to ask for what they need. If they do somehow work up the courage to ask, and they are refused, their shame at having asked is so overwhelming that they do not ask again for a long time, if ever. Sometimes people who cannot express their needs expect others to divine them—then get hurt or angry when they don't. At the opposite extreme are people who generate a constant stream of needs for other people to meet. Hypochondriacs know that medical necessity compels attention, so they live in a persistent state of emergency, no matter how many times the heart attack turns out to be gas. All in all, adult dependency needs are a minefield for trauma survivors. Problems here are a good indicator of pressure from childhood experiences.

One way to talk about relationships, whether between people or between people and their environments is in terms of boundaries, or the invisible, semipermeable borders of the self. Boundaries protect you from others and others from you. When they are functioning well, they promote healthy interdependence: robust and fulfilling relationships with other people and a rich, reciprocal experience of the world. We will talk a lot about boundaries throughout this book, especially in Part Six, where we discuss how to create and maintain healthy boundaries for life. Unfortunately, where there are dependency issues, there are always boundary issues. Someone who is militantly independent has boundaries that are too thick and rigid, making intimacy difficult, if not impossible. Someone who is over-involved with one partner after another has boundaries that are too weak, destroying the integrity and the agency of the self. Codependency literature sometimes describes four kinds of boundaries, a paradigm that is useful if regarded with the cautions I mentioned a little while ago.

The first type is non-existent boundaries, which offer no protection at all. People with non-existent boundaries may be extremely vulnerable to suggestion, like someone in a hypnotic state. They have difficulty resisting advertising and often suspect they have contracted the diseases making the news, no matter how epidemiologically unlikely. Their ideas shift depending on who they're talking to, and they may reverse themselves repeatedly without being aware of it. In relationships, they may disappear. They shape themselves around dominant partners, becoming whatever the partner desires. Or they shape submissive partners without recognizing the encroachment. When power is balanced, which is rare, enmeshment may produce a new hybrid drawing characteristics from both partners. Regardless of their power orientation, people with non-existent boundaries are socially very awkward. They cannot tell when they're imposing upon others or being imposed upon. They may lack the capacity to edit their behavior or their speech, saying or doing whatever occurs to them in the moment. Certain kinds of organic brain damage can cause non-existent boundaries, as can trauma. Children who experience extreme, persistent violation of their physical, mental, and emotional boundaries have no way to learn the difference between "self" and "not self" on which healthy boundaries depend.

The second type is damaged boundaries, which are stronger than non-existent boundaries and so offer some protection. Often damaged boundaries function well in most circumstances but fail in ways that, when interrogated, reveal a pattern that traces back to childhood trauma. Some people have robust professional boundaries but terrible sexual boundaries. Some people can fairly assess an idea but cannot resist an appeal to their sympathy. Some people are vulnerable to certain kinds of people: authoritative men or women in need of rescue or children having a tantrum. Some people have weak boundaries with specific individuals, often the person responsible for them. As with dependency problems, people with damaged boundaries may or may not be aware of the issue. They may eavesdrop, snoop on a partner's cell phone, or step into someone else's shower uninvited without being aware that most people regard these actions as intrusions. Or they may be semi-aware, as in the person who sees other people recoiling from unwanted hugs but thinks that saying "I'm just a hugger" makes it okay. Awareness also varies on the receiving end. Some people honestly don't understand why they are continually imposed upon despite the fact that they never say "no" to a request and reflexively volunteer their help any time anyone around them has a need.

Fortified boundaries are the defense of choice for many traumatized children. Having learned to associate close contact with pain, they develop the rational strategy of avoiding close contact wherever possible. They deploy a dizzying array of barriers, from physical shielding, as with fat, protective clothing, geographical isolation, and actual walls, to behavior designed to keep people at an emotional distance. Some of these behaviors are paradoxical: they appear to invite connection while avoiding genuine intimacy. Examples include hypersexuality and certain kinds of charm, both of which can present a "wall of distraction" to preempt honest, vulnerable communication and the possibility of pain. Other common walls include anger, alienation, rectitude, nonchalance, even fear. Walls can be overt or covert, immediately evident or imperceptible for months. Some people dress to advertise "keep away," adopt a menacing dog, refuse to shake hands, or refuse to speak any more than is absolutely necessary. Others appear genuinely accessible up to a certain point, which may not be evident until a relationship is well underway. As with the other kinds of boundaries, fortified boundaries may or may not be recognized by the person they protect. It's not uncommon to see a human fortress who is desperately lonely yet has no idea why.

The last category is alternating boundaries, which are sometimes fortified and sometimes non-existent. On first pass, this category may seem little different from the second category, damaged boundaries, where variation is also visible. What makes the last category unique, however, is the nature and the extremity of the variation. These are not people whose boundaries are mostly okay with some dramatic exceptions; these are people who veer between polar opposites, sometimes one day to the next. They fall madly in love, "become one" with the partner, then freeze the partner out completely, then go back to enmeshment again. With friends, organizations, ideas, and many other things, they're either all in or way out. This kind of extremity is typical of borderline personality disorder, which has strong, well-established links to childhood trauma: physical, emotional, and mental abuse, including incest, physical neglect, and systematic denial of a child's experience and perceptions. Though the mechanisms of influence are not yet well understood, some theorize that boundaries are unstable because the self is unstable due to interference with the developing child's ability to distinguish self from others. Genuine confusion about where those boundaries lie plus the anxiety of not knowing (and not functioning well because of that ignorance) prompts both the variation and the extremity. Alternating boundaries are so extreme that they don't tend to be completely invisible to the people who have them, though younger sufferers may externalize some of the symptoms, believing, for example, that other people's behavior is as variable as their own reactions to that behavior.

In addition to dependency and boundary issues, survivors of abuse may also have what are sometimes called reality issues. All human beings create for themselves a version of reality. Consisting of our thoughts, feelings, memories, perceptions, and assumptions, some widely shared with other people and some more idiosyncratic, our reality is subjective and contingent, though it should feel objective and enduring to us. Childhood abuse in the form of gaslighting can radically disturb this individual reality. When caregivers persistently deny what children perceive and experience, saying "Oh come on, that doesn't hurt at all," or "No, Mommy and Daddy weren't fighting last night," they place one important source of information (adult authority) in conflict with another important source of information (inferences drawn from observation), damaging children's trust in their own perceptions and their ability to reason. Do it often enough, and the children may become adults who don't know or trust their own perceptions and may "borrow" those of other people. This phenomenon goes beyond looking to experts or influencers for ideas, which is widespread in our culture. Trauma-related reality issues involve not knowing fundamental things about yourself: whether you like your job, whether you're hungry, whether you need a haircut, whether you've been raped. It's looking at your 85-pound body in the mirror and not being able to tell whether you're hideously fat or starving to death. Many forms of childhood abuse are accompanied by the denial of facts so obvious that an observer would consider them undeniable. But because children don't yet have the cognitive skills to challenge it, such denial sends them down a rabbit hole in which nothing is ever as it seems. Some don't come back up for many years, remaining in a permanent state of uncertainty, not really knowing what they think and feel. Others find people to reflect them back to themselves, looking for someone who "knows what I want before I do." Such reflection can form the basis of what feels like a stable reality for the "borrower." We've all seen long-term couples who live this way, though, more often, the "lender" tires of reflecting the "borrower" and of a lopsided relationship without much real reciprocity.

Some trauma survivors do know what they perceive, think, and feel but are unable to communicate it. This problem has the same origin as the last but is slightly less severe, possibly because the trauma that caused it began at a later developmental stage. Nonetheless, it's a serious problem. People who can't communicate their thoughts, feelings, needs, and desires don't stop having them, and they often expect others to anticipate and respond to unspoken wishes. In fact, they may feel that they are communicating quite well by means of hints, facial expressions, song selections, news clippings, and other signals but that other people are simply not paying adequate attention. This conviction is understandable. Trauma survivors often watch other people very carefully and read them well. At one time, their safety may have depended on being able to tell, from the sound of Dad's voice or the look on Aunt Jilly's face, whether it was okay to ask for a graham cracker or time to grab Teddy and dive under the bed. They may assume that their partners can read people equally well, which is likely not true—and even if it is, partners tire of having to study microexpressions and other semiotic subtleties just to gain basic information. "If you loved me, you'd know what I want" wears thin very quickly.

We've already touched a bit on the next set of issues pointing to childhood trauma: moderation issues. Trauma survivors seem to live by William Blake's famous words, "The road of excess leads to the palace of wisdom." They have even more difficulty than most people finding the golden mean or middle way. They swear they won't drink like their alcoholic parents then do exactly that—or marry someone who does. They eat too much or gamble too much or shop too much, but they also go to extremes in less obvious ways. They may, for example, be overly fastidious housekeepers or live like slobs or both. With their children, they may be strict disciplinarians or overly permissive pals or both. People who grow up in disordered households, where they don't know what to expect from one moment to the next, tend either to replicate that chaos or to impose a rigid and extreme order. Or both, of course.

I once had a client who grew up with a mother suffering from schizophrenia. His father coped by working all the time, and his older siblings ran wild; the household was complete chaos. He grew up with very little supervision, essentially raising himself. As an adult, a widower, he wanted to give his children the attention he had missed but had no sense of what healthy supervision looked like. Instead, he was so hypervigilant that he made the average helicopter parent seem laid-back. Then, from time to time, he swung to the other extreme, leaving the children with a paid caregiver to go off on dangerous mountain-climbing expeditions, including an ascent of Mt. Everest. This alternation between the extremes of suffocating supervision and reckless desertion is typical of trauma survivors. The *average* of his two parenting styles may have approached moderation, but he remained on the road of excess, whether of control or abandonment. Such lack of moderation affects relationships profoundly. As survivors struggle to discover what "normal" is—and to behave accordingly—other people may experience them as erratic or overly rigid or both. Lacking models and guidance, they may become controlling and/or neglectful, punitive and/or indulgent, driving away the people they most love and need. In addition to being unable to communicate their reality, as we saw in the last segment, they may be unable *not* to communicate it. They may exhibit extreme reactivity, the inability to control or temper their immediate emotional response, which is both a moderation issue and a boundary issue.

The final set of issues pointing to childhood trauma has to do with self-esteem. Popular psychology has talked a lot about self-esteem in recent decades, and the media like to sniff that we have produced too much of it by praising children for mundane achievements like coming in eighth in an eight-person sack race. The kinds of problems that signal trauma, however, are not small variations in how good people feel about themselves. They are, once again, extremes. On the high end, childhood trauma can lead to grandiosity or arrogance. These survivors don't just win the sack race; they are the best sack-racers in the whole county. One important feature of this grandiosity is that it is always competitive. Nothing is ever just good; it is better than or best. Without comparison, there is no satisfaction. Part of this stems from our culture, which fetishizes competition. But more of it stems from problems with that reality we just talked about. Lacking a clear, stable sense of self, survivors make comparisons in order to know how to value themselves: I have more money/beauty/power/friends/toys than you, so I'm g-r-e-a-t! But more than just comparison is at stake. The esteem itself *originates* outside the self; it lies entirely in the eyes of observers. If those observers cheer, self-esteem is high. If they boo or turn their attention elsewhere, self-esteem plummets. There's no core sense of personal value to temper the extremes, either the highs or the lows.

That said, survivors do tend to have a default position, and grandiosity is one. The other is abjection, a sense of being worthless. As with grandiosity, abjection is always relative, in comparison with other human beings. Growing up, I was constantly aware of how I stacked up against other children, who were good and happy and loved by God. This sense of being "worse than" or "worst of all" is unremitting and automatic. Even when not making explicit comparisons, survivors have a persistent awareness of being surrounded by people who have value that they lack. Trying to make up the deficit, they look to external sources of validation: money, possessions, credentials, achievements, honors, praise—everything from the number of their Instagram followers to the achievements of their children. Unfortunately, these ways of buttressing self-esteem don't actually work very well. They may bring a moment of gratification, but it's usually anticlimactic and fleeting. Survivors may spend years thinking, "I'll feel okay when I finally get that M.D." only to find that their self-esteem actually drops a little when they become physicians because they still feel so worthless while their expectations of themselves have grown. They've met their goal, but the self-esteem deficit is now greater than ever. There's also a mixed mode in which abjection becomes paradoxically grandiose. Sufferers come to believe that they are the most wretched people who have ever lived, that their histories are far worse than anyone else's and their dysfunction commensurately more profound. "I'm so broken that no one can help me" becomes a perverse form of bragging, often more alienating than claims of greatness.

Sometimes, we don't have to search hard for the sources of grandiosity or abjection because they lie in the lessons we absorbed in childhood. Ongoing repetition of "My brilliant girl is way too good for any school in this town" or "There's my son, the only idiot in his class who can't read," send clear messages about who we are and how we compare to others. Just as often, however, the lessons are non-verbal or need some decoding. An example is the common expression "Who do you think you are?" The message it sends is complex, challenging not just a particular self-assessment, but the child's ability to self-assess at all. It's the kind of question that, repeated over time, teaches children that they have to look to others—specifically authority figures—to know who they are and that whatever judgments they may form about themselves are likely to need cutting down. Unresponsive caregivers create related problems because, especially when they are very young, children need caregiver feedback to develop basic self-awareness and self-esteem. Raised without such feedback, they become completely reliant on whatever mirrors they can find in their environment—or they give up and disconnect completely.

At the other extreme are children who get a lot of positive caregiver attention that is conditional in some way: tied to achievement or perfect deportment or some other ideal. A well-known subtype is children who become performers—models, actors, pageant contestants, musicians, dancers, or athletes. As coaches, judges, and other witnesses veto their natural impulses in favor of dressing, speaking, thinking, and behaving in highly organized ways, these children learn to look at themselves through the eyes of the people evaluating them. If caregivers avoid overvaluing professional success, some young performers may be able to distinguish between a public image and an essential self. Many do not, however, so their self-esteem careens up and down for life depending upon what kind of attention they receive. The wrecked lives of so many former child stars attests to the danger of living this way. It's important to remember that, at both extremes, the children are drawing very logical inferences from their experience. Those with parents who are too busy, distracted, ill, intoxicated, or otherwise unavailable to supply the focal nurture children need conclude that they're of little value, even if they never hear a word of criticism. Those whose parents shower them with conditional attention also learn they're of little value and only their achievements matter. Those who do hear words of criticism take them completely to heart. Those who hear they're the greatest thing since the elimination of smallpox also believe what they're told—and face a life-long challenge to find relationships that can preserve their illusions. All are forms of emotional abuse likely to produce serious consequences in adult functioning. Physical and sexual abuse also have profound effects on self-esteem, especially when abusers transfer their own responsibility to their victims. So excessively high or excessively low self-regard, along with swings between these extremes, are signs of childhood trauma, as is over-reliance on external feedback. Adult self-esteem issues, moderation issues, reality issues, boundary issues, and dependency issues give us strong reasons to reflect on our histories and their possible relevance to problems we are having as adults. This list is by no means exhaustive; it's a starting place for reflection. I'll have much more to say about all of these issues in later chapters.

Practice: Lovingkindness Meditation

In Chapter Two, I talked about some of the causes of childhood trauma, particularly abuse. In other words, I discussed *what* to look for. Now I want to consider *how* to look. In the west, we don't often concern ourselves with the kind of attention we bring to self-examination, though we should. Cultivating certain kinds of awareness facilitates self-knowledge almost as much as the questions we ask and the information we bring to bear. I'm talking about mindfulness, real mindfulness, not the popular McMindfulness that corporations use to increase employee productivity, but sustained training in ancient techniques for quieting and focusing the mind, expanding awareness, and cultivating compassion toward oneself and others. Let's start with the last of those. In the next section, I will talk about the various ways that self-blame and self-loathing make it hard to understand what was done to us and begin to change. Our work of discovery becomes easier if we can diminish some of those negative feelings while trying to discover their causes. Unfortunately, when it comes to diminishing negative feelings, the things that work often aren't healthy, and the things that are healthy often don't work very well. You can't just decide to love yourself, tape some positive affirmations onto your bathroom mirror, make a gratitude list, and expect your attitude to change. It won't, and you may even feel worse for "doing it wrong."

Non-judgmental compassion, especially for yourself, is something human beings have to *practice*. If I could underline "practice" twelve times, I would because, when it comes to self-compassion, intention is not enough. Don't get me wrong, intention is great—it gets you to practice—but only the *doing* can lead to change. Practiced consistently over time, self-compassion will develop, increase, and feel more natural, even if the very idea seems forced and alien now. And self-compassion helps enormously with the distress of remembering abuse, so it's a very good practice for those of us with such a history. To begin cultivating compassion for yourself, try the guided meditation titled "Lovingkindness" using the sound file on my web site.[23] Try it every day for at least a couple of weeks, and see what happens. The exercise takes just eighteen minutes, and you don't have to do anything special; just get comfortable, listen, and follow my suggestions. If you like the results, add it to your daily routine, and I'll talk about other ways to develop mindfulness in later chapters.

Part II

Telling Our Stories

CHAPTER FOUR: Mr. Waldo

My second story is longer and more detailed than the first. It begins seven years after the beating that ruined my peach dress, on a sunny spring morning in my sophomore year of high school. My family now lived within the Tooele city limits, rather than on the Mack and Hack Ranch. My father had given up ranching to work as a lineman for the power company, though he still competed in rodeos—and practiced his roping skills on his children. His status as a Mormon was on the upswing, as he had not been disfellowshipped for several years and had started doing service work. The family's social health, in short, was pretty good. But its psychological health remained critical.

At a little past ten on that spring morning, I had just walked into my third-period history class when the teacher spoke words no student wanted to hear, though I had heard them often enough to mute some of their terror.

"Donna, Mr. Waldo[24] wants to see you."

I nodded but didn't turn around right away.

"Right *now*."

"Yes, ma'am," I murmured. As I turned to go, I dropped my books on a desk to establish that I would return to class very soon. I was a Mormon, after all; I understood the power of ritual.

Mr. Waldo was the school's guidance counselor with vast authority in two realms: academic and disciplinary. Academically, I was fine, an "A" student with near-perfect attendance and the admiration of my teachers—most of them, anyway. My disciplinary record was quite another matter and the reason for the skepticism of two teachers: Miss Carson and Mademoiselle DuPre, the latter name pronounced with a throat-clearing "r" that I loved to exaggerate. Miss Carson knew I was responsible for regular nocturnal invasions of her home economics classroom, a state-of-the-art laboratory equipped with every domestic apparatus, including dozens of industrial sewing machines and ten complete mini-kitchens. Such equipment may seem lavish today, but you have to remember this was Utah in the mid-sixties. Girls had to be educated to reach their highest potential: as Mormon wives. At any rate, imagine a cross

between the set of *Project Runway* and the set of *Master Chef*: that was Miss
Carson's classroom, and she prized it highly. Unfortunately for her, the locks
on the classroom windows were *not* state-of-the-art, so I often led midnight
incursions aimed at pre-setting the oven timers to go off during class the next
day or filling the blackboard with top-secret intelligence such as "Miss Carson
smokes in the closet," a revelation that reduced the home economics teacher
to tears. Mademoiselle DuPre cried too when I publicly challenged a grade
she had given me *sur un essai français*. She cried again when I lectured her on
how to deal with students like me and a third time when I converted my
assigned punishment, a five hundred-word essay on respect for teachers, into
a manifesto on respect for students. I didn't dislike either teacher; I simply
didn't spare any thought for their feelings.

These pranks were just the tip of the iceberg. With my gang of ten, a
close-knit group of girls that had assembled by seventh grade and ran
together until graduation, I initiated a near-constant stream of mischief both
on campus and off. The gang and I stole the giant foil-wrapped tire from the
front of the Goodyear store and rolled it all over town, leaving it somewhere
new every night. We were charming and popular, so no one ever criticized us,
just shrugged and rolled the tire back home to await its next hijacking. At
other times, we spray-painted our names—plus the names of our
boyfriends—on fences and walls. Our efforts weren't as deft as today's
graffiti, but we made up for clumsiness with passion and persistence. Often
we broke into locked athletic fields to play softball in the dark or broke into
the ice cream vendor's garage to steal fudgesicles from his freezer. We even
started minor fires once in a while.

On my own, I was just as enterprising. My previous visit to Mr. Waldo's
office had followed a locker-room prank: I brought in a garden hose and
sprayed the shelves of wire baskets holding all the girls' gym clothes, leaving
them to be found the next day, damp and reeking of mold. My punishment—
I always admitted guilt when asked directly—was to wash, dry, and iron all of
the foul-smelling gym clothes at home. Using my mother's three-legged
Maytag, I worked until midnight to finish the task. A few weeks later, I
brought the hose back in and drenched the gym clothes again, this time
without penalty. Whether Mr. Waldo blamed a copycat or simply abandoned
the idea that punishment would deter me, I never knew.

The second drenching was on my mind as a possible reason for his
summons, but it was behind three more likely possibilities. One was some
recent vandalism in the gym for which I was solely responsible. The
vandalism was not too egregious, though it had panache, I thought. The
previous week, I had taken a black institutional toilet plunger from the
custodial supply closet and used the bottom to make dark circles around the
top of the gym above the bleachers. The circles had faded a bit as the rubber
wore off the plunger, but they looked cool on the white cinderblock wall, very

mid-century modern. Another possibility was a lunchtime foray into Miss Carson's classroom to turn on all the gas stoves. I didn't think I had been seen, but you never know. The last possibility was the most recent and, I thought, the most likely: a group joyride across a landscaped hill outside Mr. Waldo's office. The afternoon before, my gang had piled into a Ford Falcon and driven the width of the hill, the car on a steep tilt alongside the building as it swerved back and forth, carving tracks into the manicured grass. I was sure our joyride had been witnessed, probably by Mr. Waldo and the principal, whose office was next door. Being witnessed was the point, after all. Remembering how we had honked, whooped, and waved as we careened across the hill, I was pretty sure I'd soon be explaining the tire tracks still fresh on Mr. Waldo's hill.

On my way to his office, I passed the cafeteria, where my nose told me sloppy joes were on the menu. The spicy tomato scent cheered me a little; sloppy joes were my favorite lunch. Through the open doors, I saw my mother, dressed in her lunch-lady whites, setting up the steam table that kept the food warm during service. I waved as she poured water from a plastic pitcher, but she was looking down and didn't see me. Just as well, I thought; if, by some miracle, I wasn't suspended, I'd rather not have to explain why I was in the hallway during class time. Past my mother, through the large cafeteria windows, I could see a bright expanse of sunlit grass with a few trees at the far end, and I felt a stab of longing to be outside, moving through that grass like a mountain lion or a deer or even a rabbit.

I didn't dwell on the impulse; I had preparations to make. Slowing my pace, I felt for the bulge of my waistband and unrolled my pleated skirt so that the hem fell just below my knees, rather than four inches above. I ran both middle fingers over the creases in my eyelids and under my eyes, then swiped my mouth with the back of my hand. I wasn't wearing much makeup, but I figured that, when it came to a disciplinary summons, less was more. I wasn't afraid of Mr. Waldo, but I wasn't *un*afraid. I had that queasy, anxious feeling that people call a knot in the stomach, not because he might punish or lecture me, but because he might phone my parents. As I reviewed my ranking of recent transgressions, I devised strategies to keep him from calling. Most involved making him believe that it was his disapproval I feared most in the world, that anything else would be superfluous.

Passing the girls' restroom, I contemplated ducking in but decided against it. Two or three minutes behind the grey metal door of a stall would only tighten the knot in my stomach. Every stall would bear witness to a less stressful time, as I was fond of inscribing "Donna + Len 4ever," and other eternal truths on the doors. Having found the right amount of Blue Mist on my fingers and Raspberry Ice on the back of my hand, I didn't need to check my makeup. I knew I'd see just a frosty blue tinge on my eyelids, a little mascara, and a faint layer of foundation hiding a few tiny blemishes on my forehead. And I didn't need a mirror to remind me that I was cute: a tiny, curvy blonde with huge blue eyes and an adorable smile. I wasn't vain; I simply knew what I looked like and how my appearance tended to affect other people, especially men. Any woman who was pretty as a teenager knows what I'm talking about: the way men can't help but stare, struggling to control both their gaze and their expression and generally losing the battle.

I was dressed in classic schoolgirl garb, the outfit that, thirty years later, would launch Britney Spears into the video stratosphere: blue plaid pleated skirt, white shirt, grey sweater, and knee socks. I wore saddle oxfords, rather than high-heeled loafers, and didn't tie my shirt under my breasts, but everything else was the same. It's a great look, especially for a small girl. My blonde hair was long and shiny, parted on the side. I set it at night on orange-juice cans with the tops and bottoms removed, sleeping so as not to disturb the towering row of steel cans that began above my forehead and ended at the nape of my neck. In the morning, I'd add additional cans at the side of my head, and the result was a sleek curve and lots of body that lasted all day. I finished the look with a very thin satin ribbon worn like a headband. Today's was light blue, matching my outfit and my eyes. I looked good.

At the reception desk in the main office were a secretary, who was busy with some filing, and a student assistant, "Sally." I had friends who sometimes manned the desk, as part of a for-credit class called "Office Assistance," but Sally was not one of them. She was what my friends and I called "junior varsity," girls who aspired to the popular crowd but remained on the fringes. Her dark brown hair was teased and sprayed into a huge flip, like a wig that was too big for her head. During our freshman year, I had assumed she wore a fall, a three-quarter hairpiece popular in the sixties, but this year we had PE together so I knew the hair was all hers. Every time I saw her, though, I was startled by the sheer size of her flip. I followed it to Mr. Waldo's office.

"Misterwaldodonnaleetoseeyou," she mumbled, then pushed the door open before he could reply. I wondered if a student could flunk Office Assistance.

I walked into the cluttered office, closing the door firmly behind me. Across the small room, Mr. Waldo sat at his desk in front of a large window. Though the overhead lights were on, the spring sunlight behind him was so bright that his face was, for a moment, indistinct. I couldn't see his only memorable feature: a large brown mole just below the nasolabial fold on the left side of his face. I could, however, see his only memorable article of clothing, the white, short-sleeved shirt that he seemed to wear on all occasions, in all seasons, and with all outfits. I can't swear to this consistency, of course, as I normally saw Mr. Waldo wearing a jacket over his shirt, but in the years I knew him, I watched him take off that jacket at least once in every calendar month, and every time he had underneath a white shirt with short sleeves. They weren't all lightweight summer shirts, either; some looked like heavier weight dress shirts, just without the normal sleeves. I often wondered if his wife bought regular shirts, hacked a foot or so off the sleeves, then neatly hemmed the cut edges. It's the sort of task a Mormon wife, well-trained by Miss Carson's home economics class, would relish.

Once I noticed Mr. Waldo's shirtsleeves, I developed a habit of checking for cuffs when I saw him in a jacket. As cuffless sightings accumulated, I considered alternative explanations for their absence. Perhaps his arms were disproportionately long, and perhaps he paid to have jackets tailored, because suits were a major purchase, but shirts were not. He could therefore be wearing long shirtsleeves that were a little too short to protrude. I studied his arms carefully, but they looked proportional to me. Eventually I accepted that that he probably did wear short sleeves all year 'round. Then the question became *why*. Did his arms get overheated easily? Did he own a lot of ugly cufflinks and need an excuse not to wear them? Did he have a very localized cotton allergy? The possibilities were endless.

By now some readers may be wondering why I seem so preoccupied with Mr. Waldo's sleeves. The reason is that Mr. Waldo was about to become, for me, a symbol of the kind of orchestrated oppression that occurs when dysfunction in a family aligns with dysfunction in a community. I would spend years coming to terms with what he was about to do, and I would spend a good chunk of those years forced to gaze up at him, literally gaze upward toward the lofty place where he sat exalted above most of the community. I would have thousands of hours to study the appearance and behavior of Mr. Waldo, to wonder what about him warranted such elevation, what I could discover about the Mormon Church by contemplating this exemplary figure. As a child, I had done that in a positive way by studying my maternal grandfather, who embodied the community spirit, hard work, and devotion to family that I still associate with Mormonism. Now, as a teenager, I turned my attention to Mr. Waldo. His short-sleeved shirts were information, and I would decode them.

In the meantime, I knew Mr. Waldo's sleeves as one of only two distinctive features, unless you count quintessential ordinariness as distinctive, which I don't. He was average height and average weight with a small protruding belly. He had brown hair, which he wore in a short crew cut called a butch, hair that exactly matched the shapeless brown suit he wore every day. His butch was neither flat on top nor perfectly contoured to his head; it was somewhere in between—either that or it was contoured, and the top of his skull was flat. I couldn't tell because his hair was too thick. I think he was in his forties, but at fifteen I wasn't very good at discerning adult age. He could have been thirty or fifty-five. He wore a thin black tie and black-framed glasses, not full-on Buddy Holly but close.

Behind Mr. Waldo, through the window, I could see the tire tracks from our joyride, though they were less conspicuous than I had expected, just a double wavy line of flattened grass. I wouldn't be asked to pay for any landscaping, then. Beyond the tracks and the hill was a residential street, the first of several, and just past them was One O'Clock Mountain, more hill than mountain at 800 feet but lovely in the spring when, for a moment, swathes of green appeared among its rocks and scree. Again, the longing to be out there flashed across my mind, but I put it aside.

"Sit down, Donna," he said, gesturing toward a molded plastic chair facing his desk. His tone was amiable, but he had indicated a low, uncomfortable seat. I sat, whereupon the corners of his mouth twitched slightly: a smile, in the expressive lexicon of Mr. Waldo. I smiled back, a low-wattage smile, about halfway between polite and ingratiating.

"Donna, we have a problem," he began. "That is, *you* have a problem, and *we* have a problem because of your conduct."

I said nothing. I had prepared for specific charges, not a general indictment.

"I think you know what I mean," Mr. Waldo continued. I raised my eyebrows so that I could appear not to understand without actually telling a lie. He sighed, then listed a series of infractions that included all the ones I pondered on the way to his office plus an episode I had forgotten: throwing cafeteria pizza from the window of an upstairs classroom the previous month. For a moment, I found myself impressed with his intelligence-gathering; then I began to appreciate the mess I was in and the need to launch a strong defense.

"Why am I the only one in trouble?" I asked. "You said a lot of people were involved, so why am I the one sitting here?" I tried to sound more plaintive than adversarial. I knew why I was the only one, but I wanted him to question his own certainty. He didn't.

"You're the ringleader," he said flatly.

I denied it.

"Principal Skyles and I agree: you are the ringleader," he insisted. I was sorry to hear the principal's name; I liked him.

"There's no ringleader," I insisted. "If there were, it wouldn't be me. I was the *last* to join the gang, I have the *least* power." I felt my argument building steam. "If we had a ringleader, which we *don't*, it would be someone who joined in kindergarten!" As I spoke, part of me believed I told the truth. Three of the gang had been tight since kindergarten, long before I met them. By Tooele standards, I was a latecomer, unqualified for the pinnacle of popularity that leadership of the gang implied. Mr. Waldo was unconvinced. He cared little for small social distinctions; his focus was on who authored our misbehavior. My solo shenanigans identified me as the culprit—and were themselves cause for concern.

I began to speak again, but Mr. Waldo raised his hand to cut off further protest before launching into a long explanation of a guidance counselor's responsibilities. At first, I heard it like the dog in the Far Side cartoon, "Blah blah Donna blah blah blah blah blah blah blah Donna blah blah blah Donna." I caught an occasional phrase such as "college admissions" and "truant officer," neither of which applied to me, so I became a little confused. Mr. Waldo seemed to have abandoned the topic of my misbehavior, either that or he was punishing me for it by boring me to death with a long speech. I leaned back, shifting my gaze between his black-rimmed glasses and One O'Clock Mountain, thinking about how cool it was that eyes could do that, alternate between near and far so effortlessly. Then Mr. Waldo stopped speaking, and my anxiety returned, though his upper lip was twitching in the general direction of a smile.

"I know it's hard, Donna, but some kids find it helpful to talk to me."

"About what?" I asked.

"About anything," he replied. "When a student like you engages in anti-social behavior and encourages others to do the same, there is always something wrong." "Anti-social behavior" was what grownups called "acting out" back then.

"I think I'm just high-spirited," I said in my most helpful voice. "I always have been. Maybe I should go out for cheerleading in the fall." Mr. Waldo shook his head, pursed his lips, and exhaled.

"We're going to do some testing, try to get some answers," he said after a long moment. Rolling backward in his wheeled chair, he stood, walked to a gray filing cabinet in the corner, pulled out two booklets, placed them into a manila envelope, and held the envelope toward me.

"That's not fair!" I protested. "I'm not prepared for a test!"

"Not that kind of test. You can't prepare for these." He held out the envelope further and looked at me until I took it.

"These are standardized tests, like the Iowa test. It's eleven o'clock now. Work for an hour in the library, then break for lunch, then return to the library. Sally will give you some number two pencils."

I couldn't believe it. This was my punishment? No classes for the rest of the day and some standardized tests? I had thought the Iowa test was kind of fun, so I was elated! I leapt up, eager to start, but hadn't yet reached the door when I heard my name.

"Donna, after the testing is finished, you will repair the damage you have done to school property, starting with the gymnasium wall you defaced. Mr. Nelson will supply you paint and cleaning materials. You, in turn, will supply him an apology for adding to his many responsibilities."

I felt a quick rush of shame; I liked the school custodian and had not considered the impact of my mischief on him. But shame gave way to relief as I realized that Mr. Waldo did not intend to call my parents. I even felt a small surge of admiration for the guidance counselor. He was being pretty decent, all considering. He had also shown more intelligence than I had attributed to him, both in gathering information on my infractions and in not specifying which ones I had to clean up. I would now have to remember and deal with *all* my recent vandalism, lest I miss something he knew about. Clearly I needed to review my assessment of Mr. Waldo.

Sally eyed me from beneath her giant bangs as I approached the reception desk to request pencils. I could see her weighing whether to ask about my meeting with Mr. Waldo. She wanted to know what had happened but thought it was probably uncool for the likes of her to ask the likes of me directly. It's hard being junior varsity; you're constantly having to gauge the effect of everything you say and do. When you're popular, everything you do is cool because you do it. When you're unpopular, everything you do is uncool for the same reason. In either category, you can be yourself because almost nothing you do or say will change your social status. When you're semi-popular and hoping to move up, you're constantly checking yourself: is this skirt okay? Do I say "hi" or "hey"? Should I date someone in band? I noticed such anxiety a lot, and I sometimes felt bad about it. Watching Sally waver, I almost volunteered that I had to take some tests but decided I'd rather tell my friends myself than have them get the news through the grapevine. And, if I'm honest, I wasn't *that* worried about Sally's pain. I had enough of my own.

The first booklet in the envelope was a standard IQ test, multiple choice and quite a lot of fun. It featured lots of little doodles, geometric shapes inside other geometric shapes and arrows with extra heads and flights. I looked at a pair of doodles then found another pair like it in some way, not identical but related. I looked at a series of numbers or a series of words and found the one that didn't fit. I scratched my head at the numbers a time or two, but the words were easy: horse, cow, ox, goat, sheep, pterodactyl: which doesn't belong? There were analogies and simple logic puzzles: if some Blippies were Tuggies, and some Tuggies were Razzies, then were some Blippies Razzies? Only the blue ones.

After I finished with the doodles and the livestock and the Blippies (and lunch), I went on to a very different kind of test, one I now believe was the Minnesota Multiphasic Personality Inventory, consisting of first-person statements that I had to mark either "true" or "false." Some seemed odd and arbitrary, such as "I enjoy detective stories" or "I have a cough most of the time" (both false), and some seemed to probe right to the core of my being, such as "At times I have wanted to harm myself" or "I have not lived the right kind of life" (both true). After noticing some redundant statements, I realized that they constituted a crude lie detector designed to prevent test-takers from answering deceptively. I began to worry that the test might catch me lying, then to worry even more that the fear of being caught in a lie would force me to reveal monstrous truths about myself. Having just discovered that Mr. Waldo was not the complete idiot I had always thought, I shuddered at the possibility that the test might allow him to see beyond my carefully-crafted public persona—the smart, popular girl with a defiant streak—into the dark abyss that lay beneath. I took the test in a state of high anxiety, walking the line between truth and deception like a tightrope above that abyss.

I finished about twenty minutes before the end of the school day and brought my tests to the administration's office. Mr. Waldo had said I could choose whether to go back to class or not, so I chose not to. For a few minutes, I ambled around the reception area, where Sally had been replaced by a girl I did not know, then went out into the hallway. I considered making an early start on one of my cleaning projects but instead walked the length of the L-shaped hallway over and over again without a hall pass. No one stopped me, and I was growing bored when the bell rang to release my friends for the day.

In memory, the time between my tests and my next conversation with Mr. Waldo seemed very short, just a couple of days. But I suppose several weeks is just as likely. I do recall that it was a Friday because I was wearing my gold corduroy suit, my best outfit, which I wore only on Fridays. I was standing in front of my locker, having just put my purse inside after lunch, when I heard Mr. Waldo's voice behind me.

"Donna," he said; then he waited until I turned respectfully around. I did, but just a touch slowly, out of habit. He was wearing his brown suit again, jacket on and no cuffs showing.

"Remember those tests you took?"

I nodded.

"I'd like to talk to you about the results," he said, striding off with a vague head-tilt that said I should follow. My friend Kathy was sitting at the reception desk as I swept past it in Mr. Waldo's wake; I scarcely had time to roll my eyes and grimace behind his back. Once in his office, we assumed the same positions as before: him behind his gray government-issue desk and me in the uncomfortable plastic chair. I crossed my ankles and looked down at my knees, which were slightly more taupe than usual because I always wore pantyhose with my gold suit.

"I've had a chance to evaluate your test results, Donna," said Mr. Waldo with his familiar quasi-smile and his flat intonation. I nodded but didn't say anything because I was nervous.

"I found out that you have leadership skills," he began.

Uh-oh, I thought. Was he back to the ringleader idea again? But he continued without mentioning it.

"I found out that you're intelligent, creative, and outgoing." He said some more things that were nice to hear, and I remember thinking how much they applied to my whole gang, so it made me feel good to think that they applied to me, too.

"I found out that you're an excellent problem-solver, that you like to work with other people, that you'd rather be outside, that you enjoy reading, that you're angry, and that you're depressed." He gave each adjective the same intonation, as though it were an item on a grocery list.

"I'm *not* angry, and I'm *not* depressed!" I replied. My intonation was the opposite of flat, varying dramatically in both pitch and volume. I wasn't a hundred percent sure what "depressed" meant, but I had run across the term in my reading and knew it was negative. "Angry" I knew very well. Angry meant beating your child because she dropped a cucumber slice or got too sick to finish the vacuuming or somehow offended your unerring sense of what should and shouldn't be. Angry was a dark flush in the cheeks and a grinding of teeth; angry expressed itself with shouting and swearing, with a belt and a rope and steel-tipped boots. My father was angry. I wasn't. I was very, very sure of that.

Mr. Waldo wasn't interested in my denial. He had science on his side. Besides, he had reached the crux of his analysis.

"Most students who cause the kinds of problems that you do are not intelligent. They are disruptive because they are frustrated. You, Donna, have nearly every gift a young person could possess. You can do anything in the world that you want to!"

I truly could not fathom what he was saying. My conscious goal in life was to marry my boyfriend—he was the reason I always wore my gold suit on Fridays—and have lots of Mormon kids. The idea that I had a wealth of natural gifts that could propel me toward more ambitious goals simply didn't have a place to land in my psyche, so it flew back up into the clouds. Nonetheless I was pleased. Mr. Waldo was saying nice things to me, even if I didn't believe them. More importantly, the test had not revealed my inner darkness or my efforts to conceal it. The conversation was going as well as it could possibly go! I smiled broadly at him, and he twitched his upper lip in response. Neither of us said anything for a few seconds.

"Should I go back to class now?" I asked, uncrossing my ankles to stand.

"No," he replied. "I have a few questions first." I nodded, swung my knees to the right, and recrossed my ankles in an exaggerated fashion. As I did, I felt my hose snag on a chair leg and looked down to see a tiny run forming just behind my anklebone. Drat! I needed to get out of there and get some clear nail polish on it, pronto. Kathy would have some in her purse. I smiled again to hurry Mr. Waldo along.

"So what's wrong with you?" he asked.

"What?" I replied. "What do you mean what's wrong with me?"

"Given your capabilities, why do you so often resort to vandalism, verbal aggression, theft, and other petty crimes?"

"Crimes? I think that's going a little far!"

"Breaking and entering is a crime, Donna. Larceny is a crime. Defacing public property is a crime. Endangering the welfare of a child is a crime, a particularly serious one."

"Endangering the welfare of a child?" At that moment, I decided Mr. Waldo had lost his mind. I had four younger siblings; I *took care* of children.

"Donna, you turned on all the gas stoves in the home economics room, and then you left them unattended while everyone in the school was at lunch. Do you know what could have happened? Do you know how dangerous natural gas can be? Actually, now that I know how intelligent you are, I can answer that question for you. Yes, you knew, and you turned the stoves on anyway, endangering every student who walked into that classroom for fifth period and possibly many more."

Mr. Waldo was wrong. I didn't think about the dangers of natural gas at all, just thought the prank would be funny and upset Miss Carson, which would also be funny. I wasn't trying to hurt anyone, but, yeah, okay, it was a little reckless now that I thought about it, though recklessness was typical of practical jokes in my family, which often involved firearms and broken bones. Nonetheless, I tried to see the situation from Mr. Waldo's perspective.

"Well, I think we can both see bad judgment here," I acknowledged gravely. "I guess that means I'm not so smart after all." I congratulated myself on a stunning insight that had the added virtue of modesty, and I waited for Mr. Waldo to concur. Instead he ran his hand through his close-clipped hair, from forehead to nape, sighed, and leaned back in his chair. Slowly, fear began to seep into my mind. What if my darkness was not separate from my mischief-making? I had always seen my pranks as jubilant fun, expressions of my confident public self, but what if they weren't? A couple of them were actually pretty mean, now that I thought about it. Then came a big surge of fear, like a flash flood: what if Mr. Waldo understood my darkness better than I did? The thought was intolerable, and for a moment I had trouble breathing. I tried to swim out of the flood by remembering that my whole gang enjoyed our pranks, but perhaps it just confirmed my essential evil that I was able to entice good people to do bad things.

"Let me try again," said Mr. Waldo. "Donna, when people with your abilities do destructive things, there is always a cause. Something is wrong in their lives."

I knew what was wrong: I was a very bad person. But I wasn't about to say so. I had decided after my baptism that my inner evil was between me and God, and no one outside the family should ever know about it. I had to think of something to distract Mr. Waldo, *fast*. I let him talk as I tried to come up with a tactic, and he was soon on to another topic.

"I am a guidance counselor, and one of the rules I live by is confidentiality," he said, nodding. "You can trust me absolutely. Absolutely nothing you say will leave this room, I swear to you." He folded his arms, his pale elbows sharp beneath his white shirtsleeves.

He wanted confidences then. Confidences that explained why I enjoyed driving Miss Carson crazy. Again, the answer was obvious: because I'm bad. Bad people enjoy making other people unhappy. But we weren't going there. Suddenly, inspiration hit: I remembered the song "Gee, Officer Krupke" from *West Side Story*, where the young gangsters rehearse excuses for their delinquency.

"Maybe," I ventured, it's my upbringing that gets me out of hand."

Bullseye.

Mr. Waldo's eyes popped open. Leaning forward, he came the closest to smiling I'd ever seen.

"How so?"

"Well . . . you know," I replied. I tried to inject maximum drama into the "you know," so he wouldn't press the issue, but he kept staring at me with his scrawny eyebrows raised, waiting for me to continue. Drat!

"Um," I replied. He remained patient.

"What is it about your upbringing that is causing you difficulties, Donna?"

Wait. This was a completely different question! Before he was asking me about the causes of my quote-unquote crimes, and now he's asking about the causes of my *problems*. I didn't want to answer that one either, but I had kind of opened the door with the Officer Krupke line. Drat, drat, drat!

"Remember, this conversation is completely private," he assured me. "I'm not even taking notes." He gestured toward the blank legal pad on his desk. Then he took two ball-point pens from his shirt pocket and placed them in his lap drawer. I remember that they were cheap white Bic pens with blue plastic caps. "Whatever you tell me in here," he continued, "I can't tell anyone, not your teachers, not the school board, not even your parents. You can trust me. You can tell me anything at all, and I will help you."

Still, I said nothing.

"Remember, Donna, I'm not just your guidance counselor; I'm your ward clerk. That's a sacred trust, from Heavenly Father himself. If Heavenly Father trusts me, I think it's safe to say that you can trust me too." Mr. Waldo leaned forward and took off his glasses so I could look into his eyes, which were a light, watery blue. "Is something happening at home? Someone upsetting you? Is someone . . . *hurting* you, Donna?"

Whoa, no one had ever asked me that before! In all the years I had walked around Tooele with visible bruises and welts and cuts, no one had ever inquired about their source or mentioned them in any way, even indirectly. Looking back, I recognize that a few kind people acknowledged them by treating me more tenderly, but no one actually said anything. So Mr. Waldo's question was a whole new world, and I wasn't sure how to handle it. Toughness was my go-to stance, but I was also starting to feel an odd longing to unburden myself. I decided to combine the two.

"Okay," I said. "You asked." I crossed my arms over my chest. "Yes, Mr. Waldo, someone is hurting me. My father beats the holy living shit out of me every single day."

The guidance counselor appeared genuinely shocked, sitting silent for a moment with his mouth agape.

"Can I go now?" I asked, beginning to stand.

"No, Donna, please stay. Excuse me just a moment." As I resumed my seat, he picked up his telephone, punched one of the buttons along the bottom, and mumbled something into the receiver. Then he walked around his desk and sat down next to me in a molded plastic chair like the one I occupied.

"I am *so* sorry," he said, and I believed him.

It may sound odd, but I recall very few specifics of the conversation that followed. I mainly remember the feeling of it, the sense of a giant tide of words being loosed and pouring through me, with Mr. Waldo and me like swimmers swept along. I told him about the violence at home, and there was a kind of wild exhilaration in the telling, so I told him *everything*. I told him about the previous Monday, when my father had returned from work to find me doing homework, rather than chores. Just the sight of me absorbed in an English essay had so enraged him that he threw me to the ground and began kicking me, his sharp-toed boots raising welts on my back and thighs as I curled into a ball to protect myself from the blows. I told him about other beatings and about the roping practice that bloodied my palms and my knees. I told Mr. Waldo about the constant hatred in my dad's eyes and in his brutal words, hatred that relented only when he pulled me roughly toward him for the kind of embrace no father should ever give a child.

Through it all, Mr. Waldo seemed genuinely upset and concerned. He said, "It all makes sense," and "Oh, no," and "I'm sorry, Donna." He asked a few questions, not too many. "How often does that happen?" was one, and the answer always dismayed him. He offered several times to help me, so, in addition to the sheer relief of describing the violence, I began to feel, for the very first time, a little hope that it might diminish, even end. After all, Mr. Waldo was the school guidance counselor. I wasn't sure exactly where that position sat in the hierarchy of Tooele, but it was certainly up there. Mr. Waldo was also in the bishopric of the Mormon Church, one of the bishop's closest advisors. That too was a position of power. Mr. Waldo was someone, and he wanted to help me. I was almost euphoric with the idea.

When the final bell rang, we were still talking. As students with cars headed toward the parking lot, several of my friends appeared outside Mr. Waldo's window where they pulled faces until he looked up then waved politely at both of us.

"Your friends are waiting," he said, rising stiffly from his plastic chair. I realized that we had been sitting for nearly two hours and sprang to my feet.

As I did, I felt the tiny run in my stocking sprint lightly up the side of my leg, but even a ruined pair of hose could not spoil my exuberance.

"Thank you, Mr. Waldo," I said. "I mean . . . I can't . . .." After that huge flood of words, I seemed to be completely dry. "Just thank you," I concluded and dashed out the door.

That afternoon was an enhanced version of normal. From Mr. Waldo's office, I rushed to the school parking lot, where my friends and their boyfriends prepared for the after-school ritual of dragging Main Street, the boys joking and horsing around, the girls laughing and chatting. I walked up as the crowd was beginning to sort itself into carloads, mainly couples and single-sex clusters. My boyfriend was leaning against his white Corvair waiting for me. Len was a senior and a classic dreamboat. I'm sorry to use that word because it sounds so swooningly girly, but it fit Len perfectly. A dreamboat is a boy who is exceptionally attractive and exceptionally kind, and Len was both. He was handsome, six feet tall, powerful, and lean. He practiced Adagio, a partnered acrobatic dance in which a base lifts and supports a flier through various movements and poses. It's quite beautiful. Len was the base, obviously, graceful and strong from all that lifting. He had wavy blond hair and blue eyes, a straight nose, a firm jaw, and a wide smile that carved faint vertical dimples into his cheeks. He looked like a very young Robert Redford in his television days.

I had met Len the previous year. The freshmen had their own separate school that year, but we shared a cafeteria with the high school. Though I dated two sophomores through the spring, by May, Len and I had caught one another's eye. That summer, with some of his friends dating some of my friends, we ran around in the same group. When I became a sophomore, he finally asked me out on a real date. My parents refused at first but agreed to meet Len, and he won them over. For one thing, he wasn't afraid of my father. Having moved to Tooele from Tacoma, Len didn't know my father's reputation for explosive violence, so, as he shook my father's hand, he didn't quiver with terror like the other boys I dated. My parents liked Len even more when he converted to Mormonism under my influence. In fact, my father had recently baptized him and initiated him into the Melchizedek Priesthood.

Len was kind. Len was generous. Len was patient. When my parents withdrew permission for a date, he never complained; instead, he consoled me by bringing a picnic to the house. We'd have some tomato sandwiches on the front lawn, and everything would feel okay. On special occasions, he brought gifts, extravagant in scope if not in price: candy, jewelry, a stuffed bunny bigger than I was. If I shouted at him for spending too much time with his Adagio partner, Len remained calm and reminded me that he loved me. He sounds too good to be true, I know, but that's how he was. Even though I was only fifteen, we already had firm plans to marry. Now that he was a Mormon, we could confidently prepare for a shared future in this life and the next. I would give him many children, and I would help him populate the world he would create when he became a Mormon god. Len needed my procreative power—the women in my family are nothing if not fertile—and I needed his goodness, less to counter my toxic home life than to make my essential badness spiritually irrelevant. His progress would be my progress, his salvation my salvation. Until my conversation with Mr. Waldo that afternoon, I assumed Len was my only chance at a decent life, now or ever after.

Len smiled when I approached, took my books from me, and leaned over for a quick kiss. He opened the Corvair's passenger door for me before sprinting around to the driver's side and easing the car into the queue bound for Main Street.

Dragging Main was what kids in Tooele called cruising, a mid-twentieth-century ritual in which young people rode up and down a particular stretch of road, usually not more than two miles, stopping occasionally for a soda or a snack, but mainly just riding one way, turning around, and riding back the other way, over and over again. If you've seen "American Graffiti," then you get the idea; cruising was wildly popular during the early sixties but died out in most places after the Summer of Love. It may sound silly now (not to mention environmentally unsound), but dragging Main was an important public ritual. Like the Italian *passagiata*, it facilitated and advertised social bonds: that Len and I rode together week after week with no one in the back seat established us as a couple. We were in love, serious about one another, complete in ourselves. That I was pretty and popular raised his status; that he was handsome and drove a gleaming Corvair raised mine. Dragging Main, we told ourselves and others how lucky we were, though, being teenagers, we tended to downplay the role of luck—at least until it ran out.

Main Street came into Tooele from the southwest as Route 36, turned north as Main, and continued northward through town until it turned back into Route 36 just past the giant Goodyear tire. It had only one stoplight, at Vine Street. We drove the stretch from the Hillcrest Café at the turn to the north edge of town, just over a mile. At one end of a lap, we turned around in the dirt parking lot of the Hillcrest; at the other, we just pulled a U-turn wherever traffic allowed. Len's Corvair was muscular enough that he needed only a very small gap, surging out of the turn, occasionally burning rubber, though not compulsively like the Corvette guys. We drove slowly, twenty or twenty-five miles per hour, shouting and waving to our friends as we passed. There were so many of us, especially on Friday afternoons, that Main Street grew thick with cars, but it wasn't a traffic jam, it was a parade, a celebration of being young and mobile and connected.

That Friday, the air of celebration was especially intense. When Len and I stopped at the Dairy Queen for a Coke, most of my friends pulled up within five minutes to find out why I had been in Mr. Waldo's office for so long. I didn't say too much, just that he had been very decent in not suspending me or even giving me formal detention. I explained that I had to do some cleaning and painting, but we all agreed that was a negligible penalty and rejoiced at my escape from any real punishment. They were happy for me, and they were also happy for themselves because, if I wasn't in trouble, they certainly weren't. As we drank our Cokes, our laughter was even more ebullient than usual.

Alone in the car, Len and I didn't talk much about my meeting with the guidance counselor. I wasn't sure what I wanted to reveal, not just about the family secrets I had divulged, but also about the gifts revealed by Mr. Waldo's tests. While never deliberately dumbing myself down for Len, I had spent years trying to master the qualities most valued in a Mormon woman, which did not include intelligence or leadership. I didn't see a place for such gifts in my future with Len, so why mention them now? I doubt I was consciously aware of it, but at some level I understood that acknowledging Mr. Waldo's praise could shift the balance of power between us and destabilize our relationship. He was male; he was two years older; he had to be smarter and more capable than I was. Anything else would have been uncomfortable for both of us. At any rate, I wanted to think more about what to tell him, so, as we drove up and down and up and down Main Street, we mainly chatted about other things: the friends we passed, the new rims he wanted to buy, and the tango we were rehearsing for a big performance.

We quit dragging Main, as we always did, just before 4:00 when the Tooele Army Depot let out, filling the street with commuters and parents who didn't approve of cruising. As usual, Len drove me most of the way home so my mother wouldn't see him drop me off. She liked Len but didn't approve of our afternoon ritual. About a block from my house, in front of Jonesey's Pond, he pulled over to the side of the road, took the Corvair out of gear and put on the parking brake.

"Call you around seven?" he asked. With his long right arm, he reached into the back seat for my books

"Sure," I replied. I leaned in for a quick kiss, and Len gave me two.

"I'm glad things turned out so good with Mr. Waldo."

"Me, too. I thought for sure I'd be suspended."

"No way," he laughed. "They love you at that school. But detention for sure. All you girls should get it, the stuff you do."

I shrugged, smiled, and climbed out of the car, watching as he drove away. Then, with my books in one arm, I walked happily toward my house.

As soon as it came into view, I knew something was wrong. My father stood on the front porch, home earlier than usual. He wasn't doing anything or walking around, just leaning against the wall with his arms crossed looking up and down the street. Once he saw me, he stopped looking anywhere else. Drawing closer, I noticed that he was still wearing his dirty work clothes. As a lineman for the power company, he installed and maintained cables, which involved digging dirt and climbing poles. At the end of the day, his uniform was filthy with dirt and the toxic tars used to treat the poles. Normally, he couldn't wait to take it off, shower, and put on fresh clothes. Even stranger was the fact that he was outside the house but not wearing a cowboy hat, either his straw work hat or his brown felt dress hat. My father always donned a hat when he went outdoors, even for just a moment; it was a reflex. I don't think I had ever seen him standing bare-headed on the porch, but there he was. Uneasy now, I clasped my books against my chest with both arms and plotted a course around the house to the back door. As I circled left of the porch, he pulled away from the wall with his shoulders and took a step toward me. By that point, I could see the dark blood in his face and the working of his jaw, but I kept to my course. Then suddenly he was beside me

"So you've been talking to Mr. Waldo, have you?" he said, seizing my right arm and pulling it sharply upward. When I dropped my books, he kicked one of them across the yard. "I don't know what the hell you told him, little girl, but you're not gonna tell him any more." He continued to yank my arm up and forward as I tried to keep my feet under me. My purse had fallen to where his hand was, so he ripped it off and drop-kicked it. In that split-second, I broke for the house, but he grabbed my other arm and spun me around. When I staggered in the gravel driveway, he drew his whole arm back and slapped me in the face, then slapped me just as hard on the other cheek. As my ears began to ring from the blows, he shoved me backward with both hands until I fell down. I felt the sting of gravel on my cut palms as I crab-walked to get away from what I feared most: his steel-toed lineman's boots. Of course I wasn't fast enough; I was never fast enough. But just the fact that I was trying to get away enraged him.

"You little sonofabitch!" he roared. As he began to kick my shins, I rolled myself up as tightly as I could, my face against my knees, my hands clasped behind my neck and my bent arms over the sides of my face. Blows landed all over my back, sharp and furious; he was using both feet. I squeezed myself even more tightly together, trying to become as small as possible. There was no pain, just a single thought: he's going to kill me. As he kicked, he swore and he threatened, using kicks to emphasize words as though he could physically drive them into me.

"You will *never* (kick) talk to *anyone* (kick) about *anything* (kick) *again* (kick)!" When he wearied of kicking, he pulled off his belt and used it on me like a flail. Then, abruptly, the shouting and the blows stopped. Unable to hear because of the roaring in my ears, I didn't know why, probably a car on the road. Cars had stopped him before. Slowly and very carefully, I began to uncurl my shaking body. As I did, pain bloomed where blows had landed, and my head began to throb. I lay still for a moment, tasting blood in my mouth, then pushed myself into a sitting position and forced my sore neck to move so I could look around. My attacker was gone.

I sat in the front yard for a long time, just sat there in my dirty gold suit with my legs splayed out in front of me. Though in pain, I wasn't too injured to move; I just didn't want to go into the house. My father might be in there with some unspent rage. I couldn't go anywhere else, even to my grandparents' house, because I was a mess. I could see smudges of blood, as well as dirt, on my jacket and skirt. The skirt was almost completely turned around, and the seam over the kick pleat had ripped. My pantyhose were bloody and shredded, my shoes missing. Without getting up, I located them, along with my purse and my books. My purse lay open, its contents scattered, and one book seemed to be in two pieces. It belonged to the library, so I'd have to pay for it. As I sat there, I don't recall having strong emotions about the beating or my father or Mr. Waldo or my mother, who peered out the front window a few times but didn't come outside. I felt more like a bureaucrat making a damage inventory after a natural disaster. Eventually, sometime before dark, I stood up, gathered my belongings, and went up to my room, where I removed my soiled clothing and crawled into bed.

I never did learn exactly what happened between the time I left Mr. Waldo's office and the time I arrived home. I wanted to know, a lot. Did Mr. Waldo call my father to help me or to betray me? Did he somehow believe he could stop the abuse by warning my father off? Did my father lull him into thinking that his intervention had worked or terrify him into eternal silence? Or did he not believe a single word of my story and call my father solely to report my shocking lies? I devised elaborate causal chains that diverged at key questions: Mr. Waldo did or did not believe me; my father did or did not admit the abuse; Mr. Waldo did or did not believe my father; Mr. Waldo did or did not notify church and school authorities; on and on it went, though I never did uncover facts that could help resolve any of these questions. I would have to find different ways to address them.

The following Monday I returned to school with visible bruises on my legs. I thought I might see Mr. Waldo after classes when I went to paint the gym wall, but he didn't stop by. After accepting my apology, Mr. Nelson just gave me a roller, a tray, and some paint, told me where to leave them when I was finished, and left me atop the bleachers. It didn't take long to paint over the plunger-marks, so I left campus via the hill outside Mr. Waldo's office in case he wanted to talk. For a while I stood watching as he made phone calls, put papers in piles, took folders out of file drawers, and put folders into file drawers. He sat at his desk with his back to me at first but faced the window when he went to the file cabinet, which was right up against it, so I'm sure he saw me. I was hard to miss standing alone in the middle of a grassy hill in a pink plaid skirt and a pink sweater, but he didn't show any sign that he noticed me, just opened and closed file drawers with his little shirt sleeves flapping. Finally, he left his office, so I walked home to do some more cleaning.

I rarely saw him at school after that, which was odd because I had previously seen him regularly. When our paths did threaten to cross, he always altered his to avoid me, which was easy because I also altered mine to avoid him. He never called me into his office for another chat, even when I resumed my criminal career by tossing desks from the same window that I had earlier tossed pizza. Part of me was pleased. My friends and I could resume our pranks because Mr. Waldo, for whatever reason, wanted to avoid me. In a way, that made me feel kind of powerful, like I had an invisible shield that could protect me and my friends. The feeling was exactly the opposite of the feeling I had at home, and I liked it.

"Hey, Officer Krupke!" I sang as I hosed down the gym baskets yet again, "Krup you!"

As defiant as I acted, I was also deeply ashamed. I had made a huge mistake in talking so frankly to Mr. Waldo—and not just because of the beating I received. Mr. Waldo now knew how profoundly bad I was. I hadn't explicitly told him I was evil, but I had divulged how severely I was punished for it, which amounted to the same thing. In so doing, I had brought my malignant real self into my bright social world, rather than keeping it at home, where it belonged, and secret. By confiding in Mr. Waldo, I had allowed a kind of existential pollution to occur, and now I needed to contain it and let the remnants quietly dissipate so that life could get back to normal. Avoiding Mr. Waldo while defying Mr. Waldo was the obvious solution.

I did see him twice a week at Mormon services, as I mentioned. Every Sunday, my family attended two services: a sacrament meeting in the morning and Sunday school in the afternoon. During both meetings, Mr. Waldo occupied what's called the stand, an elevated platform for members of the bishopric, participants in the service, and visiting dignitaries. He was the ward clerk, the keeper of all records for our ward, and he spent his time on the stand writing in a large brown notebook. What was he writing? I know he took attendance at services because I could see him counting, his finger bobbing as it pointed at different pews. Families always sat in the same pews, so he'd have an easy task figuring out who was absent and keeping a running tally of services missed for the bishop's annual review. He wrote a lot more than that, though. He took notes on the service: who spoke, what they said, who blessed and distributed the sacrament (torn bits of bread and water, rather than wine), what ordinances (sacraments or blessings) were performed, what announcements were made, what hymns were sung. But he wrote even more than *that*, so I assumed he also took notes on people's behavior. I was right, as it turns out; former ward clerks who have left the church report that they recorded observations such as who seemed better-dressed than they should, given the tithes they paid, and who allowed their children to play tic-tac-toe during dull sermons. All through meetings, Mr. Waldo peered and scribbled, scribbled and peered, not furtively but up on a stage where everyone who was *not* somebody had to watch him.

So I did, and, as I did, something happened. At first, my attitude toward him was the same as at school. I felt a veneer of defiance over a dense core of shame, and I wanted to put our conversation firmly into the past where I could have a hope of ignoring it. I didn't want him to see me, especially at first, so I tried to make myself small and inconspicuous in my family's pew. I didn't want to see him either. He sat at the left side of the stand, far from the central podium, so he was at the edge of my visual field, where I hoped he would soon blur and fade into insignificance, like the organist behind him. He never looked directly at my family's pew, even when counting, so it seemed we both desired the same invisibility. Then one day, apropos of nothing, I experienced a tiny change. I can't recall a catalyst, just one of those shifts that just seem to happen, like faintly jostling a kaleidoscope to reveal an entirely new pattern. It was the shirtsleeves that provided the nudge. I was mechanically checking for cuffs one morning, when suddenly I flashed on the image of Mr. Waldo in those short sleeves and thought "little boy." He wore little boy shirts between his Mormon underwear[25] and his man's suit, and he *was* a little boy. How could I have missed it? It was the key to his whole personality! Let me pause to say that, at 15, I had an unfairly low opinion of little boys, which I have thoroughly revised thanks to the example of my extraordinary son. I also knew nothing of ego states, of the younger selves whose needs and habits drive so much of our behavior. At the time, when I thought "little boy," I thought of my younger brother, whom I regarded as weak and childish, a classic stool pigeon who tried to curry favor with my father by carrying tales but managed only to lose his respect. And mine, for, though we were both beaten, I did occasionally resist or at least try to get away. Though I'm sad to recall it, such contempt for younger siblings is typical in abusive families, where the larger bully the smaller and pass on the anger they receive until even the family pets show signs of trauma.

Seeing Mr. Waldo as a little boy cleared up some of the questions I had about what had passed between him and my father. The guidance counselor had phoned to ingratiate himself with a powerful man who had married into a prominent Mormon family. He may have told himself he was helping me—subtly putting my father on notice that the school and the bishopric had received reports of abuse—but his phrasing would have been obsequious and reassuring. I could almost hear the words.

"You know how young girls are, Mr. Lee. Dramatic. Emotional. Prone to exaggerate."

At any rate, my father was not put on notice. In fact, he got the message loud and clear that the school and the bishopric would dismiss reports of abuse as girlish hysteria. I know because that's exactly the claim he would make—and church courts would uphold—when many years later he faced formal charges for the serial rape of three underage girls. That future was visible in my father's indifference to Mr. Waldo during Sunday school or sacrament meetings. He didn't look at the guidance counselor. He didn't avoid looking at him. He wasn't embarrassed, and he wasn't angry at the ward clerk, who had simply passed on some useful information, both about my big mouth and about how little it mattered.

Once I saw Mr. Waldo as a little boy, I began wondering how he could be such a big noise in the church. My grandfather Bevan was a member of the high priesthood, who outranked the bishop and the stake president, and I understood perfectly why he was important. He was strong, wise, righteous, wealthy, magnanimous, widely admired, and politically powerful. He had been mayor of Tooele for years and had sat on the Utah Power and Water Board, where he had overseen the building of dams. He even looked the part of a leader, tall and dignified, so it seemed absolutely right that he be part of the church hierarchy. But Mr. Waldo? Granted, a ward clerk stood well below a member of the high priesthood, but he still held a position of trust and authority. If the voice of church leaders was the voice of Heavenly Father, then what did it mean that Mr. Waldo's nasal monotone was one of those voices?

I focused in on one fact: he had lied. Born Mormon, I had grown up in a stark moral universe, which was one reason my opinion of my essential self was so low. Mormons don't subscribe to the doctrine of Original Sin, and that's important psychologically, especially to a traumatized child. If you believe that Adam and Eve bequeathed you a massive sin, then you have an explanation of why you might feel evil even when you're behaving really well. You're still responsible for your salvation (unless you're a Calvinist), but you didn't necessarily *do* anything to deserve that sense of badness you carry around. Badness comes with the umbilical cord. For Mormon children, the situation is much different. First of all, Adam and Eve didn't even sin, according to the *Book of Mormon*,[26] much less pass sin down. So all of the evil you have to deal with is your own doing, and you can't mentally palm that sense of badness off on some fruit-munching ancestors. If you feel malignant, as abused children often do, the church says that evil is yours. Moreover, it marks how far you stand from your earthly goal: having your heart transformed by the holy spirit so that your thoughts and your actions are always good and never evil. When Mormons call believers "saints," they aren't kidding: sainthood is exactly the standard to which every church member, even young children, must hold themselves.

So there I was, in the Fourth and Eleventh Ward Church, feeling my vast sinfulness and starting to contemplate Mr. Waldo's. I didn't have to weigh complex ethical issues, such as the balance between student confidentiality and parental rights. I didn't have to compare and evaluate shades of grey. I had simple black and white.

He had promised he wouldn't tell anyone.

He did tell someone.

I knew my scripture. "Lying lips are abomination to the Lord," said the Bible. "Wo unto the liar, for he shall be thrust down to hell," said the *Book of Mormon*. "He that lieth and will not repent shall be cast out," said *Doctrine and Covenants*. There was no ambiguity about lying in sacred texts, and there was no uncertainty in my mind. In a stark moral universe, where hierarchies are rigid and rules are absolute, one conspicuous violation becomes a lever to shift a world. Slowly, painfully, Mr. Waldo's lie shifted my world. It would take me thirty years to understand the story I just sketched, to craft a therapeutically useful version of it and to mine it for what it could teach my patients. But the process started here. During Sunday meetings, I stopped shrinking into the corner of my pew and trying to avoid Mr. Waldo's gaze. Instead I started looking at him, studying him, and I thought about what it meant that this church leader was a lying little boy. As I grew older and bolder, I glowered sometimes, taking pleasure when Mr. Waldo squirmed, dropped his pen, or made some other movement I could interpret as a reaction to the piercing glare of my hate-beams. Juvenile, yes, but at stake was how I understood myself and the universe around me. Looking back, I admire that fifteen-year-old girl glaring across the meeting room at her guidance counselor. Double-teamed by powerful men with a theocratic community behind them, physically and spiritually dominated, she was fighting back with the only weapons she had.

CHAPTER FIVE: Grappling with the Past

Recognizing abuse requires more than knowing what abuse is and how a child's perceptions might disguise it. Equally important is understanding how the adult mind can obscure or alter recognition. Research has demonstrated that an enormous amount of the mind's activity, both information-processing and memory, happens unconsciously, complicating the recollection of abuse and the recognition of its effects, either in the past or in the present. When codependency was first discovered, we believed that unconscious material resulted from repression or other self-protective mechanisms and could be retrieved through psychotherapy. In fact, one of the principal goals of therapy was to make this material conscious and integrate it into personality. The common metaphor for this kind of work is archaeology, which seeks to uncover both the treasure and the trash of the past to develop a more comprehensive understanding of the whole. But there are other views of the unconscious, increasingly visible in the academic psychology of the last twenty years, and these views expand our understanding of how childhood abuse influences adult lives. The adaptive unconscious is not so much a burial chamber for conscious material as a separate cognitive system with some duplication of effort and influence but very different methods and concerns. It's lightning-fast, compared to consciousness, but extremely crude. It's the alert system that cries "Snake!" It's also what's doing the work when you have an instant "gut" feeling about a person or a situation. Its overriding concern is survival, which is why the adaptive unconscious is so important in understanding childhood abuse and dealing with its legacies. The psychoanalytic view is important as well. Scientists don't yet understand how the two models interact, but thoughtful researchers such as Timothy D. Wilson acknowledge the explanatory value of both, as has my own experience with thousands of clients.

Keeping both models in mind allows us to understand one crucial fact: just because a process, feeling, or goal is unconscious does not mean it is necessarily painful or disturbing. Breathing is generally unconscious, as is constantly sizing up the people around us, both of which we do for years on end without alarm. We all have feelings and behaviors of which we are not aware, though our friends may see them clearly. These *can* be threatening to our conscious selves, but the fact that they are unconscious does not *make* them threatening. The adult who claims not to like animals yet always seems to have a furry head in her lap at neighborhood parties may not be repressing or denying anything; she may simply be unaware of an affinity for dogs that everyone else in the room can see. At some point, she may look down, notice that she's enjoying the contact, and revise her view of herself, perhaps even adopt a dog. While such a realization would represent an advance in how well she understood herself, it would not necessarily represent the overcoming of some kind of block or denial. This distinction is important for reasons we will soon see.

Nonetheless, blocks do exist. Children develop defense mechanisms that help them survive, and these may expunge, mask or distort memories. The most dramatic block is the least common: repression or dissociative amnesia. Repressed memory is a wildly controversial topic, one on which researchers and clinicians disagree, often vociferously. The issue is whether the mind can wall off traumatic memories and then recover them later or whether that's actually the mind fabricating new memories to please a therapist or create a dramatic back-story. I have no desire to wade into that tar pit; my professional opinion is that minds do both things. I do know for certain—and this fact is supported by copious research—that abuse in childhood may be completely forgotten or nearly forgotten or even remembered as someone else's experience. The latest edition of the *Diagnostic and Statistical Manual*, which calls this phenomenon dissociative amnesia, defines it as "an inability to recall important autobiographical information, usually of a traumatic or stressful nature, that is inconsistent with ordinary forgetting."[27]

Whatever its mechanism of action, I have witnessed this kind of radical forgetting. Many years ago, my patient "Eve," an alcoholic[28] married to a sex addict, underwent inpatient treatment for both alcohol use disorder and codependency. When she returned home after a month, she was alarmed to find her three-year-old daughter "Annie" suffering night terrors, so she brought Annie to my office, where the child revealed that her grandfather had raped her with a piece of wood. As the law required, social services and the justice system became involved at that point. Shortly after Annie's revelation, a social worker made a videotape of the child describing the assault. Yet just three months later, during her grandfather's trial, Annie replied "I don't know" to every one of the judge's questions. As a result, all charges against her abuser were dropped, and the matter rested—or seemed to rest. As I took my leave, I said to Eve, "That child will act out. Call me when she does."

Twelve years later, Eve called me. Annie, now fifteen, was acting out sexually, sneaking out to get drunk and have sex with her boyfriend. As her daughter's grades dropped from As to Cs, Eve naturally wondered whether her daughter's self-destructive behavior could be a consequence of her rape as a child. Because Annie still had no memory of the abuse, her mother and I showed her the videotape. Despite this extraordinary corroborating evidence, Annie never directly recalled the abuse. All she has are occasional flashes—split-second images of blurry details—over which she has no conscious control. That's all most survivors have. And very few can corroborate their flashes with videotaped evidence or eyewitness testimony or a confession from the perpetrator.

Dissociative amnesia may result from the split in consciousness than can accompany the experience of severe trauma. To protect itself, the child's mind detaches from reality, inhibiting perception and the formation of memories. It can also be the result of immature intelligence, children not recalling what they could not understand. Strong emotion, too, can severely disrupt memory. While fear generally strengthens memory-formation, too much fear does exactly the opposite. For these and other reasons, I generally assume that, if clients have symptoms or intimations of early sexual trauma, it likely happened.

A related phenomenon is suppression, in which a memory of abuse has been deliberately excluded from conscious awareness. Once suppressed, the memory exerts its negative influence invisibly, as in dissociative amnesia, but is relatively easy to recover—and, once recovered, relatively easy to disarm. A story will make the distinction clearer. I once had a colleague in Phoenix with unusual sexual symptoms: she needed all the lights on while making love, and she couldn't bear to be touched on or around her anus. My colleague couldn't recall anything relevant until, finally, she remembered getting pinworms, which live in the digestive tract, especially the colon. After a course of medication, her mother received medical instructions to perform nocturnal "pinworm checks." So every night her mother slipped into her bedroom, lifted the covers, and shone a flashlight at her anus, where any remaining worms would emerge. Suppressed memories can reveal very clearly the difference between a child's perception of events and an adult's. My colleague knew, as an adult, that her mother was neither cruel nor negligent in performing nightly "pinworm checks"; even today, that's what doctors tell parents to do. But the child who woke every night to a mortifying examination by flashlight knew only that something scary and disgusting was happening to her. And that's the memory she suppressed, not the more balanced view. Fortunately, once the story emerged, she dealt with the problem fairly quickly.

Denial, minimization, and delusion are also blocks to recognizing abuse. As a concept, denial is familiar enough to clients that it scarcely needs explaining, though this very familiarity can make it insidious. Those in recovery from addictions may recognize denial as a feature of their addiction, one that came sharply into focus when they achieved sobriety. And everyone recognizes denial in other people. In dealing with childhood abuse, though, people must understand whether and how their habitual ways of thinking may blind them to facts that are conscious yet not acknowledged. At the same time, as we've already seen, the workings of the adaptive unconscious can look like denial. I said a minute ago that everybody recognizes denial in other people, but I think in many cases onlookers are witnessing unconscious processes and calling them denial because they seem so obvious to observers. But the person concerned doesn't see them at all. Let me give you an example.

A colleague of mine worked with "Deena," a middle-aged woman who was emotionally abused by a narcissistic mother. Being psychologically literate, Deena was well aware of her mother's legacy but still not functioning very well, either professionally or in her personal life. She often seemed quite un-self-aware, which was odd given the amount of time she spent in therapeutic groups and general introspection. As my colleague began to probe the disconnect between Deena's self-concept and the self that other people perceived (note: there's *always* a disconnect of some kind) she noticed both denial and unconscious behavior, though they appeared very similar on the surface. In the first instance, Deena used to describe herself as a person who "hates shopping" and "never shops," yet she had a vast wardrobe, regularly sported new clothes and accessories, and talked enthusiastically about her purchases, whether made in a thrift shop or a pricey boutique. That's denial. At some level, if only when she paid her credit-card bills, Deena knew she was an avid shopper. She didn't like that about herself because she wanted to care less about material things (and save money), but she knew it. There was too much evidence hanging in her closet to completely ignore.

Deena was also convinced that she was too nice for her own good. She envied people who could get angry and wondered why she wasn't one of them when both the world and her own life were so full of injustice. My colleague reported, however, that Deena seemed quite angry most of the time, often making cruel remarks about other people, including people she loved, and engaging in passive-aggressive behavior. But, after careful scrutiny over many months, my colleague concluded that Deena truly had no idea that she either felt anger or acted angrily. She was not in denial; she honestly did not know. The negative reactions she sometimes got from people didn't supply her with any evidence; they merely confirmed her view that other people were aggressive and unfair. She was completely unable to see what my colleague would say was one of her defining characteristics.

Why does this distinction between denial and unconsciousness matter to someone trying to cope with childhood abuse? Because acknowledging the adaptive unconscious requires that we expand our therapeutic approach. If things we need to know about ourselves are perennially unconscious, rather than suppressed or denied, then they *can't* be retrieved through talk therapy alone. They can be inferred from behavior and from other people's reactions, but they cannot be directly observed without advanced training in awareness. Some scientists believe that they cannot be observed at all. Moreover, if we need to change unconscious *behavior*, traditional psychotherapy won't do it. We can't "get in there" and make discoveries or alterations; we need indirect methods that recognize how the adaptive unconscious works and can nudge it in healthier directions. We need a combination of approaches.

The adaptive unconscious draws inferences from what we say and what we do. One of the best ways to change it is to give it fresh data by changing our behavior. This insight amplifies the old twelve-step slogan: "Don't think yourself into a new way of living, live yourself into a new way of thinking." We know from cognitive-behavioral therapy that actions can change ideas. Say, for example, that you've just given up drinking, and you're convinced that you will never enjoy your favorite activities again because all of them involve alcohol. Baseball games, parties, restaurant meals: when you think about doing these things, you think about drinking. But, because you hear that slogan so often and have decided to explore new ways of living in the world, you go to a baseball game with your new sober friends. You have a little fun, so you do it again. You have more fun, and the pleasure centers in your brain get activated. No, it's not like alcohol reaching into your neurons and squirting extra dopamine onto your receptors, but it's pleasant, more and more so as you continue to attend ball games. Before long, you no longer believe that you cannot enjoy baseball without a beer or six. Your thinking has changed.

But something is happening at the unconscious level as well. Your adaptive unconscious is learning, taking in new data. The new data are weakening unconscious goals and associations that may be dangerous to your sobriety, the perverse autopilot that can direct your feet toward the beer line even when your conscious intention is not to drink. The adaptive unconscious does not change as quickly as the conscious mind. It will never have a "conversion experience." In fact, conversion experiences tend to involve the conscious mind abruptly catching up with the adaptive unconscious, as when two pals "suddenly" discover that they are in love, even though their friends have known it for years. The adaptive unconscious, though it acts faster than the conscious mind, changes much more slowly, and we cannot directly perceive the change. That lag is one of the reasons it's so difficult to make major life adjustments, even when we're convinced of the value (even the absolute necessity) of doing so. Still, the adaptive unconscious does change. Eventually, its goals will align better with conscious goals *if* it gets experiential data in line with conscious goals. In other words, to enjoy socializing without alcohol, you have to socialize without alcohol. There's no short cut, even if you radically change your thinking.

Another way to influence the adaptive unconscious indirectly is storytelling. Stories are optimal conveyances for information that must be remembered, absorbed, and put into action, which is why cultures encode so many of their values in stories. The reasons are nearly endless, but most of them start with the fact that stories are entertaining. They feature characters we can relate to in scenes we can picture. They show ideas in action, rather than just explaining them. They offer the drama of conflict, the joy of resolution or transcendence, the pleasure and insight of comedy. They excite our imaginations. Every great teacher uses stories to convey principles, and the same technique helps when we try to teach ourselves something. When it comes to influencing our own feelings and behavior, a good story is worth a thousand affirmations. I learned this lesson for myself in twelve-step programs, first Alcoholics Anonymous, then Codependents Anonymous, where I told my story, revising and refining it as my understanding deepened and my recollection improved. Unfortunately, with many meetings now so large that individual contributions must be kept brief, storytelling (in the form of "drunkalogues") has declined in twelve-step programs. Those who would recover from addictions or abuse must find other ways to tell the kinds of stories that don't just chronicle their recovery but actually *contribute* to their recovery and develop resilience.

What kind of story contributes? There are endless ways to tell such stories; how do we know which can help us and which cannot? According to Timothy Wilson, a personal narrative must be satisfying, functional, and adaptive to achieve positive self-change.[29] In other words, it must please us in some way, it must support our present life, and it must promote gradual change. If I tell a story about being abandoned at birth by my father, a Paiute shaman, and my mother, Grace Kelly, then raised by Mormons who hated me for my great beauty and my supernatural powers, such a narrative, while it may be satisfying and even vaguely functional (in explaining my discomfort with Mormonism, will not be not at all adaptive. To be adaptive, a self-narrative must be on good terms with the truth, as far as that can be known. Naturally, I recognize how subjective and contingent truth can be, and I make no claim to have a purchase on some absolute version, especially where abuse is concerned. But there needs to be a correspondence between the story, the teller, and the facts, a good-faith effort to capture, not one idealized feature of personality, but something more complex and closer to a whole human being. Even heroes need flaws to be believable. Finally, the story must subtly build in the changes it wants to promote, find their origins and their antecedents in earlier behavior. If I want to become more compassionate, for example, I can include in my self-narrative evidence of compassion, even if I was often not compassionate. But believability is important here, too; self-narration must be gently tugged toward change, not forcibly relocated. If I've actually been compassionate only once in my life, I can't make compassion the main story I tell about myself—at least until I've racked up some new behavior to keep it company.

The truth is that it's easier to demonstrate than explain how to make a self-narrative satisfying, functional, and adaptive. At the very beginning of this chapter, I told you the story of Mr. Waldo, which is a story about how I began to discover that I was abused. The version you read is a story that helped me change for the better, but it wasn't always so useful. Here's the bare-bones version, as I might have told it many years ago.

In the spring of my sophomore year, my guidance counselor, Mr. Waldo, called me into his office to discuss some pranks that I had pulled, both by myself and with a bunch of friends. We called ourselves "the gang," and we used to do things like break into the home ec room at night, steal fudgecicles, and roll the giant Goodyear display tire around town. I pulled a lot of pranks on my own, too, like hosing down the baskets in the gym locker so they really stank the next day and making dark circles on the gym wall with a toilet plunger.

Because of my solo pranks, Mr. Waldo decided that everything else was my fault too, so he gave me some tests to see why I was acting out. When the results came in, he pushed me to explain why such a smart girl did such stupid things. He said I could tell him anything because he was a guidance counselor and believed in confidentiality. He pushed and pushed, so, to shut him up, I blurted out, "My father beats the holy living shit out of me every single day." That shut him up. Afterward, for some reason, I told him all about my father. I told him *everything*.

I felt great for a while, but when I got home my father was waiting for me. He grabbed me and shouted, "So you've been talking to Mr. Waldo, have you?" Then he beat me. Nothing unusual there—he beat me almost every day—but this beating was really bad. He kept saying over and over that he was going to kill me, and I really thought he would. He kicked me and called me a sonofabitch and said I was never going to talk to anyone again.

I don't know how he found out what I told Mr. Waldo. Maybe Mr. Waldo called him, or maybe Mr. Waldo just talked to my mother, who worked in the school lunchroom. All I know is it happened really fast. As usual, the subject was never mentioned again, so I never found out anything more.

After that day, I hated Mr. Waldo. He was a liar; he had betrayed my trust. He was our ward clerk, so I had to look at him every week, sitting up front on a big platform during Sunday services. He used to wear these ridiculous short-sleeved shirts, even in winter, and for some reason they made me hate him more. I wondered how a man like that could be in the bishopric.

Even this brief version is useful because it organizes memories and feelings. In dealing with trauma, organization is important because it helps us gain control of our experience. Lists are more familiar ways we use writing to organize material—and we will use lists later in this book, several times—but storytelling is organization, too.[30] Most of us tell informal stories all the time—to amuse our friends or explain why we're late to a meeting or prove a point. Most of the time, we don't think about the process; we just do it, and our stories end up organized. Yes, we all know people who have trouble telling stories; they begin, jump ahead, wander off into irrelevancies, suddenly remember a crucial point they left out, and forget what the point of the story was in the first place. But writing will help keep them on track. When telling stories informally, we organize by figuring out the best sequence, which usually involves starting at or just before the beginning of the episode and narrating what happened in chronological order ("I had just left the grocery store and was walking down 9th Avenue when…"). Sometimes we use more elaborate strategies, such as jumping right into the most exciting moment then looking back ("To explain why Abby had punched a hole in my kayak and left me in the middle of Puget Sound, I need to go back a year…"). Sometimes we freeze time and jump around in space ("Meanwhile, back at the ranch…"). Almost always, we choose our sequence based on another organizing strategy: cause and effect. In both versions of my story, I use simple chronological order, not just because it's easy to follow, but because it makes clear how and why I was abused and how my understanding of that abuse developed.

After organizing your material, it's essential to find meaning in the story you tell. In a set of influential experiments, James W. Pennebaker demonstrated that writing about a traumatic experience improves mood, functioning, health, and even immune response.[31] Other studies have confirmed the value of writing about childhood trauma and added to our knowledge of how to enhance the positive benefits of that writing.[32] One way is mindfulness, which we'll talk about in subsequent chapters.[33] People unused to writing or unsure how to transform their chaotic feelings into a meaningful story should not shrink from this exercise. Some studies suggest that, the more chaotic their thinking in the beginning, the more people benefit psychologically from writing about their experiences. "The people who improved the most were those who began with rather incoherent, disorganized descriptions . . . and ended with coherent, organized stories that explained the event and gave it meaning."[34] Millions of people around the world write regularly in journals for exactly that reason. If I add to my bare-bones narrative even a brief comment such as "When you're a kid it sometimes seems like the whole world is against you," I find meaning in my experience, and the story begins to really help me. If I later develop more insight, all the better.

Still, to make a story satisfying, functional, and adaptive takes more than ordering and finding meaning, not necessarily more length, but more understanding. As is always the case when dealing with trauma, a therapist's help can be invaluable, not just in sorting out where your truths lie, but in determining what's a reasonable expectation of change—in other words, what's a nudge in the right direction. Self-narrative can fail by aiming too high, setting expectations beyond what your adaptive unconscious will permit, or too low, not encouraging enough healthy change—or, worse, change in an unhealthy direction. By telling too-negative stories about ourselves, focusing only on the terrible things that were done to us and leaving out the courage or the insight or the persistence we showed, we deny ourselves a chance to affirm and develop those strengths. We do the same thing by telling too-flattering stories about ourselves, substituting feel-good fantasies for the real change that can occur when our goals are realistic and attainable.

My finished self-narrative has many purposes. Several have nothing to do with the psychological value of storytelling: to introduce myself to you, entertain you a little bit, and give you a taste of what it was like to grow up in small-town Utah in the sixties. In other words, the story is far longer and more involved than required to be satisfying, functional, and adaptive. The first *relevant* purpose is to describe the abuse I suffered and identify those responsible: my father as perpetrator, Mr. Waldo as institutional collaborator, and my mother as passive enabler. I don't know for sure how the news of my conversation with Mr. Waldo reached my father, but I choose the possibility that aligns the two Mormon men and leaves my mother passively watching because that is the configuration I experienced on other occasions and is consistent with the steep gender asymmetry in the Mormon Church. When, many years later, my father faced formal charges of incest and sexual abuse in an ecclesiastical court—two different hearings, three different victims—the church excused him of all charges despite consistent and compelling eyewitness testimony. My father offered the "you know how girls are" defense, and the bishopric bought it, so in my self-narrative I put the sentence in Mr. Waldo's mouth. In short, where there is a blank in my knowledge, I fill it with a likely scenario that resonates with my other experiences. I also believe that the encouragement of the Mormon Church and the obliviousness of school officials kept my abuse going far beyond the point when the community should have intervened, so I register that belief in my story.

A second purpose of this self-narrative is to explore the process of discovering abuse: the relief of finally talking about it and seeing someone respond with concern, however short-lived. Even in its barest form, the story communicates how painful it is to taste hope then see it snatched away as abuse is renewed and intensified. But discovery is a two-step process in this story, and that's important too. The messier second discovery is the one that lasts; it's my first recognition of how abuse relates to social power, both in my family and in my community. That's a profound and hard-won insight, far beyond the capacities of most teenagers. I take the credit anyway. I acknowledge the many years I will need to fully understand my insight, but I give myself credit for getting underway. At fifteen, I'm smart, I'm perceptive, and I'm independent, and those are all qualities I want to celebrate and augment throughout my life, so they're central to my self-narrative. I also see my anger at Mr. Waldo in a positive light, as resistance. It's important to my self-concept that I stand up to bullies with a ferocity disproportionate to my small size, so, even though *factually* I'm just sitting in a church pew glowering at my guidance counselor, I present it as active dissent.

My self-narrative also emphasizes my gratitude for my social network, the counterweight to my chaotic and dysfunctional home. Throughout the story, I'm supported by love and friendship in a tight teenaged community, and that community of my peers is central to my identity, far more important than it would be if I had a healthy home life. In other phases of my life, a community of peers has been crucial to me, so, no matter when I tell this story, I want to celebrate and nurture a self that is a friend and has friends, that loves and is loved.

In the process of writing, I pushed my memory very hard but kept to the facts I recalled. I'll admit I imported material from other experiences around that time, but I did not make things up. Imported material includes general descriptions, such as what cruising was like. I remember that Len and I "dragged Main" right after my second conversation with Mr. Waldo, and that I felt unusually happy doing it, but the details are borrowed from other cruising experiences. I'm not one hundred percent sure I smelled sloppy joes on the way to Mr. Waldo's office—it could have been lasagna—but I do remember that I smelled a lunch I liked, and sloppy joes were my favorite all through high school. I'm not one hundred percent sure I was wearing Raspberry Ice lip gloss, but it's likely because I wore that color a lot and rarely owned more than one tub of gloss at a time. I do remember exactly how I was dressed, though, and a lot of other details, especially what people said. I preserved odd phrasing, such as my father's favorite "sonofabitch." I have an ear for dialogue, which is not surprising given my occupation. A good therapist pays close attention to what people say and how they say it.

Though I emphasized my strengths, I was careful not to push my self-idealization too far. I did not turn myself into a comic-book heroine or a blameless victim. I acknowledged some less appealing personal qualities, such as a lack of consideration for people hurt by my pranks. Acknowledging faults both contributes to plausibility and underscores the idea that abuse, unlike money, does trickle down. When someone exerts overwhelming power over you, you tend to enjoy a little power over other people when it comes your way. But I didn't dwell on my shortcomings. I focused on my fortitude and my insight: those were my superpowers, and survival was heroism enough for me.

The story of Mr. Waldo's betrayal is told now. It's believable, it's coherent, and it tells an important story about who I am. I could revise it at some point, but it has been more or less in its final form for many years, and constant revision of a self-narrative actually lessens its benefits. When it first began to take shape, I was coming to terms with childhood abuse and really needed the conscious understanding it provided and the nudging of my adaptive unconscious. Focusing on qualities I possessed but sought to increase created a virtuous spiral to replace the vicious spiral of self-loathing that characterized my childhood and my first years of adulthood. It became part of my psychological immune system, as did other stories about my life, some of which I'll share in subsequent chapters. I committed to those stories, assimilated them into my life, and shared them with other people, which allowed me to take my focus off myself and my history and turn my attention outward.

Practice: Writing a Self-Narrative

Choose a single episode from your past that you would like to write about. The episode can be representative, a good example of a particular type or types of recurring abuse, or it can be different in some way. The choice is up to you; just be sure to limit your focus to a single incident or scene, rather than an extended period in your life.

To begin, jot down the overall sequence of your story and some of the details you want to include. At this stage, concentrate on getting the facts right: the who, what, where, when, and how. Try to recall what was said and done, both by you and by other people. Note also what you thought at the time, even if you later decided you were wrong. If you can't recall exact details, it's fine to import recollections from the same general era. There's no need to make a formal outline; scribbles, circles, and arrows work just fine.

Write a single draft quickly. How quickly depends on the length of the episode, the vividness of your memory, and the speed with which you write. A well-tested technique is to work for an hour in three fifteen-minute bursts separated by breaks of seven and a half minutes. Some people will finish in one hour; some people will need a second hour the following day and possibly even a third.

Important notes: First, if your draft heads in a different direction than you expected, let it. The experience of writing rarely conforms to even the most careful outline and sometimes runs away from it entirely. Second, try to get the facts of the episode down, rather than talking only about your feelings or about the psychodynamics of the episode. If you find concentrating on facts difficult, try switching to the third person (turn "I" into "he" or "she") and telling the story as though you are an omniscient narrator.

Put your draft and your earlier jottings away for at least a few days. Don't even peek at them. If an idea comes to you while you're doing something else, just make a quick note and slip it into the drawer or folder or wherever you have your materials. You're trying to gain the perspective of distance.

After enough time has passed to give you some perspective, revise your draft. While revising, think about the following sets of questions:

1.   Are there facts or ideas in my preliminary notes that I'd like to include in my finished story? Are there additional features I'd like to include?

2.   What meaning can I find in the story? Does it confirm something I believe, or does it move me to question a belief? Does it offer insight into a relationship? A conflict? A mistake? Is that insight clear and straightforward or cloudy and full of contradictions? How do I feel about the story and its meaning(s)? Have my feelings changed over time? Are they likely to keep changing?

3.   What good things about myself are visible—or potentially visible—in the story? Where might a generous, compassionate person give me more credit than I'm giving myself? What personal habits, perceptions, and strengths can the story nudge in a positive direction if I focus on them a little more?

Revise until you feel that your self-narrative is not only organized and meaningful, but also satisfying, functional, and adaptive. Then commit to it and put it away, for now.

Part III

Observing Our Behavior

CHAPTER SIX: Love on Autopilot

"The past is never dead," wrote William Faulkner. "In fact, it's not even past." For survivors of trauma, daily life affirms Faulkner's famous words as patterns learned in childhood play out again and again in adult relationships, whether we recognize those patterns or not. Wittingly or unwittingly, we gravitate toward people and situations that seem familiar, delighted when we feel instant intimacy with strangers or instantly at home in a new environment. We recapitulate the past even as we try to escape it. There's an old joke in the codependency community: if you meet someone and feel as though you've known them all your life, you *have*. As a young adult, I replayed many scenes from my abusive childhood without realizing it. Over nearly a decade, for instance, I suffered a series of sexual assaults without recognizing that I had been violated. Once a child whose body was used and abused by powerful adults, I had never learned that my consent mattered. So, as a teenager and a young woman, I regarded other people's desires as irresistible, whether I welcomed them or not. Refusing an unwanted advance, even an aggressive one, would have seemed to me like refusing the incoming tide— what would be the point of such a grandiose and empty gesture? The water would come in anyway, regardless of my desires or needs. As my next story makes clear, however, by my late twenties I wasn't the only one being hurt by this pattern. I tell the story to illustrate the ways that my past became, not just *my* present, but the present of someone I loved and wanted to protect but ended up hurting.

Her name was Roxy, and she was the most broadly talented human being I had ever met. She could do anything and do it *well*. She could build bookshelves and cabinets. She could build a whole house. She could take apart a car, piece by piece, rebuild it so that it ran better than it ever had, paint it, and make it look showroom fresh. I know because she did that to my old white VW, transforming it into my new blue VW. When she was sixteen, she ran away from home and found work on a touring drag show, quickly taking charge of the drag queens' elaborate hair and make-up. Later, despite having dropped out of high school, she earned a master's degree. She could cook, really cook; she made modern foodies look like "C" students in Miss Carson's Home Economics class. She could also *teach* people to do anything well and had worked her way up to being the director of vocational and industrial education in Maricopa County, Arizona, where we both lived. She was athletic and tiny, like me, and Italian to the core, with black curly hair and an enviable natural elegance. Everyone in our group wanted her, but she wanted me.

We met at one of her legendary parties when I was twenty-six and she was thirty-one. The classic pueblo she had restored was a perfect party spot, especially with the elaborate sound system she had designed and built, which featured speakers in every room. She served food worthy of a spread in *Gourmet* magazine, including three kinds of fondue. Drinks were equally delicious: Daquiris and Brandy Alexanders with fresh-grated nutmeg. Reeling from a painful break-up, I was not in a cocktail mood and sat glumly nursing a beer outside on her screened patio. I was furtively watching my ex with a new woman, who turned out to be Roxy's ex, so we had a certain amount of smarting pride in common. Did she sit down with me to make our exes jealous? Probably. But if her flirtation was strategic to start, it quickly became earnest. Reciprocating her interest, I shook off my glumness; soon, we were deep into an animated conversation about, of all things, tractors, which she seemed to know a lot about for a city girl. I didn't realize it yet, but Roxy was interested in everything. By the time she slipped her arm around my waist and asked me to dinner the following night, our exes could have given birth to twin goats in front of us, and we probably wouldn't have noticed. We were soon dating exclusively, then living together. I moved into the beautiful pueblo, where every stick of furniture and slice of homemade bread reflected Roxy's graceful, generous style, and I basked in the warmth and beauty of our life together.

Except when I didn't. Happy as I occasionally was—or, more accurately, as I thought I should be—I often seemed bent on destroying everything positive in my life. I had a warm, solid relationship with a wonderful woman I liked, admired, and deeply loved. I had a rewarding job as the director of a center to combat sexual assault, a position in which I helped people, educated my community, and directly influenced social policy. Roxy and I had a large circle of interesting friends and high status within the vibrant urban community that was Phoenix in the late 1970s. By all conventional measures, I was thriving. Nonetheless, I repeatedly jeopardized my relationship, my job, and my friendships by drinking too much and sleeping with colleagues who were close to home or involved in long-term relationships. I had an affair with an instructor who worked for Roxy. I didn't break it off, even when he fell in love with me and wanted to proclaim it to the world, starting with his boss. I had an affair with a singer-songwriter who performed at one of our benefits; she had a long-term partner back in Ohio. I slipped out of board meetings and other professional obligations to drink on the sly, partied every night, and used amphetamines to deal with the hangover. Into a life that looked ideal, I imported more and more disruption until even I could see that I was out of control. Understand that, at this point, I had a graduate degree in social work, in the course of which I had undergone traditional therapy. Before that, as an undergraduate, I had met weekly with an excellent counselor. Now I worked in the general field of mental health and specialized in sexual violence. In other words, I was optimally positioned to understand my own behavior, yet I scarcely knew myself at all and had absolutely no idea why my life always seemed on the verge of chaos. I knew only that I was unhappy much of the time and that I couldn't find a relationship that worked, no matter how hard I tried.

After the instructor and the singer-songwriter, my next affair was with a professional colleague who was also good friend of Roxy's and mine, as was her long-term partner. In other words, dallying with Maggie could wreck my home life and some important friendships—and it certainly wouldn't help my professional reputation. I understood the danger, of course, but I didn't care. My thinking at the time was bizarre, resting on two convictions retained from childhood: that I was, at my core, a truly vile human being and that, in my life, outcomes would always be bad no matter how well I behaved. Though no longer a practicing Mormon, I still saw the world in stark moralistic terms. Good people had the capacity to shape their lives, to behave well and enjoy the fruits of their virtue. Bad people, though they might exhaust themselves striving to be good, would receive only punishment. So why bother striving? Doesn't it make more sense, while waiting for the hammer to strike, to fool around a little? I certainly thought so.

I had known Maggie since I met Roxy but got to know her better when we sat together on an *ad hoc* committee on ways to disseminate information about sexual assault. Primarily an artist, Maggie also did graphic design as a community service, producing brochures and posters to inform the public about dangers to public health and safety. Almost as soon as the committee began meeting, Maggie showed sexual interest in me: looking a little too often and letting her gaze linger a little too long, touching my arm when making a point or leaning into my shoulder when showing me design ideas. Though I recall these gestures now, I didn't see them at the time—or, rather, I saw them the way I might see an advertisement for a car wash if I didn't own a car: as an insignificant fact in a world full of much more important facts. First of all, though she was conventionally pretty, I wasn't attracted to her. She was about ten years older than I, six feet tall, and willowy, with unruly black hair and olive eyes. She always wore dresses and skirts, the more diaphanous the better, with lots of layers and uneven hems. She favored tiny, intricate patterns and olive hues, which emphasized her eyes, but professed surprise when anyone commented on the color coordination. The whole effect was a bit too fussy and ethereal for me. To be fair to Maggie, what I knew about fashion in the 1970s would fit on a three-by-five index card, so she may actually have been very stylish. I just knew what I liked in women, and Maggie wasn't it.

My own look was the opposite of fussy; I generally wore neat jeans, a snap-front western shirt, and cowboy boots. On my tiny frame, the effect was cool and feminine, which I augmented with jewelry. Well ahead of the punk-inspired curve, I had three piercings in my left ear and one in my right. In the matching holes, I wore simple gold studs with two tiny diamonds behind the left stud. I owned many necklaces, but I regularly wore two, a textured gold chain and a slender silver chain dangling the symbol for "woman." I wore two rings as well, a sturdy signet ring on my left pinkie with a bezel-set pink topaz next to it. That ring also featured two tiny diamonds and was a cherished gift from Roxy. My most dramatic accessory, though, was my hair, which had darkened just a bit since my high school days. It was now a rich gold with caramel lowlights. I wore it long and loose and parted on the left; from there it flowed straight and shining to the middle of my back. The Phoenix sun tanned my skin to match—no one wore sun block in those days—so my overall look was classic California golden girl with a cowboy edge. I attracted a lot of attention, especially when I wore any shade of yellow or light blue to match my eyes.

I was wearing a form-fitting yellow cowboy shirt with tiny red flowers when Maggie and I decided one Friday afternoon to go to my house for a late lunch. She had dropped by the center to show me some sketches just as I was heading home for a bite, so I invited her along. I often ate lunch at home because the pueblo I shared with Roxy stood just three blocks away from my office in a gorgeous Phoenix neighborhood called the Encanto. I enjoyed the noonday walk and sometimes invited friends and co-workers home with me, so the lunch itself was not unusual. What was unusual was that I would not be rushing back to the office after lunch. I had planned to initially, but, when Maggie and I stopped at a deli to pick up some bread and cheese, we also bought three bottles of wine. We told each other that we'd spend some time discussing our informational campaign, but we both knew work was over for the day. That was okay. It was Friday; we had put in some late nights over the past few weeks, so we deserved a break. Though it was barely 2:00, we were ready to party.

We walked companionably past classic southwest houses with their pale walls and terra-cotta roofs, talking about our campaign. Within a few minutes, we reached the pueblo, a single-story house with white walls and a flat roof. Bougainvillea poured over the walls, and thickets of silver-leaf cassia almost hid the bungalows on either side. High above the pueblo stood two clusters of California fan palms, one in the front yard and one in the back. Dark brown shutters framed the windows, freshly painted to match the wide wooden door in the center of the house. Even without the welcome mat, the overall effect was inviting, and Maggie remarked, as she had many times before, that she should paint a watercolor of the house.

"Roxy would love that," I murmured.

Inside, the large main room was shade-cool even though the fall day had grown hot. We crossed to an elevated dining area featuring a long trestle table with matching benches. Though slightly medieval in appearance, it fit well with the southwest ambiance, a little Catholic grandeur transplanted to the new world. Leaving a bottle of White Zinfandel and our deli purchases on the table, I gestured for Maggie to sit down then ducked into the kitchen to grab glasses, plates, and cutlery. When I emerged, she was sitting with her back to the table studying the room.

"So beautiful," she said quietly, and it was. On the far side of the room was a cast-iron fireplace with a graceful arched frame that echoed the arched doorways leading to the kitchen and the bedrooms. Near the fireplace was a huge grey sofa piled with handmade cushions, and on the floor Roxy's valuable collection of real Navajo rugs, geometrically patterned in red, grey, and brown. It was as lovely as a room in a design magazine, yet it looked comfortable, lived-in. Even just remembering it, I can feel its warmth.

I returned to the kitchen for some Seven-Up to add to my Zinfandel. Seeing the soda, Maggie smiled. I was that rarest of creatures: a drunk who could not hold her liquor, and everyone in our social circle knew it. After two wine coolers, I'd be visibly intoxicated; after three, I'd be in full blackout. I made my first cooler with lots of Seven-Up.

"Roxy will be home in a few hours," I explained. "I don't want to be too drunk when she gets here."

"We're fine," Maggie replied. "It's only a little past two." She poured herself a glass of wine, sans soda, and began slicing the baguette and the cheese log we had bought. I watched as she prepared a plate for me: chunks of bread smeared with soft white cheese and walnuts with a few olives on the side. I nibbled—the cheese log was very salty—but concentrated more on my sweet, fizzy cooler. I loved the first drink of the day, the way it loosened my tongue and the tense muscles in my shoulders, the way it turned harsh daylight to a mellow golden glow that made everyone more beautiful and vivacious. This first drink of the day, at the end of a challenging week, was especially welcome.

Having scarcely eaten any food either, Maggie soon poured herself another glass of wine.

"Liquid lunch," she explained, and we both burst out laughing as though she had said something hilarious.

"I could put the food in a blender if you'd prefer," I quipped, and we laughed hard at that, too.

"No," she said. "We just need to make it bite-sized." She picked up a tiny chunk of bread, smeared it with a dab of log cheese, and moved it toward my mouth, which I opened without thinking. "Isn't that better?"

It wasn't better. In fact, it seemed vaguely ridiculous, but Maggie kept smearing tiny chunks of baguette with cheese and feeding them to me. And, each time, I obediently opened my mouth like a child, though I did not reciprocate. After many more bites, I decided to take action.

"I have to go to the bathroom," I said, almost knocking over my bench as I leapt to my feet. Pacing back and forth from the sink to the laundry hamper, occasionally stopping to gaze through the tiny open window into the back yard, I stayed in the bathroom as long as I could, hoping that my absence would somehow extinguish the feeding-game in the other room. Finally I flushed and slowly washed my hands.

When I emerged, Maggie had relocated to the sofa, a full glass of wine on the coffee table in front of her. Next to her glass was a brand new wine cooler for me. The bread and cheese log had not made the move, I was pleased to see; in fact, they weren't anywhere in sight. Maggie must have put them away while I was in the bathroom. She stood when she saw me.

"I tried to put on some music, but I couldn't get your stereo to work," she said.

"It's custom," I explained. "Roxy built it. There are six sets of speakers all over the house, and you have to switch on the ones you want." I walked over to the console and turned a knob. "Have you heard Joan Armatrading yet?"

"No," said Maggie, so I dropped the needle on the brand new record, and the singer's staggered staccato syllables tumbled from the four speakers in the living room. "Down to Zero," my new favorite song, sounded exquisite.

Maggie sank back down onto the overstuffed sofa and patted the seat next to her. When I sat, she gazed deeply into my eyes and took my hand between hers.

"I'm so attracted to you," she said as the song surged into the bridge. I wished I had thought to play something a little less romantic—busy banjo music, perhaps. Maggie was looking at me the way a dieter looks at a large slice of chocolate cake.

"I really want to kiss you," she whispered. With the hand she was not holding, I grabbed my new wine cooler and took a series of noisy swallows, wiping my mouth on my sleeve afterward.

"Roxy will be home soon," I blurted.

"No, she won't," murmured Maggie. "It's not even three." With two fingers, she lightly brushed a strand of blonde hair away from my face then kept the fingers on my cheek as she leaned in for a kiss.

"You're so adorable," she murmured, nuzzling my face. I said nothing as she took my wine cooler from my hand, set it down on its coaster, then folded me in her arms.

When Roxy walked in ninety minutes later, we were still dressed—barely.

Though Maggie and I leapt up and began tidying our disheveled clothing, the motions were pure reflex; there was no way to conceal what we had been doing. Roxy looked from Maggie to me to the drinks on the coffee table, her face flushed and her jaw working. Spotting one of my sandals near the cast iron fireplace, she studied the shoe for a while. She was visibly angry. Finally she stepped toward Maggie and looked down at her.

"What are you doing, Maggie?" she asked, her voice low and shaking.

"I'm sorry," Maggie replied before bursting into loud sobs. "Please don't tell Olivia." Olivia was her partner of a decade and our good friend. "She'll leave me, I know she will." She continued along the same lines while Roxy walked to the front door and flung it open.

"Get *out*!" she shouted. "Get out of here *right* now! I don't want to see you *ever* again!"

I sat silently on the couch as Maggie, still weeping, lurched around the room begging for our discretion and babbling about her purse. Spotting it under the coffee table, Roxy grabbed the purse and threw it out the front door. She threw it overhand like a football, then nearly slammed the door on Maggie, who fled after it. Roxy was angry, which was unusual for her. But she did not seem to be angry at me.

She disappeared into the kitchen then reappeared with a short glass and a bottle of Jack Daniels. Sitting at the far end of the sofa, she poured two fingers, drank it off, then poured two more. Her face was no longer flushed, and she sat hunched over her glass as though throwing Maggie's purse and slamming the front door had exhausted her. When I finally glanced sideways, I could see tears in her eyes, but she did not cry, nor did she rebuke or question me. She got silently drunk on her whiskey while I sat motionless on the other end of the couch. We sat there until I got up to make myself another wine cooler, this one stronger than usual. I remember drinking half of it as the room slowly darkened, first with the failing light of evening and then with the oblivion of blackout. The next morning, hung over as usual, I pretended to sleep until Roxy left for a Saturday class. All weekend, our house was quiet and subdued; then, on Monday, I came home from work to find the stereo blasting "Stop, in the Name of Love" and Roxy dancing around the kitchen making bread. That night, she made only one reference to the episode.

"I want you to promise me something," she said, her voice soft and serious.

I stiffened but nodded.

"You'll never bring another cheese log into this house." She gave a quick bark of laughter then wheeled out of the room leaving me puzzled but relieved. She never mentioned Maggie again, and the episode soon receded into the past, just like my affair with the instructor and my affair with the singer-songwriter. At work, I saw Maggie once in a while, though we did our best to avoid one another without being too obvious about it. So it wasn't from her that I learned Olivia had dumped her. I didn't hear any details, nor did I want to. The incident was over, sealed in its compartment, not really part of my life.

CHAPTER SEVEN: Self-Reflection

This brief episode was not the worst of my betrayals, but it was, in many ways, typical—typical of my behavior before I came to terms with my childhood trauma and typical of many trauma survivors. One of the key principles it illustrates is the way childhood trauma impairs—or even destroys—a human being's ability to set, respect, and even perceive the interpersonal boundaries necessary to successfully negotiate life among other human beings, in other words, life. Because boundaries are so central to much of this book, I'd like to take some time to discuss what they are. Strictly speaking, a boundary is something that fixes a limit or extent. Traditional boundaries were physical, and boundaries are still easiest to understand in physical terms. A physical boundary may be a clear and visible sign, such as a fence at the edge of a property, or it may be variable and hard to discern. In my state, the entire shoreline, from the western Pacific coast to Puget Sound, is public property below the "mean high water line," an important physical boundary that can mark the difference between enjoying a nice, legal walk on the beach and trespassing. But that "line" isn't an actual line; it's an average of an inference based on beach debris, an average that moves over time. In fact, the closer you look at that boundary, the fuzzier it gets. Much less clear and more variable are physical boundaries between people. We don't end where our skin meets the air; normally, we claim some of the territory around us. "Personal space" is the common term for the physical distance people maintain from one another, which varies with culture, circumstances, degree of intimacy, and power relations. We constantly negotiate where the limit of you meets the limit of me, and it's not the same physical place between strangers and friends, between members of different cultures, in a crowd or in a wide-open space. On a bus at rush hour, I may sit comfortably next to a stranger with our thighs and shoulders touching; on the same bus at midnight, such proximity would be weird, even threatening.

Manipulating or breaching physical boundaries is one of the ways people try to influence one another. If I "get in your face," invading your physical space with my body, my loud voice, or my pointed finger, I seek to diminish you by shrinking the amount of "territory" you control. It's an act of physical aggression, even if I don't touch you. If, coming into a meeting, I avoid an obvious seat near you, physically isolating you in a room, I wordlessly assign you too much space. That's a more subtle snub, but it's still playing out in physical space. Businesses manipulate physical boundaries for profit in ways too numerous to mention. A bar, for example, might install "butt funnels" that force patrons into frontal contact, increasing the ambient sexual tension and making the venue a more attractive place to stay and spend money. Sometimes businesses build up, rather than break down, personal space. In a stunning book on the machine gambling industry, MIT professor Natasha Dow Schull demonstrates how video poker machines are routinely placed within design features that draw invisible lines around gamblers to give them the sense that their physical space is protected. The purpose of such "protection," of course, is to create an illusion of safety so that gamblers won't notice the more pernicious breach of other boundaries, such as the extent or limit of their discretionary income.[35]

Most of the time, most of us are adept at perceiving and negotiating physical boundaries without even thinking about it. We know where to sit on the bus so that everyone feels comfortable. We recognize when we're being encroached upon, and we step back to restore our sense of autonomy. We recognize when we're being isolated and step forward to demonstrate our sociability. We don't encroach or isolate without an invitation or a good reason. We may not immediately perceive subtle manipulation by commercial interests, but, once informed, we can recognize them. Growing up, most of us learned these skills by observation and practice, by exerting increasing control over our own physical space and having that control respected. The exceptions are people like me.

When you are physically or sexually abused as a child, you do not learn to control your physical body because it is not reliably yours to control. At any time, when you are sleeping or studying or just walking through a room, it can be co-opted by an urge that originates in another human being. It can be forced to gratify someone else's desire or absorb someone else's rage, while your desires, your rage, not to mention your terror and pain, are dismissed as irrelevant. At the most, they may briefly inconvenience your abuser, but they will not stop the abuse. In fact, they're more likely to escalate it, as the abuser retaliates for whatever slight annoyance you manage to produce. In my case, scrambling away from my father's lineman's boots tended to result in harder and more sustained kicking, though I scrambled anyway.

Until well into adulthood, I did not learn that I had a say about what happened to me physically, especially with sex. It sounds so counter-intuitive, I know, but I automatically, instinctively accommodated any desire focused on me, whether the brutality of a rapist, the passion of a lover, or the curiosity of a friend. My own desire—or lack of it—never entered my mind. All my lovers, from high school crushes to near-engagements to one-night stands, had been men and women who sought me out. I was never the pursuer, always the pursued, and pursuit alone guaranteed a positive response from me. I wasn't just easy; I was a sure thing.

So, when Maggie pursued me, resistance simply didn't occur to me. First of all, I was barely aware that I did not welcome her advances. In retrospect, I can see evidence of reluctance in my long visit to the bathroom and my occasional references to Roxy's return, but I don't recall feeling real aversion—or interest or anything at all. I was simply *there*. I'm not excusing my behavior—being there, in this case, was culpable—I'm simply trying to explain the mental state that produced the betrayal. I'd call it "thinking," except that it was not thinking; nor was it feeling or any other kind of sentience. It was a kind of autopilot that guaranteed the free exercise of someone else's will on my physical being, almost as though I had no will of my own. And I honestly didn't, right then. Though blessed with a strong will and lots of determination in other domains, when it came to sex I was compliance on legs. It was as though I had no physical boundary, no way to establish what was Maggie and what was me. For practical purposes, on that afternoon, she had no end, and I had no beginning.

As important as what I thought (or didn't think) was the automatic nature of that response. Yet another legacy of physical and sexual trauma can be a habitual inattention to the present moment, to experiences, thoughts, feelings, and physical sensations as they occur. To survive our childhoods, we devised strategies to distance ourselves from the trauma; if we could not physically get away, then perhaps we could do so mentally. I mentioned in the last chapter the full dissociation experienced by a few survivors; much more commonly, we imaginatively escape our distressing experiences by detaching from our thoughts and feelings. All human beings develop this capacity to some extent, and many of us spend a large fraction of our time mentally wandering away from whatever we're doing.[36] But there's wandering, and then there's exile. As a young woman, I didn't experience my present perceptions, thoughts, and feelings, then mentally drift away, then return to the present moment, as most people do. Instead, I checked out completely. My inattention was profound and sustained, almost like sleepwalking. Psychologists call this phenomenon depersonalization, a feeling of detachment from both inner and outer experience. It was functional, in the sense that I could walk and talk and do my job and look good doing it and have a girlfriend and make plans for my life and carry out some of those plans. But it was dysfunctional because I could not really experience that life. Moreover, estranged from my own perceptions, feelings, and thoughts, I made increasingly bad decisions—or failed to make any decisions at all—jeopardizing even the minimal functionality of my sleepwalking self. I was headed for a crash, but I was not there yet, and the truth is that survivors of trauma can remain in a state of semi-functionality for a very long time—a lifetime, in fact. To illustrate some other legacies of childhood trauma, let's return to the couch in Phoenix, where Roxy sat silently swigging Jack Daniels on one end while I sat motionless on the other.

After Roxy interrupted Maggie's and my lovemaking, I became overwhelmed with three emotions: shame, guilt, and fear. I sat, paralyzed, a vile human being wretchedly awaiting punishment. Roxy had never punished me for anything, not even my two affairs, but that fact did not register anywhere in my brain. It was irrelevant, like my desire had been. Nor was Roxy punishing me now. She had yelled "What are you doing, *Maggie?*" and thrown *Maggie* out of our house. She was visibly angry at *Maggie*, and, once my seducer had gone, her anger seemed spent. An observer would conclude, based on her slumped posture and the tears in her eyes, that Roxy was sad. Certainly a trained psychotherapist should recognize that. But there was no observer in the room, no trained psychotherapist, no *adult*. There was only a terrified child in a grown-up's body reliving a primordial trauma that had little to do with Roxy or Maggie or the infidelity of that day.

Had I been truly present at that moment, as a functional adult, the sight of Roxy's tears would have awakened genuine remorse: the knowledge that I had hurt this wonderful woman and the regret befitting such an injury. Some guilt would be appropriate, as would some shame, and maybe even a little fear that I might finally have tested Roxy's love too many times. Guilt, shame, and fear, in proportion to events, can be useful emotions, helping us avoid problems, rectify mistakes, and make beneficial changes in our thinking and behavior. To be useful, however, they have to be commensurate with our wrongs, and they have to be truly ours, not assumed or inherited. We will talk more about such "carried" feelings in chapter five; for now, let's consider how an adult might lose access to adult sentience and become trapped in the distortions of a child.

"The Child is father of the Man," Wordsworth famously wrote, acknowledging the persistence of childhood experience, thought, and personality into adulthood. Ideally a source of continuity and the basis for a rich inner life, childhood remains a potent influence throughout our lives—a joyous one, in Wordsworth's case. Psychologists have less exuberant ways of describing the persistence of childhood in the adult personality; one of the most useful, for our purposes, is the notion of "ego states," which are sets of related feelings, thoughts, and behaviors linked to particular stages of development. The theory holds that we all have multiple ego states with one generally dominating at any given moment or, for better or for worse, overall. For example, Wordsworth welcomed his Child ego state when he contemplated nature; it was the reason his heart "leapt up" whenever he saw a rainbow. These ego states, however, are not intrinsic but shaped by our experiences. When children suffer trauma, particularly over time, their Child states become "wounded" in ways consistent with the trauma. The characteristics of the Wounded Child ego state cluster around lack or loss: feeling abandoned, helpless, needy, hopeless, and worthless. In my case, physical and sexual trauma at a very early age left me defenseless and terrified, convinced I was bad and deserved horrific punishment, paralyzed by shame at my essential, irredeemable evil. As a young adult, I slipped easily into this ego state and, once there, occasionally got stuck. Many things could induce it, some of them quite innocuous. Shame is a trigger for me, even a small amount and even today. For example, if I speak sharply to a cashier who ignores me or gives me the wrong change, I feel like a terrible, terrible person. Many times, after a sleepless night, I've returned to a store, sought out the cashier, and tendered a heartfelt apology, only to learn that he or she didn't even remember the episode, it was so minor. But sexual shame was always the ultimate trigger. I mentioned a moment ago that, when Roxy caught me on the sofa with Maggie, moderate shame was an appropriate response. The problem arose when my appropriate shame triggered the global, existential shame of the Wounded Child ego state. I was no longer experiencing an emotion that might help me modify my sexual behavior but one that kept me frozen in the impotent terror of an overwhelmed five-year-old. The shame was no longer appropriate, and it certainly didn't belong to me.

A second important ego state is the Adapted Adult Child. This ego state represents an older stage of development that responds differently to trauma. It doesn't remain overwhelmed like the Wounded Child; it adapts in one or more crucial ways. It can mimic a rebellious teenager: defiant, critical, contemptuous of rules and authority. Or it can seem more like an ersatz grownup, a simulacrum of adulthood that may achieve considerable professional success and personal stature. Its characteristics often reflect common-sense adaptations to the child's traumatic environment, temporary fixes that ultimately prove maladaptive and destructive of interpersonal relationships. In its classic form, the Adapted Adult Child disowns needs and desires; seeks self-control and the control of others; reflexively judges, criticizes, and punishes; considers performance the sole arbiter of value; and has strong perfectionistic tendencies. In my story, the Wounded Child was much more prominent than the Adapted Adult Child, though the latter will feature prominently in much of the following discussion. One more very important ego state is the Functional Adult, but I'll leave discussion of that one for a later chapter.

To recognize and deal with the effects of trauma on ego states, it's necessary to develop two complementary habits: the habit of self-reflection and the habit of mindfulness. The first involves analyzing behavior retrospectively. Here, a therapist, a support group, or a lay collaborator can be very helpful, someone to ask questions, provide feedback, or offer different perspectives. I'll have much more to say about collaborative reflection in the next chapter because it's an important part of my journey and something I recommend for others. For now, I want to talk about how we can all develop tools to understand what happened to us and why we behave in the ways that we do.

Self-reflection is a very different thing from obsessive rumination. Its goal is not self-punishment or self-condemnation but self-discovery. In the last chapter, I introduced a meditation to increase the compassion we feel for ourselves and others; people who tend to excoriate themselves for their mistakes should practice that meditation regularly while engaged in self-reflection. A compassionate approach toward the self can discover more and promote more lasting change than can a judgmental approach, so compassion is practical as well as kind. A good place to begin reflection is with an incident where you behaved in ways that surprised, dismayed, or upset you. An incident worth exploring will often leave you saying to yourself, "I can't believe I did that" or "I can't believe I did that *again*." Perhaps you lost your temper or slept with someone you had vowed to avoid or bought something you couldn't afford. Chances are, you were on autopilot just as I was with Maggie, so it will take some work to excavate the thoughts, feelings, and experiences driving your behavior. Be patient, be compassionate, be honest, and be thorough; don't settle for the first answer that occurs to you, but let time, further reflection, and outside feedback test your insights.

Your goal is to find the roots of your behavior, so don't focus too much on contingencies. You want to ask "Why did I do that?" but the answer will not lie in other people's behavior, except insofar as it replicates archaic behavior that lives on in your mind. In other words, if you ask, "Why did I buy a $2,000 pair of shoes rather than pay the mortgage?" the final answer is not, "Because the sales clerk talked me into it." Sometimes contingencies can offer clues, however. If you yelled at your child because he called one of your rules "stupid," think about that bit of data. Were you in control and acting more or less like an adult until that point? What was it about the accusation that set you off? Thinking back, does it remind you of anything you experienced or witnessed as a child? Does the word "stupid" evoke strong feelings in you? When have you felt those feelings before? It can be very useful to cast your mind back to the moment you lost control and ask, "How old did I feel then?" Sometimes you'll get a mental picture or a feeling of a rough age: "little kid, really small" or "almost a teenager." Then you can ponder your recollections from that period and consider how those experiences may affect your life now. The key is not so much excavating everything you can find but excavating what's relevant to your life now, what's causing problems for you. By starting with maladaptive present-day behavior, you focus your inner work and avoid the pitfall of becoming preoccupied with your own history. If the unexamined life is not worth living, as Plato's Socrates (and my .sig file) attest, neither is the over-examined life.

The ideal is to understand and move forward.

So what kinds of adult behavior may have roots in childhood trauma? We've discussed my utter lack of sexual boundaries, and indeed versions of this problem prompt many survivors to seek help, whether from therapists, from self-help groups dedicated to sex or love addiction, or from books and other media. But there are many different ways that childhood trauma can damage sexual boundaries, depending on a dizzying number of variables, including age, type and duration of trauma, influence of other people, and the personalities of all involved. As I explained in the introduction, boundaries may be weak or nonexistent, as mine were. They may also be fortified walls that keep out everyone and everything. And they may be intermittent, impenetrable at times but flimsy or absent at other times. Some survivors act like walled fortresses with people they love but easily fall into casual relationships with people they don't like or respect. Some maintain great boundaries most of the time but submit unthinkingly to authority figures or tortured artist types. Some have difficulty allowing anyone in at all and throw up solid or intermittent "walls." These are not necessarily physical, though extra-protective clothing, crossed arms, and barrier accessories sometimes feature. More commonly, they are walls of anger, disdain, boredom, confusion, or pain, buttressed with any number of distancing mechanisms, including aggression, silence, and compulsive amiability.

Some of these mechanisms are downright ironic. Both promiscuity and excessive romanticism, for example, can be ways of protecting ourselves against the emotional vulnerability of real love. The common element is that these boundaries do not mediate between autonomy and intimacy, the way healthy boundaries do. They do not adapt appropriately to people and circumstances but ignore or defy people and circumstances. Adults with healthy boundaries are self-contained and judiciously open; they are also alert to other people's boundaries and respectful of them. Damaged boundaries pervert self-containment into isolation and openness into reflexive surrender. People who have them may not always respect other people's boundaries—and, in some cases, may not even see them.

A physical boundary issue can be a good, clear starting place for self-reflection. You need not begin with something as dramatic as a sexual crisis, though, obviously, you'll want to get there eventually. Consider minor, everyday issues. Did you try to hug someone and feel him or her shrink away? Or did someone's hug make you uncomfortable, even as you told yourself it shouldn't have? Did you show up at someone's house without calling or reluctantly admit someone who showed up at your house uninvited? Did you snoop on someone's cell phone or ignore someone snooping on yours? All of these instances are worth examining as potential breaches of physical boundaries, especially if they happen regularly. The behavior may indicate that, as a child, you had little privacy or little say in whether or not to express affection, which does not make you cold or impolite or nosy or a doormat, just someone who needs to take more care in setting and observing physical boundaries.

In addition to physical boundaries, there are psychic boundaries and a lot of overlap between the two. Sexual boundaries, for example, are often both physical and emotional—and sometimes mental as well. To simplify this discussion, I'll confine my classification to three categories, physical, emotional, and mental, with the caveat that these are not so much distinct divisions as categories of convenience, with many boundaries spanning all three. If someone shows up uninvited at your house, for example, they cross more than a physical boundary because home invokes a complex web of thought and emotion, from feelings such as comfort, safety, and love to deeply personal ideas about identity, with home typically being the domain of a more private self. My point is not to further demonize drop-in visitors but simply to underscore the intricacy of what might seem, at first glance, the fairly straightforward concept of crossing a line.

Emotional boundaries involve our sympathies, our antipathies, our hopes, our fears, our desires, our aversions, our joys, our sorrows, and innumerable other feelings. In our emotions lie our energies for living, as well as a lot of what we consider essentially "us," which is why it's so important to set and maintain emotional limits, to control what comes in and what goes out. These boundaries are largely internal, though they may have external catalysts, corollaries or symbols, such as an emotionally manipulative mother's homemade chocolate cake, baked to contrast her own selfless devotion with her child's monstrous neglect. People with weak emotional boundaries may be easily influenced, even moved to action, not just by other people, but by advertising and commercial design, film and other media, and political rhetoric. People with weak emotional boundaries may also intrude on others, criticizing, offering unwelcome advice, asking personal questions, making inappropriate sexual comments, stirring up guilt, shame, anger, or fear in any number of ways. In contrast, people who are emotionally over-fortified have difficulty feeling sympathy or empathy. They may not recognize emotional responses in other people, whether those responses are positive or negative. Even if they are not physically isolated, such people can end up emotionally isolated, unable to attune or connect in any meaningful way with the people around them. We all have the experience of feeling "alone in a crowd" once in a while, but for survivors with emotional walls, the feeling is commonplace. As before, damaged emotional boundaries can be mixed: at times impenetrable, at times nonexistent, at times even vaguely functional. There may be particular situations or character types or emotional responses to which we are vulnerable, as I am to shame.

Just as the body is often the vehicle for physical boundaries, speech is often the vehicle for emotional boundaries, so self-reflection in this domain often involves looking at the ways we speak—or, more generally, communicate. Do we, for example, speak sarcastically to avoid revealing anything about ourselves and keep people at a distance? Do we instead reveal too much too soon? Given the culture's collective fascination with the intimate details of people's lives, the idea that there is even such a thing as "too much" may seem quaint and old-fashioned, yet "TMI" remains a frequent online rebuke—and a good indicator of weak or missing emotional boundaries. Over-disclosure takes many forms beyond revealing too much private information too soon. It may also involve being unable to keep someone else's confidences or feeling constantly obligated to explain everything we do. It can be spontaneous, or it can be prompted by leading questions, and a truly telling sign that you have allowed an emotional boundary to be breached is asking yourself, "Why on earth did I answer that question?" Again, it's necessary to find the root answer, not the easy excuse, "Well, she asked, and I didn't want to seem rude." As with weak or absent physical boundaries, weak or absent emotional boundaries often trace back to experiences in which the child's feelings were criticized, mocked or completely disregarded.

Spotting patterns in the ways we communicate will aid reflection. Some habits—shouting, name-calling, and mocking people's weaknesses, for example—are obvious breaches of emotional boundaries—the shouter's the target's, and those of anyone in earshot. But there are many more subtle forms that may be harder to recognize. Patronizing or habitually correcting people, for example, can be the emotional equivalent of crowding them physically; it nudges a psychic boundary to enlarge one party and diminish another. Interrupting or finishing other people's sentences functions similarly. Yes, people with healthy psychic boundaries sometimes do both when excited about a shared passion or project, but under most circumstances such actions disparage another's feelings and ideas while inflating our own. That interruption has become a staple of political debate, especially among television pundits, is due precisely to this effect; a weaker position seems stronger to many viewers when its advocate verbally encroaches on other speakers. Sunday morning news shows often look to me like boundary-shoving matches in which substantive issues are merely convenient pretexts (and early casualties).

In addition to habitual speech, relationship patterns can reveal emotional boundary issues. We've already discussed romantic and sexual relationships, but there are many others that can be traced back to childhood trauma. One obvious category is relationships with parents, former caregivers, and their surrogates. Advice columns are full of anguished letters from people whose partners seem over-involved with members of their family of origin. The "momma's boy" and "daddy's girl" are familiar cultural clichés, adults whose primary relationship remains with the opposite-sex parent even as they enter into marriage or long-term romantic partnerships. I don't mean to suggest that close relationships between parents and their adult children are intrinsically suspect; I have such a relationship with my grown son, and it's a source of great joy in both our lives. But he's not my first call in a crisis or a moment of celebration; my wife is. And his primary confidante is his wife, not me. Our roles in one another's lives are clearly defined, not by a formal set of rules but by our everyday behavior. If I know he's having a special dinner with his wife, I don't phone, for example, and he accords my wife and me the same courtesy.

Problematic relationships often muddle the roles of parent (or caregiver or sibling or friend) and partner. Because these roles are complex and vary between cultures, communities, and families, it's difficult to determine exactly where one role encroaches on another, but we can point to a few constants. The first has to do with intimacy. Partners commit to sharing themselves and their daily lives. Ideally, this sharing involves sex, affection, trust, and self-disclosure, as well as a unique language of words, gestures, and symbols emerging from the partners' history together. Much of that sharing *must* be private, so if someone outside the partnership regularly receives full reports of the couple's intimate behavior, including conversations, that's a clear breach of an emotional boundary. Moreover, while it's difficult to quantify intimacy, it's not uncommon to find partners more intimate with outsiders than with their spouses or lovers. Not long ago, an online newspaper printed an exemplary letter from an anguished girlfriend; I have edited it for brevity but preserved its essential message:

[My boyfriend] lives with his female best friend and doesn't seem to have many others. Their lives are so entangled it's like they are married: they share a computer, home and vehicle; she is estranged from her family and has been "adopted" by his; she chooses his clothes etc. He assures me they are just friends, but she [walks] around naked. I believe they are hugely codependent, but he can't see it and is very defensive of her. I really like him and thought we had something, but it seems he'll never be free from her. It may sound as if we are teenagers, but we are in our mid-40s.[37]

The letter appeared in a regular column that publishes reader's responses, and many of those responses said, in one way or another, "I've been there too." In other words, the unacknowledged triangle is a common phenomenon, a conclusion my practice would support. There are three parties to this problem, and all of them may have damaged emotional boundaries. The boyfriend has intermittent boundaries; he's too well-defended against his girlfriend but lacking limits where the roommate is concerned. The roommate may even be part of his defense against the girlfriend (certainly, his *defensiveness* about her is), though he could also be completely oblivious to the whole triangle. My own experience shows that such ignorance can afflict even intelligent, well-informed people. As for the roommate, wittingly or not, she's breaching multiple boundaries, not only enmeshed with the boyfriend but encroaching on the prerogative of the girlfriend in multiple ways, not least by stripping off her clothes. She may well have weak or missing emotional boundaries—and possibly physical and sexual boundaries, too.

The big question mark is the girlfriend. She wrote the letter, so she's aware that her romantic situation is fraught. I would urge her to reflect upon her attraction to this man. Did she know about his enmeshment with his roommate but move ahead anyway? Does she believe the roommate is the problem and, once he's "free of her," the relationship will thrive? Does she have a history of choosing partners who, for various reasons, do not offer her true intimacy? Partners who need fixing? A "yes" to any or all of those questions suggests that she too has boundary issues, not just in failing to limit other people's encroachment on her emotional well-being, but in encroaching upon theirs. After all, trying to "fix" other people is a radical intrusion, no matter how dysfunctional their lives may seem.

Let's pause for a moment to consider enmeshment as a boundary issue that can be traced back to childhood trauma. Simple enmeshment can happen any time two people with weak emotional boundaries become involved: they lose their distinctiveness, their independence, and begin behaving more like one another, spending increasing amounts of time together, even adopting one another's habits and perceptions. Usually, in such enmeshment, there's a stronger personality that dominates the shared reality, but both parties must experience boundary failure for the dynamic to work. More profound enmeshment usually traces back to a traumatic relationship with a caregiver, usually a parent. As we grow up, we normally begin to turn away from our families of origin toward our peers for companionship, friendship, and romantic love. As sexual interest begins to stir, we may accept information and respond to inquiries from our parents (or, more commonly, flee from such conversations as from swarm of killer bees), but we will normally undertake the majority of our investigations—and all of our hands-on experiments—with our peers. What can disrupt that process is a parent who treats us like a partner in some way. Physical incest is the most conspicuous example of this phenomenon, but emotional incest is its less-known psychic analogue, and it too can do considerable damage.

With emotional incest, a child is called upon to meet an adult's or older child's relational needs. The most common form is spousification, a dynamic in which a caregiver treats the child as a surrogate husband or wife, often because the real partner is absent or emotionally distant. Such children may assume adult responsibilities, participate in adult activities and discussions, even dress or act like adults. They may become their caregivers' closest friends, confidantes, and emotional support systems at the expense of their own social development. I'll admit that, whenever I hear a teenager say "My mom/dad is my best friend," I always hope they're just buttering up the parent to ask for a bigger allowance. Unfortunately, children have no way to resist spousification; they're naturally enmeshed with their caregivers. Worse, many children feel thrilled to be given adult roles, whether as the "man of the house" while daddy is away or as the keeper of mommy's secrets. At times children perform adult duties very well, better than the available adults, making them seem comfortable and happy in developmentally inappropriate roles. "She's an old soul," a father may say as a way of explaining why his teenaged daughter spends every weekend antiquing with him, rather than hanging out with her friends. Of course, healthy children do enjoy sharing their parents' activities; the question is whether these activities take the place of peer interactions and whose needs they meet. Children should not become responsible for the emotional well-being of their parents, no matter how rewarding it feels.

The effects of childhood spousification are hard on adult relationships. When spousifying parents remain alive and reasonably proximate, they rarely relinquish their privileged status without a battle, whether any parties acknowledge it or not. In fact, the biggest fight can be establishing that a problem exists. I once had a client I'll call "Emma," who married "John" right after they both graduated from college. While they were dating, Emma noticed John's close relationship with his mother but thought well of him for his gratitude to the woman who had brought him up. She believed that John's devotion made it more likely that he would be equally loyal to her and responsive to her needs, a claim she had read in women's magazines. And he was, it turned out, a loyal and dutiful husband. Unfortunately, his mother remained the center of his life. She had a key to the house and would come and go while the couple was at work, cleaning, stocking the fridge, or cooking dinner for the three of them. In return, she asked that John perform "men's jobs" around her house, from raking the leaves to changing light bulbs. Mom did not keep a list of tasks that John could do on a single weekend morning; instead, she called nearly every day with an urgent request, which John immediately leapt up to fulfill. What bothered Emma the most, however, was the intimacy of mother and son. Their jokes were private; their conversations were murmured; even after a decade of marriage, they would break off speaking when she entered a room and say "you wouldn't understand" if she asked to share the joke. She tried, calmly and gently, to explain that she felt like a third wheel in her own marriage, but both John and Mom treated the accusation as crazy.

"Any other woman would be grateful to have so much help!" they both said, and many of Emma's friends agreed. Emma felt very low, especially when Mom discovered that she could no longer drive after dark and needed even more of John's time and energy in the evening. Finally, after many years, Emma cracked.

"I want a divorce!" she cried. "Go live with your mother! You're more married to her than you are to me!"

That's when I met John and Emma. Fortunately, to save his marriage, John became willing to "divorce" his spousifying mother, though it took him a very long time even to see that their relationship was a problem. And Mom never did see it, not too surprisingly. In her mind, her "man of the house" had grown up to marry a selfish shrew who begrudged him the manifold joys of a mother's love.

There are many other ways that emotional trauma in childhood may lead to boundary issues later on, ways that we learn to feel emotions that aren't ours and learn not to feel emotions that are. Some of these appear in in the appendix, but no such summary can be comprehensive. Such lists should stimulate, not limit, your reflections. If you find yourself wondering whether your thoughts, words, or behavior hint at a problem with emotional boundaries, consider what healthy boundaries are supposed to do: control what comes in and what goes out so as to facilitate interaction with other people and with the environment. That's the goal, and falling short is reason for reflection, however different the lapse may seem from my examples.

In addition to emotional boundaries—and overlapping with them—are mental boundaries. The way we understand the world and ourselves is very much shaped by other people, by people we know who have taught us and by many more people we don't know who influence us in ways too numerous and subtle to describe. That said, we normally construct views of the world and ourselves that feel authentically ours, that constitute our sense of what is real and true. Our convictions may include verifiable scientific facts, disputed religious or political beliefs, and a host of ideas in between. They may change dramatically over time, or they may remain relatively constant; they may be coherent, or they may be scattered and contradictory; they may be conscious or largely unconscious. We may regard our perceptions as individual and contingent, or we may insist that they represent some form of absolute truth; regardless, they shape our thoughts, feelings, and behavior to an astonishing degree. Good mental boundaries help us navigate among ideas and concepts, allowing in those with value and excluding those that are harmful or irrelevant. Good mental boundaries are more important than ever in this "information age," when one click of a mouse or a television remote can expose us to us to more new ideas than our great-grandparents encountered in a year.

Perceiving our own mental boundary issues can be extremely difficult because we're using our minds to examine our minds. The complex of ideas, opinions, and perceptions we regard as our "reality" seems normal to us, so in many cases we must draw on other people's input, whether the advice of a friend, the collective responses of many people, professional opinions, published research data, or any number of other sources. Unfortunately even getting to that point can be a tremendous struggle. For example, we're all familiar with the eating disorder *anorexia nervosa*, which disproportionately afflicts young women. A common feature of the disease is a body dysmorphia in which sufferers see themselves as overweight despite a low number on the scale, visibly protruding ribs, or anxious comments from friends. They perceive these raw data but interpret them differently than do the people around them: as encouraging signs, perhaps, or goads to redouble their food restriction. Regarding the shape of their bodies, their mental boundaries are fortified walls, their sense of reality fixed on the notion that they need to lose weight despite considerable input to the contrary. Sufferers benefit enormously from locating the roots of these mental boundary issues.

Some roots clearly lie in trauma, including both abuse and neglect, physical and psychic.[38] Much more pervasive is psychic trauma, specifically, injury to a child's sense of self. As we've seen before, such trauma does not imply deliberate abuse or neglect; it can be caused by well-meaning parents seeking the best interests of their children. For example, parents may over-direct a child's educational, recreational, or social choices, deciding for the child that she will become a doctor or join an elite dance group even if her native talents and inclinations lead another way. Sometimes this influence is subtle, amounting to little more than reacting with pleasure to some accomplishments and ignoring or disparaging others. Because children want to please their parents, they tend to repeat actions that gain parental approval. If that's winning an honorable mention at the school science fair, rather than first prize in a national skateboarding competition, they get the message quickly: be *our* version of you, not *your* version.

Children who are spousified may also develop self-concepts based primarily upon the needs of other people and lacking integrity or autonomy. A related phenomenon, which we have touched on but not described, is parentification, in which children take on roles belonging to a parent, often heavy caregiving responsibilities. Large families typically require older children to supervise their younger siblings, but babysitting is not parentification when the sitter's duties are carefully delimited and developmentally appropriate. An eight-year-old, for example, can "keep an eye on" a three-year-old who is playing house in a cardboard box in the living room, if Mom or Dad is close by and ready to respond to a shout. If Mom's at work and Dad's passed out upstairs, then the same eight-year-old is parentified, particularly if sole responsibility for the toddler is commonplace. With parentification, there's often a dual role reversal; the children become parental, and the parents become childish, often requiring care themselves. Such "generational boundary distortions," which also include spousification, occur frequently in alcoholic family systems and show a clear correlation with eating disorders—and with other pathologies stemming from damage to children's self-perception.[39] Anorexia offers a chilling example of how sufferers can exhibit both flimsy and excessively fortified mental boundaries, especially in regard to their self-concepts. They can be, at the same time, both deeply enmeshed with parents and impervious to those parents' pleas to eat. The one place where their trampled mental boundaries suddenly become stone walls is, tragically, the place they most need to see through others' eyes.

Anorexia is a complex problem deserving much more time than we can devote to it, but it does introduce perhaps the most important mental boundary issue affecting the lives of trauma survivors: the perception of the self. As survivors, our ideas about ourselves tend to be variable and extreme. We may be grandiose, convinced of our very special place in the world, confident in the respect, admiration, and envy of others. We may be abject, convinced of our utter worthlessness, confident that we deserve only loathing and contempt. We may alternate between the two extremes or, paradoxically, combine them to become, as they say in twelve-step meetings, "the piece of shit at the center of the universe." What's common in all these formulations is that we derive our self-esteem from somewhere outside ourselves, whether by preserving an archaic remnant imparted by our parents or by constantly looking for external feedback, from the salaries we earn to the success of our children to the number of our Instagram followers.

In my case, after my infidelity with Maggie, I had to deal, not just with inappropriately extreme emotions, but with an atavistic self-concept, an idea I had inherited from my parents' version of Mormonism. On its own, the Church of Latter-Day Saints is famous for maintaining sky-high standards of behavior. "Be ye therefore perfect," says the gospel of Matthew, "even as your Father which is in heaven is perfect," and Mormons consider this verse a commandment with the force of "Thou shalt not kill." Perfection is expected, not just in religious life, but in every other realm: education, work, marriage, even the performance of simple, everyday tasks such as chopping an onion. Not surprisingly, a recent study found that seventy-seven percent of young Mormon adults described themselves as perfectionists, and within that group about two-fifths (or thirty percent of the total number surveyed) qualified as "maladaptive perfectionists," meaning that they accepted the church's high standards and felt continually diminished when they fell short.[40] Many reported a disabling fear of sin and of divine punishment, as well as persistent guilt and shame. Obviously, I can relate. My parents added a twist, however. First, they obscured the difference between divine punishment and the earthly punishment my father dealt out on a regular basis. My father became God's deputy—not that God couldn't devise His own punishments if He wanted (and I did fear that possibility), just that He had a habit of relying on fathers to handle children. Second, my parents promoted a backward logic of punishment, maintaining that, if I were being beaten, I must have done something wrong. In other words, the sin didn't produce the punishment; the punishment retroactively produced the sin. Trained from a young age, I accepted every tenet of this system of belief so thoroughly that, even in my late twenties, even after renouncing the Mormon Church, I still saw myself as an abject sinner awaiting richly-deserved punishment. My mental boundaries were strong against evidence to the contrary but nonexistent against corroborating evidence. Even healthy adults have some of this tendency—it's called "confirmation bias," and it refers to our habit of noticing only data that support what we already believe and ignoring all other data. Survivors of childhood trauma, however, have an extreme and virulent version, as we saw in the case of anorexic self-image.

And it's not just ourselves about which survivors can hold some unusual ideas. In extreme cases, we may have difficulty perceiving the behavior of other people or understanding our environments. For example, some survivors have trouble recognizing aggression directed their way. Often such people seem admirable, peace-lovers who remain calm and positive despite provocation. I agree that choosing to ignore aggression is an honorable and healthy response, one we should celebrate. But I'm talking, not about consciously de-escalating, but about being unable even to see a threat. In a competitive business, for example, the inability to spot an offensive play may limit advancement, not just because the undetected play could succeed, but because failure to counter it could look like indifference or naïveté.

In reflecting upon our own behavior, we should consider what we fail to do, think, or say, as well as what we do, think, or say. If we notice that other people seem more perceptive in some regard—more able to spot aggression, for example, or more able to tell when other people are in love, we can try to identify our deficit and trace it back to its roots. A common discovery is the habitual denial or misrepresentation of childhood perceptions. Some children hear their parents fighting every night yet are told that it did not happen, that they must have dreamt or imagined it, that Mommy and Daddy never fight. They see their parents' angry faces, hear the brutal language they hurl at one another and the alarming sounds of struggle, yet are assured that Mommy and Daddy love each other very much. When children are told that they don't see what they see and that they see what they don't see, they can become adults who struggle to maintain a coherent, functional, reasonably accurate view of the world, an individual "reality" to ground their experience. As adults, they doubt themselves, not just their capacities but their most basic perceptions. A sad example is the adult who becomes the victim of a crime such as an assault on a crowded subway but fails to fight back or flee or even say "stop" because, as they later reveal, "I couldn't believe it was happening."

A related boundary problem, one I've mentioned before, is susceptibility to commercial persuasion. In this case, debased self-worth may combine with weak or intermittent mental boundaries to allow uncritical assimilation of manufactured desire. Advertisers and producers spend prodigious amounts of time, energy, and money figuring out how to engineer maximum boundary collapse in the shopping public. They hire social psychologists and behavioral economists; they commission research to discover, not how to build a better mousetrap, but how to market a cheaply-made mousetrap to as many people as possible, whether those people have a mouse problem or not. Some industries, such as the global alcohol industry, spend far more on marketing than on product development—so much so that competing brands sometimes market the same beer under different names.[41] The people who sell us these products are master-influencers, and all of us have succumbed at some point, spending too much money on things we didn't need or even really want. That said, some people seem especially vulnerable to commercial persuasion, whether in a brick-and-mortar store or online. For such people, careful self-reflection is essential because compulsive shopping may have roots in many different kinds of childhood trauma, including a form of perfectionism that implies it can be reached through material means. Children raised to pursue an ideal of physical perfection (impossible standards of appearance, dress, or grooming) or social perfection (impossible standards of popularity, reputation, or success) may keep looking for the products or services that will finally get them to that ideal. Other possibilities, according to the very limited research on childhood trauma and compulsive shopping, include all the categories of trauma covered in the last chapter, especially emotional trauma.[42] It's essential that we carefully investigate specific purchases so that we can trace what they represent to us now (whether that is part of the product's "brand identity" or something completely different), what we thought and felt when we bought it, what feelings we might have been trying to *avoid* by buying it, and where we might have encountered any of those feelings in the past. Again, a great help to such investigations is to think about the experience of losing control and ask "how old did I feel?" It's a powerful question, and it needs to be asked over and over until patterns begin to emerge and understanding begins to develop.

CHAPTER EIGHT: Mindfulness

To fully understand the past, to function more effectively in the present, and to optimize the future, survivors of trauma should develop mindfulness, which begins with practicing meditation. In the last chapter, I mentioned that mindfulness training has lately become fashionable, showing up in some surprising places, such as hospitals, schools, corporate retreats, prisons, and the military. The reason for its surge in popularity is simple: it helps people in a wide variety of ways, ways we can now observe and measure scientifically. For forty years, we have been aware that meditation reduces stress and cultivates equanimity. We use the name of an ancient meditative tradition, Zen, to refer to these benefits, saying "Bob is very zen" to mean that Bob is calm and non-reactive, that he manifests a quality like serenity, only cooler. A much more recent development is the ability to measure the effects of meditation on the human brain. With the emergence of technology that can watch the brain in action, scientists can now explain *how* meditation promotes physical health and emotional well-being, as well as a range of other beneficial cognitive and neurological effects. Scientists studying long-term meditators have found measurable changes in the structure of their brains, changes suggesting that meditation can positively influence processes thought to be automatic, such as aging and the body's fear response.[43] Even a little bit of meditation helps, as beginners also show reduced reactivity to stress and inflammation. In fact, the science far outstrips most of the claims made by meditation's proponents, with the possible exception of yogic flying. What was once fuzzy and "alternative" is now solidly evidence-based.

What matters more for our purposes, however, is the growing consensus about the value of mindfulness in the treatment of trauma.[44] A recent review article concluded that most of the published research is preliminary but very encouraging.[45] Much of it focuses on the reduction of post-traumatic stress and the facilitation of post-traumatic growth by cultivating skills such as focused attention and the ability to disrupt automatic judgments and reactivity. Most clinician-researchers see mindfulness training as an adjunct to traditional therapy in the treatment of trauma;[46] a few contend that mindfulness training alone may relieve symptoms.[47] The major reference work in the field of trauma therapy marshals compelling evidence for both positions,[48] which for me simply underscores the importance of mindfulness in any program of recovery from trauma, whether guided by a therapist or undertaken independently. In short, mindfulness is the foundation of resilience.

So what is mindfulness? It is no more and no less than radical attention that is focused on the present moment, on experience as it happens. By "experience" I don't necessarily mean events; experience includes physical sensations, emotions, thoughts, and sensory perceptions as well. A nose-itch is an experience, as is hearing a motorcycle roar by. Thinking "I wish I had a motorcycle" as the roar fades away is an experience, as is the chorus of "Born to be Wild" that suddenly plays in your head. When you are mindful, you notice the itch, the roar, the thought, and the song as they arise. Then you notice the next phenomenon—a distant dog barking, perhaps—and your mind lets go of the motorcycle. What you seek to avoid while practicing mindfulness is letting that motorcycle hijack your attention and take it far away from the present moment. Normally, that's what minds do: one thought leads to another, then another, a wish to a hope to a full-blown fantasy to a memory to a regret to a mental reminder to an elaborate daydream to another memory and so on and so on. Before long, you're planning a motorcycle camping trip in the Canadian Rockies or wondering whether Netflix has "Sons of Anarchy," and you've completely lost touch with the present moment.

Learning mindfulness is learning to return to that present moment, over and over again. It's normal for your attention to get hijacked, especially at the beginning, when your mind often behaves like a monkey on a sugar high. It does not want to pay attention to the present moment; it wants to swing wildly from tree to tree while pounding Laffy Taffy and screeching excitedly. It can, however, be trained to pay attention, at least some of the time, and I want to stress above all that mindfulness is not a talent some people have naturally but a skill we all must learn through practice. So how do we learn it? Those who have been practicing the Lovingkindness meditation have already begun. They have begun learning to focus their attention inward, and they have begun developing the self-compassion that will help them to master other basic techniques. Why is self-compassion so important? Because learning a new skill always involves making mistakes, lots of them, and the more gentle and patient you are with your own mistakes, the more quickly you will learn. Say, for example, you mentally climbed aboard that motorcycle a few minutes ago and rode it all the way to Banff before remembering that you were supposed to keep your attention focused on the present moment. As soon as you catch your mind wandering, you have a choice: you can criticize yourself for not being mindful or you can let the lapse go and renew your effort. Monkey-mind wants to do the first because thinking about how bad you are at meditation is being distracted from the present moment, especially if the criticism launches a litany of failure and self-doubt. But self-compassion helps you to just let go, which is by far the more effective strategy.

Our second meditative technique aims to develop concentration. We do that by focusing our attention on one object for a set period of time. That object can be external, such as a candle flame, or it can be internal, a part of the body, a physical process, or an image in the mind. People with a religious tradition may use a sacred object; people with a reverence for nature may use a flower or a rock or a mountain, but the truth is that you can focus your attention on almost anything. There are some categories that tend to be less effective, such as objects with negative associations, objects that move erratically, and photographs of family members, but most things work just fine. The classic focus for meditation is the breath, which is a very practical strategy, if only because the breath is always handy. In addition, because we pay so little attention to our breathing most of the time, the experience of focusing on the breath trains us to pay attention to something we normally take for granted, which is useful in developing mindfulness. Another benefit of the breath is that it is both constant and constantly changing. It speeds up and slows down, it deepens and becomes more shallow, yet it is always there, embodying both change and continuity. Finally, our breathing is typically not something about which we have a great many ideas and feelings.[49] It can be easier to focus on the present moment, especially at first, when your object of focus isn't overly embedded in a network of thought, emotion, and belief. That said, everyone is different, and some meditators benefit from linking their mindfulness practice to their core convictions. In addition, some survivors of physical and sexual trauma may initially be more comfortable focusing their attention on something outside their own bodies. I recommend trying the breath as a focus but being prepared to switch if that's distressing in any way. As to what sort of external object would offer the same benefits as the breath, try something that reflects or emits light: a sunlit wall, a stream, a glass of water, a spoon, a candle. You needn't carry an object around with you; just think "light" and look around wherever you are for a good object. Light works well because, like the breath, it both persists and subtly changes. And it's also something that we tend to take for granted.

To focus mindful attention on the breath or on another object, sit in a stable position.[50] If using a chair, choose a sturdy chair with a flat bottom. It should be deep enough that you can sit away from the chair back with your spine straight. It should be the right height to allow your knees to bend at a ninety-degree angle and your feet to rest flat on the floor. A thin cushion or folded blanket may be added for additional height or comfort. If sitting on the floor or a mat, place a very firm cushion under your buttocks and sit cross-legged or in a half-lotus position, with one foot resting on the opposite thigh. (If you can sit in a full lotus position, you're probably an experienced meditator and can skip the following instructions.) The cushion should be high enough to angle your knees down a little, increasing your stability. Your knees and the cushion form a tripod, a stable base for your upper body. You should not feel teeter-y or unbalanced; if you do, shift your weight around or try another position. If you look online you will discover alternative positions for meditation, such as kneeling, and equipment that offers physical support for them. Some of this equipment is useful. If you want to sit in a half-lotus on the floor, a nice firm meditation cushion will make that position much easier. If you want to sit cross-legged but your knees are too stiff, a little meditation bench will help. Beyond that, you can spend thousands of dollars on special chairs and other accessories, but they won't help you meditate any better. Only practice will do that, and practice doesn't cost anything.

Once your lower body is stable on your cushion or your chair, make sure your upper body is aligned by imagining that you have a string attached to the crown of your head and that someone is gently pulling that string from above. Yes, it's the same string your ballet teacher or track and field coach asked you to imagine, so dig it out and put it back into service. With the string taut, your chin should tuck in slightly as your crown rises toward the ceiling. Keep your mouth closed but your jaw relaxed, and let your tongue rest behind your front teeth. Leave your eyes open but unfocused and slightly cast down. If you are meditating on an object, such as a glass of water, make sure it is where you can see it from this position or choose another object that you can see readily without moving your head. Finally, place your right hand palm up in your lap and your left hand on top of it palm up. Both hands should be close to your abdomen and slightly cupped. Gently bring your thumbs together so they are just touching.

Why all of this attention to the right chair and the right posture and the right hand position, to what the body is doing? Surely mindfulness is about the mind and can be achieved in any position! Yes it can, for people with experience. But, when learning a new skill, you want all the support you can get, including support from your body. And, in truth, your body is more than support for mindfulness; it's one of your best teachers. Let me continue to describe the process, then if you still want to meditate while lying in a hammock with your eyes closed or hanging upside-down from a trapeze, then be my guest!

To begin meditating, simply focus on your chosen object. If that's your breath, then pick a site where you feel yourself breathing, such as the diaphragm that controls the action, the lungs that fill and empty, or the nostrils where air enters and exits. To some degree, you'll be aware of all of them, but try to focus mainly on one. Don't try to control your breath or gather information about it, just observe. If your object is a pond or a crystal ball or a flower, let your gaze and your attention rest gently upon it. Don't try to commit it to memory or figure out what it's made of; don't try to scrutinize it in any particular way. As with the breath, you're not looking to gather information about your object, just observing it.

This kind of observation requires a balance between effort and ease. You have to try but not strain. You have to relax but not grow slack. A common metaphor for the effort involved in meditation is the tension on a violin string: too tight, and the string breaks; too loose, and it won't make a sound. Only between those extremes do we find music. Whether on your breath or an object, your focus should be alert but also have a kind of softness to it, as though your attention held something precious and fragile. You don't want to crush it by holding too tightly, but you also don't want to hold it so loosely that it falls. Through practice, you will learn how to focus "just right," and before very long that balance will become natural.

A huge part of that "just right" effort is how you handle lapses in attention. As I've said a couple of times now, lapses are frequent, sometimes almost continuous, especially as you're starting out. In fact, novices are often surprised to find themselves unable to go more than a second or two without succumbing to one distraction or another. That's okay. It's normal to be besieged by thoughts, feelings, sensations, and more thoughts. They're not going to magically disappear when you learn to meditate, so forget anything you may have heard about meditation "emptying the mind" because it doesn't. What happens is that you gradually learn not to get swept up in the thoughts that arise. The key to that process is kindly but diligently returning your attention to the breath or the object whenever that attention wanders. I've mentioned the need for kindness already, the importance of not reading yourself the riot act every time your mind slips away for a little attentional holiday. Chastising yourself, questioning your ability to meditate, wondering whether meditation is just a giant waste of your time: all these are just more distracting thoughts taking you further away from the present moment. But forgiving yourself for lapses does not mean becoming lax. You still have to try to maintain your focus in the next moment. In other words, self-forgiveness must be accompanied by renewed vigilance, or it's self-indulgence, not self-compassion. Once again, you have to achieve balance: try steadfastly to keep focused but move on quickly and kindly when you fail.

Believe it or not, your body can help you achieve that balance. The seated meditation postures I sketched a few pages ago both foster and reflect the equilibrium between relaxation and alertness. Whether in a chair or cross-legged, you're comfortable enough to sit for a long time yet holding yourself upright. Your eyes are open, taking in your surroundings, yet unfocused. Your jaw and tongue are relaxed yet not slack. If you start to slump or your head falls forward or your eyes close or your mouth opens, you may be getting too relaxed. If your chin rises or your back becomes rigid or your eyes squint or your teeth clench, you may be straining too much. Even the position of your thumbs can reveal a loss of balance; when you're too relaxed, they tend to drift apart, and when you're straining, they tend to push against one another. They should be just lightly touching.

Two final notes, and you're ready to begin practicing focused awareness, or basic meditation. Regardless of your object, you may want to add a little structure to your practice, especially at first, by counting your breaths. Count "one" at the end of the first exhalation, and count each subsequent exhalation up to ten, then start again at one. If you get distracted and lose the sequence, start again at one. Some people find, even if they're meditating on an object other than the breath, that breath-counting helps them stay focused, and they do it for many years. Some don't. Some report that breath-counting is a technique they use when they feel particularly distracted, regardless of how experienced they are. At any rate, it's easy to add in and may help, so it's worth a try. The final consideration is duration: how long should you meditate? My answer is that sitting regularly is more important than sitting for a long time, so start with a length of time you can commit to every day. If that's ten minutes, then sit for ten minutes. Ideally, you'll notice some benefits and *want* to increase the time, but, for that to happen, you have to meditate regularly.

To support and encourage your practice, you could join a meditation class or group. With mindfulness so popular these days, there are a lot of them, which is both a good thing and a not-so-good thing. Because there is no way I could screen the available options, all I can do is offer some suggestions about how you might find a good one. Excellent places to look are traditions with a long history of teaching and encouraging meditation, as well as organizations derived from them. The latter include the national program called Mindfulness Based Stress Reduction (MBSR), which is offered in hospitals, medical centers, and, lately, mindfulness centers all over the country. MBSR is an introductory meditation course founded by physician Jon Kabat-Zinn, who adapted Buddhism and yoga to a western, scientific context. Some people might prefer to go to the horse's mouth and check out Kabat-Zinn's teachers, who include Thích Nhất Hạnh, Sharon Salzberg, Jack Kornfield, and Joseph Goldstein, all of whom also have students of their own teaching all over the world. Many Zen and Vipassana (Insight Meditation) centers offer meditation instruction and support for practitioners of any religion—or no religion. Some may feature a bit of chanting in Pali or Japanese, but none expects adherence to (or even knowledge of) Buddhist philosophy, and all warmly welcome beginners. My own feeling is that it's better to learn and practice meditation with experts, even if some of them dress a little strangely, than gamble on a facilitator who may have no training and only a little more experience than you do. As your meditation deepens, you will appreciate the guidance and support.

If you Google "meditation," you will see that I'm leaving out dozens, if not hundreds, of kinds of meditation, including some very well-known ones, such as Transcendental Meditation. Useful as these may be, they are not as overtly focused on mindfulness as the types I've mentioned, so the research I've cited does not apply to most of them.[51] One exception is well worth investigating, though it deals with movement more than sitting meditation. Called Trauma Sensitive Yoga, it cultivates mindfulness primarily through attention to the body, a slightly different approach to the same goal: learning to pay attention to the present moment. Trauma Sensitive Yoga is fairly new, but it was developed by trauma specialists with rigorous scientific testing and high standards for certification.[52] I fully expect it to become widely available within a few years.

What can you expect after practicing meditation for a while? Specifically, how does it benefit survivors of trauma? First, even beginning meditation elicits a measurable relaxation response, which deepens with accumulated practice. Relaxation helps ease stress and stress-related illness, which are more severe in survivors of childhood abuse than in the general population.[53] So stress-reduction alone would make meditation worth the effort for survivors. But stress-reduction is just the first of many gifts. The second is increased self-knowledge. I mentioned a moment ago that, if you practice meditation diligently, you will become less prone to having your attention hijacked and taken on long journeys far away from the present moment. When it is hijacked, you'll catch the diversion more quickly. Eventually, for short stretches then longer stretches, you'll be able to watch your thoughts come and go without getting caught up in them. For a moment, you will see how a thought arises and generates another thought—or feeling or memory or physical sensation or fantasy or recollection. You will start to understand how your mind works in the moment, as it's happening, rather than just retrospectively.

The third gift is an easing of the depersonalization that results from childhood abuse. Being attentive to the present moment is reconnecting to your own experience, and even a few minutes of reconnection every day can begin to ease the persistent sense of detachment that many of us feel.[54] The more we can sustain mindfulness in meditation—and eventually outside of it—the less alienated we will feel from our inner and outer reality. A fourth, related gift—in truth, all these gifts are related—is decreased reactivity. As we calm down a bit, learn how to stay in the present moment, and begin to understand better how our minds work, our responses become less automatic. Mindfulness slows our perception of time,[55] and, at this more gentle pace, we begin to perceive a gap between action and reaction, between hearing words, for example, and having a feeling about those words. The gap allows us to make a choice, not just about what to do or say, but even about what to think or feel. We become less locked into habits conditioned by our negative experiences and more able to choose better ways of responding moment by moment. These choices may be minuscule at first, but they are huge in their impact, especially if we have resolved to make positive changes in the past but failed when the rubber met the road. For trauma survivors used to replaying old scripts or running on autopilot, as I was, even just perceiving the gap is a revelation. It loosens the bond between stimulus and response; it promises that we can use the understanding cultivated by reflection proactively, in real time, not just after the fact. The gap, in short, creates freedom, and mindfulness creates the gap.

Those four gifts are just a beginning. With sustained effort, each will expand and diversify: stress reduction into reserves of calm; increased self-knowledge into self-acceptance; decreased self-alienation into personal integration; and decreased reactivity into emotional regulation. Add to these the many well-documented health benefits, from lowered blood pressure to lighter respiratory infections to protection against mental illness, and mindfulness meditation seems almost magical, except that the only wizardry required is persistence.

How much meditation do you have to do to get such results? There's no formula, obviously, especially for survivors of childhood abuse. Nonetheless, one small pilot study does offer some encouraging numbers. In the study, twenty-seven survivors of childhood sexual abuse took the eight-week MBSR program I mentioned earlier then followed it with daily home practice. After twenty-four weeks, they received three refresher classes. At the end of the eight-week program, participants showed a sixty-five percent reduction in depressive symptoms as well as all symptoms of PTSD, with the greatest reduction in avoidance and emotional numbing. These results persisted through the last assessment at twenty-four weeks.[56] Two and a half years later, the research team reassessed twenty of the original subjects and found "significant long-term improvement in depression, PTSD, anxiety symptoms, and mindfulness."[57] If one basic instructional course and some independent meditation practice was that helpful, imagine the results you could achieve with more vigorous effort!

In the last chapter, I ended by returning to the opening story and explaining why I told it in the way that I did. This time there's little need because I didn't alter or embellish much. The names are changed, of course. Roxy is alive and blameless, so I wanted to spare her any possible embarrassment my story might cause. I did add a few minor details, such as the music that was playing when Maggie made her move, which I don't actually recall. Joan Armatrading is a good guess, though, as I played her first album over and over that fall, and I still enjoy it. But most of the other description is accurate, down to the red flowers on my yellow cowboy shirt. My memory for detail is pretty sharp, especially regarding that era, my twenties and thirties, most of it spent in Phoenix. I can still see clearly the houses, the neighborhoods, the people I knew, the city and the mountains beyond. I enjoyed revisiting it in my imagination and sharing a little of it with you.

Still, telling that story was uncomfortable. The twenty-six-year-old Donna who two-timed her amazing girlfriend is a lot harder to like than the fifteen-year-old Donna who defied her guidance counselor. As I described making out on the sofa with my colleague and friend, I was aware that some readers might have negative reactions, particularly if they've been on the receiving end of sexual betrayal. I thought perhaps I should tell a different story to illustrate the effects of childhood trauma on adult thinking and behavior, one in which I'm a bit more sympathetic. I went so far as to begin a second story, one about being forcibly raped by my piano student and not realizing, even afterward, that the attack was rape. I had set the scene: my student and I sitting side-by-side on the piano bench as I demonstrated the difference between *allegro* and *moderato*. I was just about to describe the way he pulled me off the bench by my hair when I realized that this more sympathetic story would deprive me of a valuable opportunity to demonstrate habits that we must develop if we hope to mend the damage caused by childhood trauma. The first is obvious, and I've said enough about it that I'm sure you understand its value: honesty about ourselves. Without being willing to accept a few ugly truths, we remain stuck.

The next is sympathetic understanding, how we feel when we trace our behavior back to its roots in childhood trauma. I don't excuse my infidelity, but I see how my early experiences created the conditions that gave rise to it. I feel tenderness for my own confusion and pain, for the many things I did not know, both about myself and about other people. Sympathetic understanding is the fruit of reflection, and it's one of the ways we know we're being both honest and compassionate as we examine the experiences that shaped us.

If sympathetic understanding proves challenging, the practice of mindfulness meditation will help generate the necessary compassion. Even the focused attention we learned in this chapter makes us more compassionate, both toward other people and toward ourselves. But we can also aim our compassion more specifically toward difficult aspects of ourselves and our histories. When you become comfortable with the Lovingkindness Meditation and able to do it on your own without guidance, try adding a step. Imagine a part of yourself or your life that you consider difficult. This figure can be a memory of yourself at a particular time or a character you create: the self that rages, for example, or the self that fades into the woodwork. After you send good wishes to the usual suspects, you will send them to this difficult figure, and the practice will help generate compassion for aspects of yourself that may be hard to love.

Finally, the story illustrates abundantly the need for mindfulness, because the entire sequence of events issued from my lack of it. Had I been aware of my thoughts and feelings—and of the obvious signals Maggie was sending out—the afternoon would have unfolded very differently, whereas my piano student's attack would likely have proceeded with or without my awareness. The episode reminds me to stay connected to my experience, moment by moment, to both my outer experience and my inner experience. Paradoxically, the more mindful of my own experience I become, the more I feel a part of everything that exists. Henry David Thoreau had it exactly right when he wrote, "You must live in the present, launch yourself on every wave, find your eternity in each moment."

Practice: Breath-Counting Meditation

The previous chapter offered detailed instruction in basic meditation. Some of you will want to try it solo, which allows you to proceed in your own way at your own pace. Others may prefer to have some audible prompting at first, so I have recorded a guided meditation focusing on the breath.[58] The meditation takes ten minutes, a good starting length. After you've used it for a while, you may begin to find that the sound of my voice distracts you, draws your attention away from your breath. You may even find the sound of my voice annoying. Take that as a sign that you are ready to meditate on your own, at least some of the time. Guided meditation is a wonderful tool, an optimal way to cultivate resilience, but it works better if you practice solo meditation along with it. So consider this sound file a valuable set of training wheels. It will help you develop the balance you need to meditate—the physical balance, as well as the balance between effort and ease—until one day you discover that you've outgrown it!

Part IV

Finding Support

CHAPTER NINE: My Executive Retreat

My next story picks up just a few months after my tryst with Maggie. Though Roxy had forgiven me, my life continued to unravel as I watched, helpless and confused. Every night I got blackout drunk, and every morning I tried to chase off the hangover with a handful of white crosses, the Adderall of its day. Once in a while, the hangover wouldn't budge, so I stayed home, lying glassy-eyed on the couch between painful bouts of retching. Though still committed to the fight against sexual abuse, I no longer brought my best self to work. I missed meetings or slipped out for a beer during breaks. I started to delegate more. I was often distracted, not by anything in particular, but by a vague, persistent dread, like a shadow I could see only in my peripheral vision. I knew something was desperately wrong with my life, but I didn't know how to fix it. I was sure I knew what it was, though: seepage from my core of evil. What I didn't understand was why I was losing the ability to insulate other parts of myself from that evil, as I had once done so successfully. I wasn't completely incapacitated; I could still pull myself together to meet major challenges, such as a public lecture or a meeting with a state representative. But, day to day, I held myself together with spit and rubber bands, and I wondered why the people around me didn't see that. I was about to learn that some of them did.

On my birthday, I decided to kill myself—not right away but a few months later so I would have time to make arrangements. My death would be a belated birthday present to myself, as well as to others, so I chose the day carefully: April 14, 1978. Having worked for years in hospital emergency rooms, I knew what would kill me efficiently—and what might bungle the job. I made a short mental list of necessary tasks and started at the top. The morning after my birthday, as Roxy and I enjoyed a leisurely Saturday breakfast, I scanned *The Arizona Republic* for reports of crime in our neighborhood. There wasn't one, but I did find a brief article about a mugging in Glendale. I read it aloud. The next day's paper featured a murder in Sunnyslope, so I read that one aloud too. The next weekend, I found a few more violent crimes in the newspaper and did the same thing. After a month,

I broached the idea of buying a gun. As two small women living in a dangerous city, I argued, we needed the protection. Roxy was lukewarm about my proposal, citing the fact that guns harm their owners more often than they do intruders. She reminded me that we both had advanced training in self-defense and could take care of ourselves. But I was ready for her objections. We were not hapless neophytes who would accidentally shoot ourselves, I pointed out. She worked with dangerous tools every day, while I had fired guns on my parents' ranch. (I didn't mention that they were BB guns.) And self-defense training was no match for an armed intruder. She was not convinced, so I pulled out my strongest ammunition: my own history. Six years earlier, I had been working alone in a Salt Lake City gas station when it was robbed, once by a man with a knife then again, five days later, by the same man. The second time he had brought an accomplice and a gun. Both times I was assaulted, the second so violently that I expected to die. Roxy knew the story well, so I needed only a few words.

"Yeah," Roxy murmured. "I get it." She was such a compassionate person; I felt terrible playing on her sympathy.

In early February, we bought a gun. The process was even easier than it is now; we just dropped into a gun shop, filled out a form, and walked out with a Rossi .38 Special Snub-Nosed Revolver and a box of bullets. The gun was bright silver with a wooden grip, smaller than I expected but still a bit large for both our hands. But the sales clerk discouraged us from buying a "ladies' gun," saying they didn't have enough "stopping power."

"You shoot a bad guy with one of those toys, he may bleed to death," the clerk explained, "but he'll have plenty of time to kill you first." Roxy looked a little pale, so I quickly paid for the .38 Special and hustled her out of the store.

That weekend we took the revolver out to the desert to practice shooting. We brought along green wine bottles and brown beer bottles but had trouble finding a place to line them up. In the movies, there's always a convenient wall or a horizontal branch, but we had to make do with a small, lumpy rock, and the bottles fell off more than they were shot off. As usual, Roxy turned out to be far more skilled than I, even though I was the one who had grown up around firearms. She shot most of the wine bottles and all of the beer bottles, which didn't bother me because the only target I cared about would be very easy to hit. Besides, the more Roxy liked shooting, the less likely the gun would go back to the store. I praised her marksmanship effusively and deemed the purchase a great success. One task down, three more to go.

The second task took several months. Between December and April, I wrote letters: to family members, ex-girlfriends, ex-boyfriends and close friends. I wanted to make very clear why I was taking my life. To make sure I would be understood, I typed each letter when I had finished drafting it. My handwriting was messy even then, and I didn't want people struggling to make out the words of a suicide note. I did the typing in my office on the weekend and kept the letters in a large manila envelope marked "Commercial Cleaning Estimates." My purpose in writing the letters was to explain to each person individually that I wasn't trying to hurt or shame them. I knew well the guilt that survivors feel, the self-lacerating questions that hound them: why didn't I see it coming? What could I have done to prevent it? What might I have done to *cause* it? I wanted to preempt as much of that questioning as I possibly could by explaining that everything began and ended with me. All my life I had been fundamentally bad, and nothing I had done—or could ever do—would change that fact. I had tried to change, to do the right thing and become a good person who could be happy. As a Mormon, I had struggled hard for perfection but fallen far short, over and over again. As an agnostic, I no longer held myself to that impossible standard, yet my sense of failure and unworthiness had not diminished. The upshot was clear: no matter how low I dropped the bar, I wouldn't be able to clear it. I could never be happy because I didn't deserve to be. I honestly believed that my suicide would be a gift to friends and family, and I hoped they would accept it in that spirit. After I finished explaining my decision, I thanked each person for the joy and love they had brought into my life, mentioning a few of our best times together. Then I wished them well, and signed off, in pen, with "Love always, Donna."

The third task was what the movies call "getting my affairs in order." I paid bills and returned library books. I checked my planner and plumbed my memory to be sure I had kept all my promises, even the ones that are mostly hot air, like "Yes, we must do lunch." I did lunch, read a colleague's master's thesis, and had a yogic foot massage. I listened to mixtapes made by one of the center's volunteers, and I made sure all of my files were orderly and up-to-date. Though I was doing a lot more than usual—and still drinking every night—I was surprisingly calm and efficient. Driving me was the knowledge that I didn't have to maintain this pace for long; just one strong push, and it would all be over.

My last task was repaying Roxy for her kindness, which I hoped to do with equal kindness. I broke up with the instructor and avoided further sexual entanglements. If anyone showed even slight interest, I stayed away from him or her. Eager to throw myself into activities Roxy enjoyed, I proposed painting the house. She reeled me in by asking for my help with an ugly thrift-shop cabinet she wanted to refinish. The cabinet had so many layers of old paint that just stripping it took a whole weekend, but I found something deeply satisfying in soaking and peeling and scraping and finally getting down to the naked wood. Stripped all the way down, the cabinet was beautiful, and I once again marveled at Roxy's ability to see that. As I spent more time with her, my love for her intensified, but along with it came the renewed conviction that she deserved someone better than me. Much as I treasured our dwindling time together, it was only possible because it was dwindling. In other words, I deserved her love—and could enjoy it—only because I was about to free her.

The evening of April 13, Roxy and I went to a production of the erotic musical revue *Oh! Calcutta!* We had a glass of wine before the show and another at intermission, but I deliberately avoided crossing the blackout threshold. I didn't want to be hung over the next morning. The evening was close to perfect. The infamous play turned out to be hilarious, brimming with deft slapstick and clever songs. We knew half the audience, it seemed, including most of the people sitting around us. During intermission, a steady stream of friends joined us as we drank our wine, including Annie, a member of my board of directors. Annie was a psychologist in her forties, a woman of formidable intelligence. I didn't know her well, but I respected her. In truth, I was surprised to see her at *Oh Calcutta!* as she was what we used to call "uptight." For the same reason, I was a little surprised when she approached the boisterous group around Roxy and me. As she walked up, we were all laughing about the last skit we had seen, which featured a couple having sex in a research facility while scientists in lab coats observed, probed, and occasionally joined in. Suddenly I stopped laughing and assumed a fierce expression.

"I don't know what you're all laughing about," I growled. "At the University of Utah, we did that kind of research all the time!" I explained that Mormon scientists were on the leading edge of orgasmic research because the church wanted members to have a lot of children.

"How do you think we *do* that now that polygamy is illegal?" I demanded, keeping my face serious. Finally, I joined in the laughter, and even Annie cracked a smile. Then someone else said something clever, and the merriment continued. Maybe it was the slapstick of *Oh Calcutta!* and maybe it was the emotional push-pull of spring, but everyone seemed funnier than usual. When I think about that night, I remember the sound of general laughter and the sound of my own laughter rising above it, and I remember that, by the end of the evening, my cheeks and my belly were sore from laughing.

The next morning, I awoke to find that Roxy had left early for work. For a moment, I felt a wave of panic about not saying goodbye one last time; then I reminded myself that I had been saying goodbye for four months, and my letter to her would say goodbye again. After dressing in jeans and a sweatshirt, I made myself a cup of Irish Coffee with a generous slug of whiskey. I retrieved the revolver and the box of bullets, half-empty now, from the high shelf where we kept them, grabbed the manila envelope marked "Commercial Cleaning Estimates," and took my supplies and my coffee to the screened porch behind our house, where I placed them on a pine-plank picnic table. Then I pulled the hallway phone out the back door as far as its cord would reach, about six feet shy of the picnic table. I put the phone on the concrete floor—not ideal, but it would do. I would call the police just before I shot myself so Roxy wouldn't come home to find my body.

I sat down at the picnic table and gazed through the screen into our beautiful back yard, admiring the gold-and-green streaks of our palo verde trees and the pink-purple clouds of bougainvillea against our back wall. The air was warm and so still I could hear children in a schoolyard blocks away and knocking on a neighbor's door. Sipping my Irish Coffee, I glanced over at the hot tub where Roxy and I liked to relax, and I realized that I felt good. Relieved. The porch was a good place to die. But when I glanced up from the hot tub I saw Annie standing right outside, staring through the screen door at the gun on the picnic table in front of me. Dressed in a severe brown suit, she didn't belong in our beautiful garden with her tight bun and her huge brown handbag clutched to her chest. I felt a rush of annoyance. Neither of us said anything for a few minutes.

"May I come in and have coffee with you?" she asked finally.

"I'd rather not," I replied. "I'm busy right now." Rude, yes, but it was the truth. I glanced at the screen door latch, which was unlocked, as usual. Damn! I was wondering how fast I could get to it when Annie pushed the door open and stepped inside, still staring at the gun on the table. I was looking at the gun, too, and we were both thinking that I could easily grab it and shoot myself before she could get halfway across the porch. Complicating her assessment was the knowledge that I could also shoot her, however remote the possibility. Complicating *my* assessment was the knowledge that I couldn't shoot anybody because I hadn't loaded the gun yet. As Annie stood frozen, my mind scrambled for options. I could grab the gun and the bullets, race into the bathroom and lock the door, then shoot myself quickly before the police arrived. If I failed, I'd be locked in a psych ward within the hour, and, having been committed several times in my college years, I knew how terrible that would be. If I succeeded, I'd have made exactly the kind of mess I was trying to avoid. Suddenly I felt an avalanche of despair: I was so rotten that I couldn't even kill myself properly. Slumping, I silently indicated a seat across from me at the picnic table. Annie quickly sat, pushing the gun down the table out of my reach.

"What are you doing?" she asked. When I looked at her instead of replying, she added, "Yeah, stupid question." We both sat silently for a moment; then Annie cleared her throat and began again.

"I see two options for you today. One, I call the police and they take you to Maricopa County Hospital."

"No," I said, my voice low but urgent. "I *mean* it. *No.*"

"Two, I drive you to a place in Wickenburg called The Meadows. It's a . . . retreat center where . . ." —and here she paused to scratch the side of her nose—"where executives go for a while to . . . regroup." She promised she would not just drive me there but bring me home again after three days. I picked up my Irish Coffee, now cold, and drained it. This choice was a no-brainer: a squad car ride to a mental hospital versus a weekend at an executive spa. The Meadows it would be. Annie made a murmured phone call while I packed an overnight bag with clothing, toiletries, and some white crosses from Roxy's stash. While Annie banged around in the guest room—hiding the gun, I surmised—I filled a thermos with more Irish Coffee. Within a half hour, we were speeding northwest on Route 60 toward Wickenburg.

Neither of us said much during the trip. I fidgeted with the radio for a while but snapped it off when three stations in a row played "Shadow Dancing." I was not in the mood for disco. Annie showed no reaction when I poured myself another Irish Coffee, nor when I asked her to pull off at a rest stop twenty minutes later. She simply answered me with kindness when I spoke to her and kept silent when I didn't. I later learned that she had been worried about me for many months. In addition to my declining performance at work, she had noticed me slipping out of board meetings to drink and had begun to intuit the nature and scope of my problem. Being an experienced psychologist, when she observed my hilarity at *Oh! Calcutta!* she saw the possibility of suicidal intentions, as people planning to kill themselves often feel joy and relief at the imminent end of their suffering. She had stopped by my house that morning hoping we could have a private conversation before work then grown alarmed when I didn't answer the front door. We were never particularly close—before or after that morning—but her act of kindness saved my life.

When we arrived at The Meadows, I discovered that Annie had told the truth about one thing: the place looked like an executive retreat center. Everywhere I saw men, mostly middle aged. They wouldn't all turn out to be executives, but they would turn out to come mostly from the oil industry, which learned early that it makes better business sense to fix broken employees than to fire them. Seeing all the men walking around, I suddenly wanted to stay in the car and have another drink, in case The Meadows turned out to be a retreat center that believed in fasting and calisthenics and the kind of massage that left bruises.

"I'm going to finish my coffee before we go in," I said.

"Okay," said Annie, "but please eat something too." She handed me a packet of peanut-butter-filled crackers that she had bought at the rest stop then moved back the driver's seat and stretched out her legs while I poured and sipped and occasionally munched.

"Not many women here," I said finally.

"No, not many," she agreed.

"Everyone's wearing leisure suits. I should have brought mine."

"You have a leisure suit? A *men's* leisure suit?"

"Sure do." The previous year, I had bought a classic beige polyester, sharp of collar, flapped of pocket, and flared of trouser. I wore it more proudly than ironically.

"Where'd you find one that fits?"

"Sears. Boy's department." Having exhausted that topic, we fell silent again until I finished my coffee and two of the cracker sandwiches. I was surprisingly un-drunk, given my low tolerance and the four stiff drinks I had consumed that morning.

"Look, there's a woman," Annie said finally, pointing to a slender figure entering the building. The woman had a high brunette ponytail and wore a navy pantsuit with white shoes. "Come on, it's time to go in."

"I think she works there. Her outfit looks like a uniform."

"You could be right," Annie agreed.

I was right. When Annie and I entered, the woman was sitting behind a desk in a small office. Seeing us, she smiled and beckoned through her open door. Annie gave me a quick squeeze and said goodbye.

"You'll be back in three days, right?" I reminded her.

"Absolutely, if that's what you want." She walked out the front door before I could ask about that "if."

The woman in the navy pantsuit beckoned again, so I walked into her office. Closer up, I could see that she was pale, delicate and pretty. She smelled sweet too, like a field of clover, and I was suddenly aware that I smelled like a distillery. Tough, I thought. Besides, I'll bet a lot of executives come in smelling boozy.

Dropping heavily into a chair, I waited for her to hand me a menu of relaxing activities. Instead, she took a medical history followed by a lot of really nosy questions.

"How much do you drink?"

"Not much," I replied. "Except for today, I mean. In general, I'd call my drinking very average."

"Average being . . . what exactly?" she pressed. "How many drinks per day?"

"Well, that depends," I answered. She was starting to annoy me.

"On what?"

"On the day of the week, the season of the year, where I am, who I'm with, what's going on—you know, the usual."

"Ballpark it. How many drinks on an average Saturday?"

"There is no average Saturday. I don't live that kind of life."

"How many drinks this *past* Saturday?" She smiled ever so slightly, but her voice remained soft and uninflected. What was wrong with the woman, I wondered. Why was she so nosy? Was her ponytail too tight? I squinted at the badge clipped to her collar. She had introduced herself, but I didn't recall her name. Now I saw that it was Daisy Harmon, R. N.

"I don't remember, *Daisy*," I sneered. "How many drinks did you have last Saturday?"

"None, but we're talking about you. Try to remember how many drinks you had last Saturday. Guess if you have to."

"Okay, three."

"Three what? Beers, cocktails, bottles of wine?"

"Wine coolers," I said. The woman wrote something on a form.

"How about yesterday?" she continued. I was thoroughly annoyed now. Why was this woman so obsessed with the minutiae of my life?

"Also three."

"Wine coolers?"

"Yes."

"And about what time of day did you drink the first wine cooler?" On and on the questions went until I began to think I would have to describe every drink I had ever taken, all the way back to the fifth of Black Velvet I had downed on a dare when I was fourteen. Finally she ran out of questions.

"Is there anything you'd like to add?" she asked.

"God, no."

"Okay, I think we can move on."

"Finally," I muttered to myself—at least I *think* it was to myself.

"What about drugs?" she asked, and we were off to the races again, counting every pill I had ever taken. What would she want to know next: all the sandwiches I had ever eaten? What happened to my executive retreat? The glow of my last Irish Coffee had faded, though I still felt vague and muddled. I wasn't sure whether I needed a few white crosses or another drink, but I knew I needed something.

"May I use your bathroom?" My question interrupted a question about marijuana, which I hardly ever used because it made me paranoid. I told her so, and she directed me to a restroom down the hall.

"The purse stays here," she added, when I reached for my macramé shoulder bag. I raised my eyebrows but said nothing. The white crosses were in my overnight case anyway.

Halfway to the bathroom, the events of the morning suddenly caught up with me, and I suddenly felt like I was trapped in a free-falling elevator. I had failed to kill myself and, in the process, had been caught trying. Whatever competence I had managed to feign was gone—at work, at home, in my community. By now, Annie had talked to Roxy and who knows *who* else, and I was well and truly finished. Rather than relieving the misery I had caused my loved ones, I had multiplied it. Sure, I could have a nice rest in this . . . whatever it was . . . but when Annie picked me up on Monday, I'd be mired in a much worse mess than before—without the sure-fire exit strategy I had when I woke up that morning. In the bathroom, I splashed water on my face and tried to push the thoughts away.

"I'll figure something out," I told myself. I *have* to figure something out." But I didn't believe myself. Very slowly I walked back to Daisy's office and resumed my seat.

"Feel better?"

"No," I sighed. "I could really use a drink."

"That's been working for you, has it?"

"It's the only thing that works at all," I grumbled. "But I suppose I'll be drinking spinach nectar and goat's tears for the next few days."

"If you like," said Daisy. "Now, about your experience with marijuana . . ."

By the time she finished, my stomach was growling and my head was starting to pound, yet I also felt too queasy to eat. So far this executive retreat was a complete failure, and all I wanted was to be taken to my room so I could nap. I said as much.

"Soon," replied Daisy. "First, someone's going to show you around." She left the office and returned a moment later with one of the executives, a solidly-built man of about fifty who looked like a former defensive lineman in plaid pants. His oiled grey hair was combed back from a shiny red face, and he smiled as he offered me a handshake.

"Ralph S," he said.

"Ralph is graduating tomorrow," said Daisy. "He'll help you get oriented."

"After you ma'am," said Ralph. Those could be fighting words in the late seventies, but I wasn't up for a spat. I just wanted to get the tour over with and go lie down.

When Ralph and I stepped outside, however, I felt slightly better. Since my earliest years, I have loved the landscapes of the American west, especially the mountains and the deserts, which, no matter how ravaged my life, always managed to soothe my soul just a little. The Meadows had a stunning view of the Hassayampa River Valley and the Bradshaw Mountains. This spectacular scenery was one reason Wickenburg had become the dude ranch capital of the US, a place where stressed-out businessmen and glamorous movie stars came to experience Arizona's wide open spaces. The Meadows, until recently a dude ranch called the Slash Bar K, consisted of a central lodge, eight small cabins, some outbuildings, and a pool. As Ralph guided me around the property, he talked a steady stream, but I barely listened. Nonetheless, just walking around, I began to feel better about the weekend. The pool, especially, looked inviting on this warm April day, and I wondered why no one was swimming. Some more alluring activity, probably. When I saw stables at the edge of the property, my heart soared. For all his brutality, my father loved horses and had passed that love down to me. I was beginning to forget Nurse Daisy and her long, odd interrogation and to feel a little less panic about the mess I had made back in Phoenix. Maybe a weekend of riding and swimming—and very likely some hiking, too—would offer perspective and help me figure out how to cope.

When Ralph led me back into the central lodge, I smelled food cooking but didn't see a dining room. Nor did I see anything that looked spa-like or even vaguely recreational, aside from a small stack of board games on a shelf in the lounge: Scrabble, checkers, and Monopoly, topped with six or seven decks of playing cards. Next to them was a small shelf of hardback books, most exactly the same size and the same color, dark blue. I didn't see a television or stereo, and I wondered how the executives and I would pass the next three evenings. I asked Ralph.

"Meetings," he replied with a broad smile. "Sometimes we go into town, but usually there's one right here. Fridays we have a speaker, so you picked a good day to show up. Friends of Bill come from all around: tourists from the ranches, locals, lots of different people. Right in here is where we'll be."

"Who's Bi—" I began, but he was already charging down the hall.

Perplexed, I followed him into a modest room that perplexed me even more. There was nothing relaxing or entertaining about the room. It looked like a hundred meeting rooms I had seen in my life—and not one of the nicer ones. In the front was a beige linoleum table with metal legs. On it, slightly askew, sat a small podium; behind it stood a portable blackboard. Most of the room was filled with metal folding chairs, also beige and arranged in wavy lines.

"It's not much to look at, I know," said Ralph, "but this room will change your life." I doubted that the room could change my socks, but I kept the opinion to myself. Ralph was obviously crazy; either that or this was some kind of spa prank, and soon he would smile and take me to the sauna, where we would have a good laugh about the drab storeroom he had just shown me. Instead, he steered me to the center of the room so I could see a large poster hanging in the middle of the front wall. Then he gestured toward the print with both hands, as though it were the Mona Lisa. It was an unremarkable poster, a black-and-white printed list titled "The Twelve Steps of Alcoholics Anonymous." When I saw the title, I exploded.

"What is this place?" I shrieked. "It's not an executive retreat! What is it?"

"The Meadows is the best kind of retreat," Ralph said calmly. "It offers recovery from the disease of alcoholism."

"What?" I shrieked again. "I'm not alcoholic!" I'll spare you the full scope of my protest except to say that it was loud, vehement, and often vulgar. I was seething, and I did nothing to curb or conceal my anger as Ralph steered me back to Nurse Daisy's office. Several times, as I raved, I clipped him with violent gestures, and once, when he touched my elbow to steer me away from a collision with a food cart, I shook his hand off so forcefully that I hit him sidearm in the stomach.

"She scares me," Ralph said to Daisy when we finally made it back to the nurse's office.

After he left, Daisy gave me a long appraising look. I had spent most of my rage and was starting to calm down.

"You scare people, huh?" she asked finally. When I nodded, she grinned with delight, and a friendship was born.

It would take a few days to bloom, though, because first I had to go through withdrawal.[59] Withdrawal from alcohol, for those who don't know, ranges from a little shakiness to full-on delirium tremens. At the extreme end, it's a life-threatening medical emergency, and no one with a serious alcohol habit should ever just stop drinking without a doctor's supervision. Unfortunately, even some doctors don't know that. Fortunately for me, I was surrounded by people who *did* know that—many from personal experience—so I was well cared for. I was sick, though, with a thoroughly unpleasant combination of nausea, exhaustion and extreme nervous agitation. I was sick for long enough that Monday came and went without my uttering a peep about why Annie hadn't shown up to take me home. And, in truth, I was sick enough to entertain the possibility that I belonged at The Meadows. As I sweated and heaved and shook in my bed, I began to suspect that, yes, perhaps I too was an alcoholic.

At first the idea was revolting. You have to understand: before 1978, public perception of substance abuse was very different. To most people, an alcoholic was a Skid Row bum passed out on a sidewalk next to an empty bottle of Thunderbird and a puddle of puke. An addict was the same bum, only with a filthy syringe in place of the wine bottle. If you wondered why I got so upset when Ralph showed me the Alcoholics Anonymous poster, that's why. Nowadays, when celebrities regularly acknowledge stints in rehab and interventions are presented as television entertainment, it's hard to imagine a time when addiction was so profoundly stigmatized. But it was—and the only comparison I can make is to the way we regard pedophilia now: as pure moral depravity for which there is never any excuse. All that began to change just five days before I went to The Meadows, when former first lady Betty Ford announced she was entering treatment for addiction to alcohol and prescription drugs in California. Mrs. Ford was poised, successful, and likeable, one of the most popular first ladies in recent years. For the first time, the public saw that "nice" people, even women, struggled with addiction, and the old stereotypes began to erode. That erosion would take a while, though; meanwhile, I was stuck with yet another reason to condemn myself.

Treatment at The Meadows consisted mainly of several Alcoholics Anonymous meetings per day and the first five steps of the AA program, which involve admitting an addiction, submitting to a higher power, and confessing shortcomings. In recent years, the facility has diversified its approach to substance abuse, but the AA core remains, as it does in more than ninety percent of American inpatient and outpatient treatment. My guides through this process were my counselor, Joan, and my fellow patients, mostly men from the oil industry who were considerably older than I. Also involved were a second counselor and four nurses, including Daisy. Most of these people were not educated or credentialed therapists, so some were intimidated by my experience and my advanced degree. Instead, they were sober alcoholics, in some cases *really* sober alcoholics. Between them, the two counselors had fifty years of sobriety, which averaged out to twenty-five years each. As someone who barely had twenty-five years of *life*, I simply could not fathom how that was possible—and, in my more churlish moments, wondered why anyone would celebrate decades spent *not* doing something. I thought it was a little like celebrating not leaving the house for a quarter-century; sure it's hard, and I supposed there was some honor in that difficulty, but only the world's most boring people would want to try.

My attitude changed, fortunately. One reason was that people were very kind—Joan and Daisy hugged me constantly—so my surly veneer softened a bit. But the main reason was something my counselor Joan said a few days after I finished detoxing.

"You're not evil or mentally ill, you know. You're just an alcoholic and a drug addict." She said the words very matter-of-factly, as though she were saying, "You can't sail over the edge of the earth, you know. You just keep on sailing." To her the idea was obvious, no big deal. To me the idea was completely mind-blowing. Of course I was evil; my life-long efforts to be good had failed completely. And I was mentally ill as well, quite severely so, or I wouldn't have spent so much time in psychiatric hospitals as a college student. As to whether I was an addict, the jury was still out. The idea had never occurred to me until withdrawal forced me to consider it, but it didn't feel very natural. I decided that the best I could do was welcome it into the realm of possibility, so I stuck a "maybe" in front of Joan's comment and, very tentatively, tried it on for size. "Maybe I'm not evil" was radical enough.

There's a lot more I could say about my treatment at The Meadows and my many years in AA, but this is not, strictly speaking, a book about recovery from addiction; it's a book about recovery from trauma. The two topics overlap because addiction is one of the main ways survivors cope with trauma's effects, so I will have much more to say about addiction in this chapter. But my final emphasis will be on how recovery from addiction supports recovery from trauma. For example, I believe very strongly that survivors who struggle with addiction must get well and truly sober before they can deal with their trauma. Sobriety is so essential that I do not accept Legacy clients until they have been sober for at least a year. What I don't have strong opinions about is how clients achieve that year. Inpatient treatment and AA worked very well for me, but twelve-step programs don't help everybody—or even most people. Fortunately, addicts who want to get sober have more therapeutic choices now than ever before. Though most inpatient treatment centers still emphasize AA, more and more of them also provide other tools, such as mindfulness training and biofeedback. Even some promising medications are in development, after years of being condemned by abstinence-only purists. There are also new outpatient options, as well as a range of new support groups, including Refuge Recovery for Buddhists and a whole slate of online groups. Addiction treatment still has a long way to go, especially for lower-income patients, but it has also come a long way in just a few decades. One recent victory: in 2008 and again in 2014, laws mandated parity between coverage of physical health and mental health, including treatment for addiction. We are well on the way to taking addiction seriously as a medical condition and treating it accordingly.

Once I was over my initial misgivings, my recovery from substance abuse was speedy. I was lucky to land in one of the best—and, at this point, one of the *few*—addiction treatment facilities in the world, where I received excellent care from knowledgeable and compassionate professionals. I was lucky to have that care relatively early in my drinking career, before I did too much damage—to myself or others. I was lucky to enter treatment just as Betty Ford began to de-stigmatize addiction. I was lucky to feel a strong affinity for AA, which, at that time, was the only game in town. I admired the organization's loose, horizontal structure, its lack of rules, its radical democracy, and above all its emphasis on finding the truth in our own experience. I enjoyed the meetings: the candor, the camaraderie, the self-effacing jokes, the great storytelling, the small rituals, even some of the clichés. There was only one potential snag for me: the "higher power" on which so much of the AA program relied. Having rejected my Mormon faith, I found the notion of a punitive, voyeuristic deity off-putting, to say the least. I recoiled at the idea of someone "up there" watching my every action, even the most intimate, monitoring my thoughts and evaluating each in turn. That omniscient old guy with the white beard would not work for me. That guy would not keep me sober; that guy had kept me drunk and miserable. I even prayed about it, though I wasn't really sure who or what I was praying to.

Then, about a week after I arrived at The Meadows, I walked outside after a meeting. I gazed for a while at the Hassayampa River shining in the distance; then I looked down to see a Hopi rattlesnake coiled in the sun, its head lying on the outermost coil. Its skin was lovely, peachy-pink with regular patches of caramel brown like jagged blazons the length of its body. It didn't have many rattles—a young one, then—but it was beautiful, and I watched it for a long time. As I returned to the building, I spoke softly to myself.

"Everyone tells me my higher power can be anything outside myself, bigger than myself, stronger than myself. That, for me, is nature." I remembered all the times I had sought refuge in the mountains or the desert; I remembered lying in bed as a girl imagining myself as a cheerful rabbit or a cool, graceful mountain lion. Nature, my refuge and my strength, was as vast a power as I could imagine, and it would help me stay sober. Fitting nature into the AA paradigm did take some work. Asked to pray to it, I used to wonder why I couldn't just go outside and walk around in it, but I got used to making the adaptation. And, over the years of my sobriety, nature would prove a strong, nurturing, and endlessly adaptable higher power.

Almost right away, my recovery from addiction began to set in motion the long, slow process of recovering from trauma. As I entertained the possibility that I was an addict, rather than evil or mentally ill, I could feel other certainties starting to loosen, as though furniture that had always seemed built-in might actually be moveable. It was more a feeling than an idea until a single conversation brought it into focus.

The occasion was the last of the five AA steps that I did at The Meadows. The fourth and fifth steps go together: in the fourth, you compile your own "moral inventory," and, in the fifth, you share it with another person, in my case Father James, a priest who worked with The Meadows. I had labored for days on my fourth step, chronicling even minor misdeeds in painstaking detail, quickly filling up one spiral-bound notebook and nearly exhausting a second. Though ready to believe I was not mentally ill or evil, I still believed that everything I had experienced was my fault. In addition, I wanted to do a perfect fourth step, so I saw the call to be "thorough and searching" as a call to be "exhaustive and prosecutorial." When it was time to share my magnum opus, I read it to the priest over the course of several hours. After I finished, he took both my hands and looked me in the eyes, his face drawn with sorrow.

"None of this was your fault," he said, and I could hear a slight shaking in his soft, deep voice. "There's nothing wrong with you." I felt confused at first, sure I must have misheard him.

"Pardon m—," I began.

"You had terrible parents," he continued. "You were in a terrible situation. All of this"—he gently pulled the two notebooks from my hand and held them up—"is your parents' fault, not yours." I felt a physical jolt, like landing after a long free-fall. He repeated his words over and over with minor variations, and slowly I began to absorb them. Then he finished with a soft laugh. "Your eighth and ninth steps should be the shortest eighth and ninth steps *ever.*" I was still new enough to AA that I had to look back at the step numbers to understand that he meant I had very few amends to make. As King Lear says of himself, I was "more sinn'd against than sinning." I sat quietly for a while, stunned by this revelation. I was not to blame! There is no language to convey the relief I felt. I had come into the room lugging my encyclopedic fourth step and certain that it would be one of the most disturbing the priest had ever heard—not because my individual sins were so shocking, but because they were so many and so relentless, like the drip-drip-drip of a sewer pipe that quietly turns a clear pond into a cesspool. Instead, he had lifted them from me, not by saying, "I absolve you," but by saying, "These sins were never yours to begin with." When Roxy arrived for my graduation from The Meadows a week later, that was the first news I told her, clasping her upper arms and shaking her before folding her in a rapturous embrace.

Before that graduation, though, there was one more way—once crucial way—that The Meadows helped me begin to recover from childhood trauma. After my acute withdrawal was over, I did not immediately feel fine. I felt better, a lot better, but one big problem remained: insomnia. Even as a child, I was a bad sleeper, doubtless because of the sexual abuse I endured. I learned very young to fear the predator who crept around my house at night, so I always slept very lightly, waking at the slightest sound or stirring of the air around me. Sometimes I lay rigid under blankets that I pulled as tightly as I could, hoping to make myself inaccessible. As an adult, I still slept "with one eye open." The past few years, drinking had sent me quickly to sleep at bedtime but woken me in a jangle of nerves several hours later. Now, deprived of my evening sedative, I wasn't sleeping at all. It didn't help that I had a roommate, who both kept me from sleeping and kept me from being able to switch on a lamp and read. So I had begun prowling the halls in the wee hours, hoping to find another insomniac who'd be up for a chat or a game of Scrabble. My first night of wandering was socially unproductive. I ended up in the lounge, where I read all the personal stories in the back of the AA "big book." The next night, I found two men playing cribbage in the lounge. They invited me to join them but then couldn't remember how to play three-handed. I watched for a while, hoping to pick up the game, but their explanations confused me, so I got bored and left. The third night, finding no one in the lounge, I fixed on the idea of a walk outside. I knew it wasn't a great idea, given the venomous inhabitants of the Arizona desert, but, on balance, I feared pacing the halls all night more than I feared spiders and bark scorpions. A flashlight was all I needed, so I headed for the nurse's station to cadge one.

I was surprised to find Daisy on duty; I had thought she worked days. She smiled broadly when I walked up and asked me how I was doing. Feeling a little embarrassed about my behavior in her office the week before, I shrugged and answered "fine."

"Can't sleep, huh?" she asked. I shrugged again. "I couldn't either, at first" she replied, and I realized that Daisy was yet another staff member with a history of substance abuse. "Truth is, I still don't sleep very well—one reason I don't mind working nights."

"I never was much of a sleeper," I admitted, "even as a kid."

"Having too much fun to sleep?"

"*Someone* was," I mumbled, "but it sure as hell wasn't me.

"Sit," Daisy said, glancing at the chair next to her.

I sat, eager for conversation.

"So whose fun kept you awake?" she said.

Confiding was a different matter. In my experience, telling people about the terrible things that had happened in my childhood was a bad idea. After getting burned by Mr. Waldo, I had tried again with the leader of the Mormon Church, President Spencer W. Kimball, who had set me on my knees for almost six hours, demanding that I confess my "sexual sins." Someone was having fun then, too, and it sure as hell wasn't me. Daisy noticed my hesitation.

"Some other time," she said, giving my hand a quick squeeze. "How's your first step going?" I told her I was starting to entertain the possibility that I might be an alcoholic and addict.

"I call that excellent progress," she laughed. Then she told me about her experience coming to the same realization and how hard she fought it and how much relief she felt when she finally admitted it. By the end of our conversation, I was a little further down the road to accepting that I wasn't crazy or bad, just addicted to a couple of drugs. Even better, I felt that I had found a companion on that road.

Daisy worked nights for the rest of that week and the next week. Most nights, I went to bed around ten with the rest of the patients, but I generally managed only a light doze, if that. By one, I was typically sitting with Daisy in the small office behind the nurse's station drinking the first of many cups of decaf. By two, we were deep into a conversation that often lasted until the sky was grey and full of birdsong. Those discussions were extraordinary. I've been a talker all my life, and I'm in one of the most conversation-based professions on earth, so deep dialogue is familiar to me, even commonplace. Yet, looking back, I still marvel at how fresh and penetrating our discussions were. Within a few nights, we evolved a conversational style marked by candor, balance, and reciprocity. She did not condescend to me because I was her patient, and I did not condescend to her because she was not a professional therapist; instead, we discovered that our perspectives were complementary and could lead us to unique insights. Sometimes discussion felt like trapeze artistry, one of us somersaulting through the air, the other swinging forward just in time to make a spectacular catch. I'd catch Daisy, then Daisy would catch me; we were not therapist and client or nurse and patient but fellow explorers. We made discoveries together that neither of us could have made alone—or with any other companion. It wasn't long before we revisited the topic of my insomnia, and this time I was ready to share. I told her everything I knew, and her gentle, probing questions helped me discover things I hadn't known. Then she told me why she had trouble sleeping, and together we began excavating her past.

By the time Daisy returned to the day shift, we were friends. More importantly, we were collaborators. Our project was not just sobriety, though it began with sobriety. Our project was understanding, at the deepest possible level, why we drank and used drugs. The moral language of AA, valuable as it could be, did not penetrate the mystery at the heart of our addiction, which was what we were trying to escape or numb or annihilate with chemicals. By the time Father James told me "None of this was your fault," I had someone in my life who knew what that revelation meant, who could help me radically revise my understanding of myself, my history, and the world around me. Daisy and I rolled up our sleeves and got to work.

That work did not end with my graduation from The Meadows, for, on that day, the director offered me a staff position. I was thrilled to receive the vote of confidence, which confirmed my own impression that I had made unusually swift—and *real*—progress in sobriety. I was also thrilled that Daisy and I could continue our conversations. My new job involved conducting psycho-social assessments. Immediately after patients emerged from detox, I took their histories—family, employment, social, any history that could shed light on their problems and contribute to possible solutions. I administered the Minnesota Multiphasic Personality Inventory, the psychological test Mr. Waldo had given me, which measured traits such as anger, cynicism, and self-esteem. Then I turned all the information over to our staff psychologist, who devised a treatment plan. Still so newly sober, I was grateful not to be doing therapy just yet, merely soliciting information. At the same time, I was learning a great deal about a population that hadn't been studied much: alcoholics and drug addicts. I quickly began to perceive a clear link between addiction and childhood trauma, a link that my own practice and a solid body of academic research would eventually confirm.[60] But my experience had already confirmed it, as had Daisy's. The more we talked, the clearer it became that our very different backgrounds had produced some startlingly similar feelings and behavior. Over the next few years, we found commonalities that surprised us, not just our shared addictions, but habitual ways of perceiving and responding to the world.

We had some obvious superficial similarities. We were both attractive young women. We were both intelligent, middle-class professionals dedicated to helping people. Our backgrounds, however, seemed very different. Though both from large families, we were at the opposite ends of the pecking order: I was the first of five children, and she was the last of four. I grew up mostly on a farm or a ranch, close to nature and accustomed to physical labor; she grew up in various midwestern suburbs, where nature is domesticated, and labor is a day in September. I was raised Mormon, every facet of my life dominated by the church, its representatives, and its principles. She was raised to check the "Episcopalian" box on forms but had little experience of any religion. Despite living in a sparsely populated region, I grew up among lots and lots of people, many of them related to me. Daisy was much less geographically isolated but grew up without an extended family or a strong sense of community. We both went to several different elementary schools, but my family settled down after that, whereas hers kept moving. My parents, being Mormon, were teetotalers; Daisy's parents were drunks.

Our adult problems initially looked very different, aside from the substance abuse. But even that we did differently. Though both polydrug users—alcohol plus other pharmaceuticals— our "others" were different, and we used them to different ends. I've already explained my habit of getting drunk in the evening then taking speed the next day to deal with the hangover and give me some extra oomph. Since high school, my life had been rigidly compartmentalized, and I used different drugs for different compartments. In my addled way, I was trying to prop up my professional self, the self that was acceptable to me, and annihilate the self I saw as evil. The fact that the two selves lived in the same body kept this strategy from functioning optimally, to put it mildly.

Daisy didn't rocket up and down the way I did; she used drugs and alcohol to try and keep herself on an even keel. As a nurse in the 1970s, when hospital inventory control was lax, she had access to a wide range of pharmaceuticals. During the day, she used a combination of opioids and benzodiazepines to maintain a "slow glow," to which she added alcohol at night. She rarely became visibly drunk or high; in fact, she wasn't chasing euphoria, just trying to feel okay and tamp down the low-grade panic that had been her life-long companion. Not surprisingly, increased tolerance meant bigger doses and more panic when their effects subsided, driving a downward spiral that affected her job performance. A DUI, which I had somehow escaped despite multiple nights of blackout driving, had unmasked her problem, and her employers had sent her to treatment.

We had ostensibly different patterns in our social lives as well. I was a lesbian in a committed relationship but a serial philanderer with both sexes on the side. In my late twenties, I was starting to think about children but had none yet. I had a lot of friends—a few men but mostly women. Daisy, in her early thirties, was navigating the end of her third rocky marriage and had four children by two husbands. She was a devout heterosexual who *married* philanderers. These men did more than betray her, though; they beat her and criticized her relentlessly. Nonetheless, she was male-oriented and had very few women friends.

Initially, our backgrounds didn't seem to line up with our adult experience. One of psychology's maxims is that we gravitate to what is familiar, yet Daisy and I didn't seem to be doing that, exactly. I was beaten as a child but not at all drawn to physically abusive women or men. She was *not* beaten as a child but ineluctably drawn to abusive men. At the same time we were puzzling over this seeming discrepancy, we were both noticing almost daily that the people coming into The Meadows—and later into the Nevada clinic where I specialized in treating addiction—had horrific backstories covering many different kinds of abuse or neglect. What emerged was a clear correlation between childhood abuse and adult addiction, though it was rarely a correlation the addicts themselves perceived. Often they would mention a devastating experience in an off-hand way, as a fact with no significance, like the kind of toothpaste their family preferred. The same thing happened as we got to know people from our respective AA groups. In the "drunkalogues" I mentioned in chapter five, speakers would sometimes recount a bit of adolescent misbehavior in great detail, then barely mention a disproportionately harsh punishment, a brutal beating or confinement in a locked shed without food or water. Sometimes we could hear the pain as someone mentioned going to bed hungry every night or being sent to boarding school at age seven. More often, as these fleeting admissions came and went, we heard comic bravado or no inflection at all. That last was Daisy's mode, and it took me a while to realize how much hurt lay beneath that seeming lack of affect.

Our conversations were varied and wide-ranging. Sometimes discussion was focused on events in our lives, their roots, their dynamics, and their resolution. Daisy, not surprisingly, had complicated, volatile relationships with spouses and children. Sometimes discussion was more abstract as we tried to wrest general principles from our experiences and those of our friends or patients. Always discussion was heuristic, not swapping rehearsed opinions, but exploring barely-understood phenomena, developing new perspectives and therapeutic approaches as our comprehension evolved. Sometimes discussion was hard work, but more often it was comforting, energizing, and even exhilarating, especially as patterns began to emerge and prove useful to us and other survivors.

We talked for years: in person and over the phone. Daisy remained at The Meadows as I moved around the west: Nevada, back home to Utah, then back to my adopted home of Phoenix. In Phoenix, I maintained a close professional association with The Meadows, counseling its staff and running aftercare groups for its graduates. Perhaps my most important job, however, was as a consultant, helping develop techniques and programs as they diversified from the twelve-step-focused treatment model with which they started. Working with Daisy and the director, now her husband, I helped develop a coherent program to help addicts deal with the trauma that led them to use drugs, including alcohol. That program became the Survivors Workshop, which remains an integral part of addiction treatment at The Meadows, as well as a free-standing course available to anyone, regardless of the issues that prompt them to seek help. That program also became Legacy, the four-day therapeutic intensive that I brought to Seattle a quarter-century ago. Between Legacy and the Survivors Workshop, Daisy and I have helped thousands of people understand and overcome their childhood trauma.

At the same time, I was helping develop a complementary approach, a group called Codependents Anonymous (CoDA), which had its inaugural meeting in Phoenix in 1986. CoDA is a recovery program for people with a spectrum of interpersonal problems that generate dysfunctional relationships. This meeting was the result of intense conversations among a small group of friends in recovery who together had discovered both the value and the limitations of Alcoholics Anonymous and similar programs. I've spoken at length about their value, but the truth is we had begun to wonder why, after working the program with courage, rigor, and unstinting effort, we weren't feeling better—as much better as we thought we should be, anyway. With the help of books such as Claudia Black's 1982 best-seller *It Will Never Happen to Me*, we began to discuss problems beyond addiction, just as Daisy and I had been doing for some years. Through these discussions, we became convinced that a twelve-step approach could be useful in dealing with unresolved childhood trauma and its damaging effects upon adult relationships. When we resolved to found such a program, CoDA was born. Soon afterward, my personal life took me to Seattle, so I was not involved in the writing of the book *Codependents Anonymous*, or, as it's familiarly known, the CoDA Book. Nonetheless, my history is included in the "personal stories" section, as are the histories of friends and co-founders. Its place there, one story among many, testifies to the critical importance of community in recovery from childhood trauma.

CHAPTER TEN: Collaborative Reflection

My relationship with Daisy underscores the value of deep dialogue in developing resilience. Resilience, remember, is something we create through our actions, not something we naturally possess. And one of the best things we can do, as survivors, is talk with others who can understand our experience and whose experience we can understand. I was lucky to find such a person—and to watch our collaboration bear fruit for many years. As I've mentioned, our discussions inspired a therapeutic program that has helped thousands of people. They also inspired at least three books: this one, of course, and several by Daisy. In fact, I distinctly recall the conversation that generated her second book. For months, we had been discussing her rocky relationship with her fourth husband who, unlike her previous husbands, avoided confrontation. The more he retreated, the more Daisy tried to provoke him, so they were locked in a dance that we had analyzed at length. Daisy thoroughly understood the dynamics of this dance but danced it anyway. Now, as we sat on the balcony of my apartment in Phoenix, she told me about the latest *pas de deux*. It was a late summer evening shortly before I moved to Seattle, and the low red sun burnished Daisy's hair, now bobbed, as she described an argument over her husband's attention to another woman. As always, it was an argument in which she had done all the arguing. We had been over this ground many times before, so I responded more bluntly than usual.

"Daisy, honey, he's not doing anything but sitting there in silence, which makes you look like an idiot," I said. "You want him to be something that he's not, so you come at him again and again, and the result is always the same: no comprehension and no change. Still, you come back for more. That's love addiction."

It was dialogue that finally got through to Daisy, and many times it was dialogue that got through to me. In the next chapter, I'm going to present a crucial conversation between Daisy and me, a phone call that changed my life.

But first I'm going to talk generally about the kind of dialogue we developed, which is one of the most useful tools available to trauma survivors, a tool I call collaborative reflection (CR). In CR, two or more people investigate an experience in the hope of understanding it more deeply than they could on their own. It differs from informal discussion in its intensity and focus on one participant at a time. It requires active listening as a starting point, though its goal is shared discovery, rather than conflict resolution. The term "collaborative reflection" comes from the college classroom, where two or more students investigate a text together, building on (and sometimes questioning) one another's insights to yield a richer interpretation than they could produce individually. When Daisy and I engaged in CR, our histories of abuse and our present-day thoughts, feelings, and behavior became the "texts" we pored over together, and there is no question that our cooperative understanding far outpaced the insights we gained working alone. I urge you to remember this "textual" metaphor because it is can be very liberating, both emotionally and intellectually.

CR is a way for two or more people to learn something together—from one another and with one another. It's not therapy, and participants must be careful not to slip into roles more appropriate to a counseling relationship or offer mental health advice. CR is also not twelve-step sponsorship or mentorship or any relationship in which one party guides while the other follows. It's a joint expedition to which all parties bring insights gained from experience, observation, or study. The goals of the expedition are discovery and support, which will require that all participants lead sometimes and follow at other times. What's crucial is that collaboration be genuinely democratic in the long run. Though not therapy, CR should be therapeutic in the sense of being beneficial, restorative, and productive of insight. Though it may not be comfortable every single moment, it should feel safe and supportive.

A good collaborator will be someone for whom you feel affinity but not psychic twinship. Ideally, you'll be similar enough to engender sympathy yet different enough to offer one another genuinely fresh perspectives. Beware of power asymmetries, particularly if you're prone to dysfunctional ones. The relationship has to be one of equals, or it won't work. That said, consider people who are not like you demographically; don't automatically assume you have to stick to your own ethnic group or age cohort. Gender can be a little tricky, especially if you have a history of sexual trauma. Many people find it easier to open up with people of their own gender, and that's generally what I'd advise, but consider your own gender identity, sexual orientation, and personal history in making such a decision.

Where do you find potential collaborators? You may have friends with histories similar to yours, and you may already have discussed those histories at some length. Think about those people and consider how interested they might be in a slightly more structured, more purposeful discussion. In addition, given the statistics about childhood trauma and addiction, twelve-step or other therapeutic groups are excellent places to look. If you belong to such a group, you can listen (or, online, read) what people share about themselves and gauge their potential interest in working together. Among twelve-step groups, Codependents Anonymous, (CoDA), which I mentioned a moment ago, and Adult Children of Alcoholics (ACA) are specifically dedicated to survivors of childhood trauma. In many ways, those groups attract a population ideal for CR; just make sure you approach people who are open to new methods, genuinely interested in other human beings, and ready to change.

To get started, you may want to take a structured approach with a clear separation of functions. One person at a time will speak; the other(s) will witness and then offer feedback. For clarity of pronoun reference, I will treat the speaker as female and the witness as male, but I could just as easily have done the opposite. The speaker should choose a story to tell from her experience. It's probably best to start with a story that is low or moderate in intensity but that is nonetheless important to the speaker. Before beginning, the witness should make a point to remind himself that neither the story nor the feelings it evokes are his. I often tell workshop participants to check their boundaries, and that's exactly what the witness should do before beginning and any time he feels uncomfortable. At the end of this section, I'll introduce a boundary meditation that is very helpful here, along with a way to invoke its benefits on the fly. One way or another, the witness must "boundary up." Empathy does not mean being triggered.

A second, very important, preliminary is a commitment to confidentiality. Both the speaker and the witness should explicitly affirm that they will never, under any circumstances, divulge one another's confidences without permission. This affirmation can, if necessary, take the form of a written non-disclosure agreement, which would make it legally binding. Much more commonly, it will be a spoken vow, something simple, such as: "I promise never to repeat what you tell me in confidence or share your private information with a third party, unless you specifically ask me to." A formal vow may seem unnecessary, particularly among old friends, but I believe it's important. It frames the collaborative process as special, closer to legally privileged communication than to everyday conversation and worthy of similar respect. A formal vow is also a boundary-setting ritual and a clear commitment to boundary maintenance in the future. However it's handled, it should be a regular part of CR.

Before beginning her story, the speaker should offer essential background information. This material will diminish over time, as the collaborators accumulate knowledge of one another's lives, but at the beginning it may be substantial. It may include information such as who was involved, how old the speaker was, where the family was living, what were their circumstances, and any other facts necessary to provide a context for the story. This material cannot and will not be comprehensive, but it should prevent the speaker from having to stop repeatedly and fill in necessary information. When the speaker finishes giving background information, the witness may ask a question or two if the information seems thin, but this is not a general fact-gathering opportunity for the witness.

The speaker should then tell the story in as unhurried a manner as possible. She should convey, as best she can, three things: what happened, how she felt about it at the time, and how she feels about it now. The witness should listen as attentively as possible. He should have the means at hand to make a few notes, but I strongly discourage the use of a laptop, tablet, or smart phone for this purpose. In the last year, research has demonstrated that even the presence of such a device nearby erodes the owner's concentration. The speaker deserves the witness's full attention, so use paper and an old-fashioned writing implement to make an occasional note.

As the speaker is telling her story, the witness should try not to prompt or ask questions *unless the speaker requests such help*. If the speaker has great difficulty telling the story because of its emotional magnitude, the witness should remain patient and attentive. It's fine to be solicitous—to offer water, for example—but the witness shouldn't try to soothe the speaker or calm the atmosphere in the room. On occasion, the speaker may ask for help in telling the story. If that happens, the witness may offer prompts such as "And then what happened?" or "How did you feel about that?"

After the speaker finishes, the witness should offer feedback. This feedback must not be a critique of the story or a comment on the severity of the trauma it described. We are all different, and something merely irritating to one person may be shattering to another. The witness should not pass judgment but should help the speaker understand her experience more fully. Often the most helpful way to frame responses is in the form of questions. These should not be questions about the intent of parents or caregivers, questions such as "Do you think he meant to hurt you?" Questions of intent, while essential in a court of law, are meaningless when it comes to understanding the effects of trauma. As I've said, over and over, a caregiver can do tremendous damage in good faith, driven by love and concern. "It's for your own good" has motivated many a cruelty. The most helpful questions aid the speaker in gaining perspective on her experience. If, for example, the witness notices that the speaker blames herself for her own suffering, he can ask questions that gently challenge that view.

"How, *exactly*, did you cause the situation?"

"At five years old, what could you realistically have done differently?"

"If you saw a five-year-old in the same situation today, what would you think? How would you feel?"

Sometimes statements can help as well, especially first-person statements of feeling.

"When you described what your mother did, I felt such fear for that little girl!"

"As a five-year-old in that situation, I would have felt sad and lonely." The witness is not telling the speaker how she should feel; instead he is giving her a way to "try on" a different perspective and see how it fits. Questions may also solicit additional information that might be relevant.

"Where was the rest of the family when all of this was going on?"

"Did anyone ever acknowledge what had happened?"

Whatever the witness can do to introduce new perspectives will be valuable. Sometimes it's useful to identify a kind adult the speaker knew as a child—a grandparent, a teacher, a neighbor—and make him or her a hypothetical witness.

"If your grandpa had been there, how do you think he would describe that punishment?"

"What would Mrs. Garcia have said if she knew you were locked in the attic all weekend?" This technique offers a compassionate perspective on the past via a known personality from that era and is particularly useful early on, when the witness's compassion is less familiar and meaningful. Because compassion is so important to this exercise—as it is to dealing effectively with childhood trauma generally—a further elaboration of the lovingkindness meditation you learned may help to foster it. In this modification, after extending good wishes to your benefactors and yourselves, extend good wishes to your collaborator(s) and receive the same in return.

As the witness offers feedback, he should not expect to see obvious changes in the speaker's understanding. In other words, he should try as hard as he can to be helpful without looking for a particular result, either in the short term or over time. One reason for asking a lot of questions is that, when people figure things out for themselves, new ideas are less alien and more easily accepted. Still, people often need time to think them through and integrate them with beliefs that may be powerful and deeply-held. Some of the reflection in "collaborative reflection" happens outside the conversations that generate it.

After finishing with the first story, the speaker and the witness(es) exchange roles and repeat the process. How they proceed after that depends upon how they want to handle the material from their stories. One option is to write them down in a way that both testifies to the trauma in the tale and amplifies the strength of the teller, as I did in chapter two. Here the partners can help each other enormously, both before the writing begins and during the process of drafting and revision, Beforehand, they can help identify opportunities to enhance positive qualities in each other's stories.

"When you hid under the bed, that showed courage and quick thinking!"

"Though your mother called the kitchen a disaster area, I saw a loving, creative child who wanted to make other people happy."

As they write early drafts, their knowledge of each other's stories will let help them make acute observations about the direction the writing is taking. Again, these are often better framed as questions.

"What made you decide to leave out what your father said to you afterward?"

"What made you decide to start the story when your mother threw the plate, rather than when she got home?" Some comments will have to be framed as statements, though they should ideally be "I" statements and be accompanied by an explanation.

"I thought it was important that your older brother was in the room watching TV and laughing—not to blame him, but to show how unremarkable violence was in your home."

Because these stories constitute a lasting witness to our experience, the contributions of an actual witness are invaluable in shaping them. Moreover, because the stories can shape the way we see ourselves—and even what we *become*—they must accentuate what is good and strong in us, which is something not all trauma survivors do well, at least not naturally and not right away. While we're developing those capacities, we can help each other because we generally find it easier to see positive qualities in others than in ourselves.

In the next section, I will describe a performance-based way to use the material gained in collaborative reflection. I will also transcribe an example of another way to use it: as the basis for free- and far-ranging ranging conversation about your experience as survivors of trauma. Because we were similar in some ways and different in others; because we were interested in each other's experience and in the larger dynamics of trauma; because, outside of our conversations, we took every opportunity to learn about how human beings functioned in the world; because we respected one another but were not afraid to ask the hard questions, Daisy and I were able to deal with our own trauma and to help other people deal with theirs. I wish no less for you.

Practice: Boundary Meditation

Many of the guided meditations in this book are based on standard instructions from programs such as the University of Massachusetts's Mindfulness-Based Stress Reduction (MBSR) and the University of Washington's Mindfulness-Based Relapse Prevention, which are themselves based on the practices of teachers such as Thích Nhất Hạnh, Seung Sahn, S. N. Goenka, Pema Chodron, and Sharon Salzberg. I have adapted those instructions specifically for survivors of childhood trauma, but they are firmly rooted in mainstream mindfulness practices. In contrast, this Boundary Meditation is a new practice. Using the technique of visualization, which is common in many meditative traditions, I designed a practice to reinforce your conscious efforts to establish and maintain healthy boundaries. It's an excellent addition to your regular practice and a fitting preliminary to work requiring boundary maintenance, such as Collaborative Reflection. After you practice the meditation for a while, merely calling to mind its central image will help you to quickly "boundary up" when necessary.

To give you some variety, as many mindfulness programs do, I tapped my assistant to record the Boundary Meditation.[61] She has been practicing Zen meditation for thirty years, but her tradition celebrates "beginner's mind," so she's an apt guide to a complex new practice. It is a bit longer than most in this book, lasting just over twenty-four minutes. Unlike the others, which can be done in any stable meditative position, Boundary Meditation is practiced lying on your back. Your spine should be straight, your legs slightly apart and relaxed, your toes to the side, your arms slightly away from your sides, and your palms facing up. Those of you who practice yoga will recognize Corpse Pose, which is ideal for this type of meditation. When meditating lying down, there's always a chance you'll doze off. If you do, don't fret; you probably needed the rest. Try again after a good night's sleep.

Part V

Lightening the Burden

CHAPTER ELEVEN: I Return to the Scene of the Crime

The next story jumps ahead nearly twenty years. I'm leaping over major life changes, including my entry into private practice, my pursuit of a Ph.D., my relocation to Seattle, and the most important of all, the arrival of my son, James. I could write a whole book just about James's childhood, which taught me more about human development than any psychology course I ever took, but, for our purposes, the crucial change in my life was learning—through observation, study, collaborative reflection, and constant practice—how to cope with the trauma I had suffered as a child. Working with a therapist, supported by Daisy and dozens of friends in AA, CoDA, and the community of recovery professionals, I made steady progress for a decade. Then, when my son was born, my desire to provide him with an optimal upbringing lent my recovery new urgency. After years of working with dysfunctional families, I knew how important it was to insulate James from the effects of my own childhood trauma, to "break the chain" through which suffering is passed down the generations. I redoubled my efforts to understand my history and replace old ways of thinking and acting with new, healthy responses.

At times, I saw dramatic progress. Perhaps the most visible change lay in the way I experienced anger. In the early years of my sobriety, explosive anger remained a real problem. To cite just one minor example, shortly after I moved to Seattle, a driver, heading west into the setting sun, failed to see me stepping into a crosswalk and came within inches of hitting me. Enraged, I chased his car to the next stoplight and pounded on his passenger-side window screaming, "How dare you? *How dare you?* You could have killed me, you sonofabitch! Who do you think you are?" Looking straight ahead, he did his best to ignore my pounding as he waited for the light to change.

"Open your window, goddamn it!" I screamed, still pounding. When he continued to ignore me, I looked around for a rock or a brick to smash the window. I would make him listen to me! Spotting a chunk of concrete on the ground nearby, I lunged for it, only to watch the car speed away as the light turned green. I remember shaking with anger and making plans to return to the following day with a baseball bat. He wouldn't get away with nearly hitting me! I knew what his car looked like! If he thought he could drive down my street again without paying for his recklessness, he had another think coming! On and on churned my fantasy of revenge. I imagined my bat smashing through his windshield, sending bright nuggets of safety glass flying and forcing the smug, oblivious driver to gasp with fear the way I had just done in the crosswalk. I imagined other drivers looking on with approval as I struck a literal blow for pedestrians everywhere. I needed a long time to calm down that afternoon, and, for several days afterward, just thinking about the episode renewed my rage.

Over time, I gained control of that anger. The first step, of course, was recognizing its sources. A small fraction was natural and appropriate. The driver had entered a crosswalk at a high rate of speed with the sun in his eyes. I knew that because I had glimpsed the sunlight on his face and because I had often driven the same stretch of road late in the day. For most of the block, a driver heading west at that time of year could see little but searing light. In such dangerous conditions, drivers should slow down, no matter how urgent their errands. That driver didn't, so a brief and transient feeling of indignation falls within the range of acceptable responses. Most of my anger, though, had little to do with the speeding driver—or anything else happening in my life. It was not situational but primal, exploding out of my unconscious when triggered by the driver. It manifested automatically and ran furiously on its own momentum before my conscious mind even registered the near-accident, much less began to respond.

That primal anger had two main sources. One was childhood anger I had bottled up. Over and over, adults had done serious injury to my body, and I had been unable to express—or even feel—much natural anger about the assaults, though I had passed a little of it along to my younger siblings. There were many assaults, so there was a lot of anger, but anger was dangerous to express in my family because it provoked my father into greater cruelty. So most of mine was stifled. Now along comes an anonymous driver threatening to do what my father did, hurt me for no reason other than that I was in his path. He wasn't a source of retaliatory rage, like my father; in fact, he seemed a little afraid of me. That put the shoe on the other foot, for once. Looking back, I see a kind of exultation in my fury, as though a part of me relished the power to scare an adult male who subordinated my life and safety to his own inscrutable impulses, as my father had so often done.

Another piece of the anger was learned behavior, pure "monkey see, monkey do." All of us imitate our caregivers, even those whose example we consciously reject, and I was no exception. For seventeen years, I watched my father exercise power with his fists, boots, and insults, not just within the family, but out in the community too. His public brawls sometimes landed him in hot water—he was regularly "disfellowshipped," or formally shunned by the Mormon Church—but, for the most part, he successfully used anger to dominate other people without consequence. (He didn't even mind church discipline; it was the family that felt embarrassed.) Much as I consciously loathed his brutality, my unconscious absorbed the lesson every tyrant teaches: there is power in rage.

Both sources of anger are what we call carried feelings. These are emotions that originate in someone else's experience, affective legacies that can be passed down many generations. At any point in their transmission, they may be felt or unfelt, acknowledged or unacknowledged. For example, a father who sexually abuses his daughter may or may not experience the shame that would naturally accompany an act so widely abhorred. Whether he feels his own shame or not, his daughter will likely feel it, either because he has explicitly assigned it to her or because, consciously or unconsciously, she has assigned it to herself. It's tragic, but sometimes children pick up terrible emotional burdens simply because the adults who ought to carry them cannot or will not. Mechanistic as this dynamic sounds, family systems theory demonstrates, over and over, that children compensate for the perceived deficiencies of their caregivers, which includes doing emotional work they may not even understand.

In general, carried feelings can be recognized by their nature, their intensity, and their effects. They are always excessive. Carried shame is mortification; carried sadness is despair; carried anger is blind rage. When I was screaming and pounding the window of that poor driver who had almost clipped me in the crosswalk, my rage far exceeded justifiable anger. It was overwhelming and alien, less like strong emotion than like possession by a malign spirit. In the last chapter, I talked about how relieved I felt when Father James told me that the sins I had lugged around for so many years were not actually mine. The relief was almost as intense when I grasped that this rage wasn't mine either, that it had come from someone else and that I could give it back.

As my next story begins, carried anger was no longer a problem in my life. More than a decade had passed since I chased that car down the street or felt any urge to retaliate for the inevitable petty insults of life. Over the years, I got better and better at catching anger as it was triggered and pausing to choose whether—and how—I would let it rise. In addition to general mindfulness, which helps prevent the cognitive hijacking that unleashes rage (and other carried feelings), I used specific techniques to stay in control. One was simply asking "Whose anger is this?" Another was a reality check to remind myself of the functional adult I had become.

"I am Dr. Donna Bevan-Lee," I would begin. "I am a psychotherapist and the mother of a ten-year-old son. I am standing on Beach Drive in Seattle, Washington." On I would go in that vein. Rehearsing the essential facts of my adult life, which I still do occasionally, brings me quickly back to the present moment, to a healthy ego state. It allows me to deal appropriately with any strong emotion that is rising—or to walk away until I can.

I recently learned another technique that does essentially the same thing. With this method, you meditate to prepare in advance for the inevitable triggers you will encounter as you go about your daily life. This meditation uses the attention you've been cultivating, along with your imagination, to create a refuge of stability you can use in a moment of distress, anger, or fear. To practice it, you assume your usual meditation posture and picture a mountain you can visualize clearly.[62] I envision Mount Kilimanjaro, which I summited a decade ago after a week of hard climbing. Rising nearly four miles above the Maasai Steppe in Tanzania, Kilimanjaro is ideal for two reasons: it's the world's highest free-standing mountain, and it's host to five different climate zones. For this meditation, it's good to choose a mountain that's easy to picture in your mind and that has some diversity in vegetation and weather patterns. I could happily use King's Peak, the highest mountain in Utah and another favorite climb, or beautiful Mount Rainier, which I see in the distance nearly every day.

After clearly visualizing your mountain, you contemplate both the myriad changes visible on its surface and the stability of the geologic mass beneath. (So it's probably not a good idea to choose an active volcano!) After you have thoroughly absorbed this model of surface transformation and inner stability, you imagine yourself *as* that mountain. Seeing yourself as the mountain reinforces the idea that you're fundamentally stable and strong despite superficial changes, no matter how dramatic they may seem. The exercise is beneficial while you're quietly doing it, but it's also a valuable resource at more challenging times. Through practicing the meditation, you create a mental image that evokes calm, strength, and stability, and, after a while, all you have to do is imagine your mountain-self to gain a some perspective on whatever emotional storm is starting to rage—around you, inside of you, or both. Your functional adult stays in charge, and your anger remains commensurate with whatever provoked it. Appropriate anger, like all emotions, comes bearing gifts: energy, focus, clarity, and purpose. I don't ever want to banish natural anger, one of the world's great engines of positive change. But carried anger brings only pain and embarrassment, and I was thoroughly glad to be rid of it.

I was not rid of all my carried feelings, however. As I was about to discover, I had some I didn't even suspect, despite all the work I had done on mine and on other people's. Such is often the case with carried feelings, which can be entirely unconscious. By this time, I had been conducting Legacy workshops once a month for almost five years, helping a steady stream of clients discover and cope with their childhood trauma. I justly thought I had made excellent progress with my own history and devoted increasing attention to new goals, such as being an optimal parent to a pre-teen son. Year by year, I saw myself as more mother than daughter, a survivor who had refashioned a devastating legacy of abuse into an instrument of change. In other words, I was defined by a strong sense of agency that may have obscured some of the more subtle effects of that abuse.

The episode began when two medical crises hit my family at the same time. The first was anticipated and planned for: my father had hip replacement surgery. His years as a rodeo rider had been hard on his joints, and his hips were badly arthritic. Otherwise healthy and active, he was promised an uneventful surgery and quick recovery. He would be back in the saddle by Labor Day, barely two months away. The second medical crisis was a complete shock: my mother had a heart attack, a near-fatal one, the day after my father's surgery. Slim, active, relatively young, a paragon of Mormon abstinence whose lips never even touched coffee, my mother might have been called one of the world's least likely cardiac patients. Little did we know she had a single mutated gene that wildly elevated her serum cholesterol, eventually blocking her cardiac arteries.[63] The attack came in the middle of the night while she slept alone in the bed she normally shared with my father. Though unable to speak, she managed to pick up the bedside phone and dial my sister, who called the sheriff who summoned the ambulance that saved her life. Less than twenty-hour hours after my father's surgery, he and his wife lay in two different hospitals twelve blocks apart. My father was doing well, but my mother was in the ICU, and nobody yet knew whether she would survive. When my sister called with the terrible news, I notified all my clients that I had a family emergency and rushed to Salt Lake City.

When I arrived at the ICU, I found a waiting room full of worried people. On every couch, bench, chair, and table perched a friend or relative of my mother, all nervously awaiting news. Under the harsh fluorescent light, they murmured in small groups or read tattered copies of *People* magazine or sat jiggling a leg and staring into space. When I arrived, I was immediately conducted to her room. She looked terrible, frail and helpless, a pale fly caught in a vicious web of tubes. Medication had bloated her face and made slits of her eyes; at first, I couldn't tell whether she was even awake. As I entered, a cardiologist was explaining that she needed a quadruple bypass immediately.

"No," she whispered. I approached the bed, not sure whether she could see me, whether her eyes were open or closed.

"Mom?" I began. "We need to do what the doctor says. We can—"

"Go away," she said weakly.

"Mom, it's me, Donna," I said. I began reaching for her hand, but stopped when I saw a tube taped to it.

"Go away," she repeated. I didn't take offense. My mother is a modest woman; I knew she wouldn't want to be seen as I was seeing her.

"Well I'm here, Mom," I replied, "and so are a lot of other people, all out in the waiting room, all hoping you're okay. They're expecting me to report back in a minute, so I'm gonna tell them you're ornery enough to tell me to go away, and I believe they'll see that as a good sign." She smiled very softly at my little joke.

Within hours, my mother had the bypass surgery. She had initially wanted to wait until my father was well, but that really wasn't an option; she was far too ill. For several days, she remained in the ICU, and the crowd returned to the waiting room every day. Only immediate family were allowed to actually see her—and only one at a time—so my siblings and I took turns delivering minutely-observed reports, even when all we could report was that she was sleeping. In truth, our bulletins may have become a little competitive toward the end, as each one tended to be more elaborate than the last. Having worked in a hospital emergency department for several years, I specialized in medical terminology, but my brother David specialized in ornate description of humdrum details.

"She's snoring," concluded one of his reports. "It sounds like a woodpecker drumming on a breadbox."

On the third day of our vigil, my father turned up, surprising everyone. Almost no one from the ICU waiting room had made the twelve-block trek to his sickbed, so he brought the sickbed to us. Shortly before lunchtime, he rolled off the elevator in a wheelchair pushed by my youngest sister, Julie. He was dressed oddly: in jeans and a hospital gown. Instead of a jacket, he wore a white terrycloth bathrobe, and I think the whole ensemble was to remind everyone that he too was ill. When several people rushed forward to help him, he directed them to the largest couch in the waiting room, which was filled with my mother's well-wishers.

"I'm afraid you'll all have to get up," said my father with mock-regret. "Must keep the leg elevated. Doctor's orders." With a great deal of grunting and groaning, the helpers began to lift him from the wheelchair. I tried not to roll my eyes. Many patients were up walking around on crutches hours after a hip replacement, yet my fit, youngish father needed the help of three men to manage a wheelchair transfer.

"Wait," I said to the men, then turned to my father. "Shouldn't you stay in the chair so you can see Mom?" Murmurs of agreement rose from the helpers as they lowered him back into the chair.

"Later," said my father. "Doc says I shouldn't move around too much. The hip is giving me terrible pain." He emphasized "terrible" with a grimace worthy of a Civil War soldier enduring a battlefield amputation. Then he asked for a drink of water so he could take some medication and swallowed several white pills.

"Nice touch," I murmured, assuming the pills were part of his performance. "Vitamin C?"

"Painkillers," said my father with another grimace, this one worthy of a medieval heretic on the rack.

"Whatever you say, Dad" I replied.

Once settled on the couch, he announced that he had left his hospital against medical advice to support his ailing wife. As he spoke, my sister Julie looked surprised but said nothing. His support for my mother consisted of asking people to fetch him things: water, coffee, ice cream, Doctor Pepper, sandwiches, french fries, more ice cream, magazines, information, and still more ice cream. He insisted my mother's physicians stop by to consult with him, though his only question was when she would be able to resume her normal domestic duties, as he expected to be convalescent for quite a long time. To my chagrin, my mother's chief concern, once she awoke from surgery, was exactly the same.

He never made it into the ICU to visit his wife that day. As darkness fell and the waiting-room crowd began to thin, Julie took him to her house then brought him back the following morning after the waiting-room crowd had returned. He had swapped the hospital gown for a checkered cowboy shirt but kept the terrycloth robe, claiming it was more comfortable than a jacket and could be washed in hot water, in case of emergency.

"Emergency?" David whispered to me. "What emergency?"

"Ice cream spill," I replied. "Chocolate stains are worse than blood!"

We both laughed as my father took another handful of white pills. That day unfolded much like the previous day. My siblings and I took turns visiting our mother and reporting back to the assembled crowd. We also took turns bringing my father food from the cafeteria, one snack at a time. In the early afternoon, my mother's cardiologist finally delivered the good news we were waiting for: she had turned the corner! She would have a long convalescence, but she would recover. People who had been at the hospital for days cheered and began to drift back to their normal lives. When my father finally rolled down the hall to visit his wife, pushed by his favorite grandson, his five children faced facts. I spoke the words no one wanted to hear.

"They both need nursing, and we'll have to do it." We quickly decided that the fairest thing to do was each take a week. One by one, we would move into their home and see to their needs. By the time all five of us had done our stint, they'd be able to take care of themselves. I had the most experience in a hospital setting, so I would take the first, most dangerous, week. During my mother's last days in the hospital, I raced home to reschedule commitments and talk to clients. Within a few days, I was back in Utah, not in Salt Lake City this time, but on my parents' remote ranch seventy miles to the southwest.

The ranch was in Faust, Utah, which is too small even to be considered a town, so the mailing address was Vernon, a bustling metropolis of 181 people five miles south. Faust exists because it was a station on the Pony Express established by part-time rider Henry J. Faust, but the town never really caught on, so Henry and his family moved to Salt Lake City soon after the Pony

Express folded. The land around Faust is dry and flat, though there are mountains in every direction except due north, where the Great Salt Lake is. It's scrubland, where the plants are like me: small and tenacious, able to bloom without much in the way of nurture. Desert grasses and creosote bushes predominate, though there are large patches where nothing can grow. Whether you like the landscape depends on your tolerance for wide open spaces, dusty roads, and the thin dry air of the high desert. I think Faust is beautiful, though outsiders typically see all such landscapes as desolate, one reason they test weapons and dump toxic waste there. The doublewide in which my parents lived was familiar from many visits but much more cramped than I was used to as an adult. Moving in for my week, I felt conflicting sensations: inside I felt hemmed in by the limited space and lack of privacy, but all I had to do was step out onto the deck to feel profoundly isolated.

My parents and I arrived at the ranch on the first of July. Getting started was easy. My time working in emergency rooms had familiarized me with what could go wrong after surgery—and what to do about it—so I felt none of the anxiety families sometimes experience when bringing loved ones home from the hospital, even though I had two of them to deal with. I had also nursed two people through serious illnesses at home, so I knew what needed to be done and how to do it with cheerfully. I set about organizing the house for optimal efficiency and establishing routines that my siblings could take over or adapt as our parents regained their health. The routines weren't difficult or complex. My mother had to eat and walk around and take her medication and have her bandages changed and strengthen her lungs with an incentive spirometer, a tube attached to a cylinder with a ping-pong ball inside. Using the spirometer involved coughing, never an attractive prospect for someone with a chest incision, but absolutely essential to clear mucus and avoid pneumonia. Nonetheless, her care seemed straightforward, and I anticipated few problems. My father, deprived of his waiting-room audience, took a swift turn for the better, so I wasn't worried about him at all.

Within hours, it became obvious that neither patient would be easy or straightforward. My mother complained constantly about severe pain. Cutting deep into the body hurts, of course, but open heart surgery is considered one of the less painful of the major procedures, so her doctors predicted that she'd soon be able to manage her pain with Tylenol. Not likely, I thought; the woman seemed to be in agony. The only relief she got was right after she took a Percodan, and even that wasn't much. Were her doctors simply wrong? I wasn't sure. On the one hand, my mother had never coped well with pain or illness. As a very young child, I remembered her bedridden and weeping for many months after the birth of my youngest sister, which was complicated and traumatic—but not *that* complicated and traumatic. On the other hand, when I changed her bandages, I could see extensive bruising from the rib-spreader, and it looked plenty painful to me. Like me, my mother is a tiny woman, and surely there's more tissue damage when instruments built for big people are used on small people. But her doctors all said there was no medical reason for severe pain, so I crossed my fingers and hoped she'd feel better back in the familiar surroundings of home.

She didn't. She remained in agony. Moreover, she was obviously suffering postoperative depression, which is extremely common after heart surgery. Coming home to the ranch, rather than lifting her mood, just reminded her of all the things she could no longer do and made her feel worse. She didn't want me to help her in any way and snapped at me when I brought her a glass of water or offered the incentive spirometer. She didn't want any assistance, comfort, or food. She didn't want to rest. She cried most of the time, and, when she cried, we had the same conversation over and over.

"What's wrong, Mom?"

"I don't know."

"How can I help?"

"You can go away." She meant it, too. And I wanted to oblige her. Unfortunately, the only thing she wanted to do was walk—without assistance, of course—so I was terrified to leave the room completely. I compromised by moving a few feet away and pretending to read the *Tooele Transcript Bulletin*. Hour after hour, over the same newspaper page, I watched her pace the floor with shuffling baby steps, ready to dive across the room to break her fall, should she teeter too far in one direction.

My father's convalescence, on the other hand, became downright miraculous. Barely able to manage a wheelchair transfer in the waiting room, he was quickly up on crutches and moving around the house with alacrity, if little grace. I still had to wait on him, of course, because none of that new mobility could be squandered on fetching a Doctor Pepper; it had to be preserved for following me around so he could evaluate my performance of specific tasks and suggest improvements.

"That's a stupid way to fold towels. Everyone knows you're supposed to start lengthwise."

"She needs to blow so that the ping-pong ball is right in the middle. Don't hold it so far away, you idiot!"

"That salad dressing is crap! Why did you buy that crap? The orange kind is the only good kind! Get the orange kind! Put it on your list right now!" Between my mother's weeping and my father's criticism, my week was growing longer by the minute.

The nights were the worst, even though they afforded a break from my father, who, fortunately, was able to sleep. My mother had far too much pain and emotional distress to sleep, so I stayed up to keep her company, sitting at the end of the couch where she lay and rubbing her feet when she would let me. I was exhausted, though, and more than once dozed off while fully upright, waking to feelings of guilt for "abandoning" her.

"What's the point?" she muttered when I inveigled her to eat.

"You'll feel better. And you'll heal better."

"No, I won't." Then she wept. When I knelt by her and tried to take her hand, she pulled it away then struggled to her feet and resumed her feeble pacing.

"What can I do to help, Mom?"

"Nothing. Just go to bed. You keep falling asleep anyway."

The pattern persisted for several days then got worse on the morning of July fourth, when my father arose in an unusually foul mood. The first sign was a familiar glower: a dark look I remembered from childhood. Face flushed, eyes narrowed, jaw working, he stared at me as he emerged from the master bedroom and made his way into the kitchen, where he continued to stare at me over the counter that divided the kitchen from the living room. I felt a tiny ripple of fear, which I quickly dismissed it as a meaningless atavism, a reflex that belonged to a time when his moods ruled my world. As I watched, he spilled pills into his hand and clapped the hand to his mouth with a "pop" I could hear from the couch. Then he picked up a carton of grapefruit juice, unscrewed the top, and drank noisily from the carton. I began to wonder why he had not abandoned his fake medication when he gave up the rest of his invalid charade.

"Go make him some breakfast," said my mother, interrupting the thought. "Leave me alone for a while."

"Morning, Dad," I said, walking toward the kitchen. Sit down, let me make you some breakfast. What can I fix you?"

"I would rather die of starvation," he growled.

"Suit yourself," I replied. As I scrambled an egg white in olive oil for my mother, he noisily prepared a bowl of Frosted Flakes with milk then ate it standing at the counter rather than accept my help carrying it to the table. I had a strong impulse to roll my eyes but didn't. In fact, I was pleased that he had not managed to rile me even once, not with his attention-seeking in the waiting room of the ICU and not with his hostility at the ranch. At any rate, the Frosted Flakes seemed to sweeten him up a because he soon stopped glaring and crutch-swung to the living room, where he began reading the latest issue of *Guns and Ammo*.

A few hours later, though, he resumed his glowering. Ignoring it, I made him a tuna salad sandwich and set it on the dining table along with some apple wedges and a glass of milk. Instead of sitting down to eat, he swung into the kitchen, where I saw him begin his customary pill-taking performance. This time, however, he frowned at his open palm, returned a few pills to the vial, and bellowed my name.

"I'm almost out of my medication," he hollered. "I need a refill." I may have rolled my eyes this time, but I did play along.

"Phone the pharmacy for a refill," I called from the living room. "I'll go into town and pick it up tomorrow."

"No refills," he called back. We have to call the doc.

I stood up and walked into the kitchen, where I found him leaning against the counter holding a small prescription vial. How long would he keep this charade going?

"Let me see," I said. Though I was only a few feet away, he threw the vial so that I would have to dive for the catch. I did not dive but let the vial fall and roll under the refrigerator.

"You never could keep your eye on the ball," he growled. I said nothing but used the handle of a broom to retrieve the vial. I looked at the label expecting to see the faded name of an old antibiotic. What I saw instead was Vicodin. Studying the vial, I suddenly felt the kitchen floor shift under me: the excessive pill-popping I had witnessed over the last week wasn't theater at all. To catch up, I read the label carefully, counted the pills in the vial, and did some math in my head. He was taking more than twice the prescribed dose; no wonder his mood was up and down.

"It's the Fourth of July," I said finally. "We can't do anything today."

Independence Day seemed to drag on for a week. When evening finally trudged into view, I made steak and potatoes for those who were eating and poured an Ensure into a glass for my mother. She drank less than half of it but managed to keep it and her pain pill down, so I was grateful for that.

I had brought a skyrocket with which to celebrate. For those used to lavish fireworks displays, one skyrocket may seem a paltry celebration, but the ranch in July was dry as a bone, and the last thing I needed on top of my ailing parents was a brush fire.

"Let's go outside on the deck to celebrate the Fourth," I suggested after dinner. We can have a drink and watch the sun go down; then I'll launch our firework." I got my parents situated on the deck, my father with a Doctor Pepper and my mother with a tiny glass of water, which was all she felt up to, and I was just about to sit down with my own glass of water when my father made an unexpected request.

"Go get my gun." Not wanting to upset him, I fetched his twelve-gauge shotgun. When I returned, he was leaning against the front rail of the deck, his crutches leaning beside him. Taking the rifle brusquely from my hands, he fired into the front yard four times, sending up a small explosion of dirt and dry grass each time. The fourth time, a gopher exploded along with the dirt, flying about two feet into the air before landing on its side, where it began to convulse.

"Take that, you sonofabitch," he growled. The creature's limbs continued to jerk.

"Finish it, please," I said softly. My father raised the shotgun to his shoulder and fired twice more. I don't think he hit the gopher again, but, mercifully, its spasms stopped. Still cradling the gun, he gave me a hard look, his face as dark as it had been that morning.

"See what I did to that sonofabitch?" he demanded. I turned to look at my mother, who was staring down into her glass. After a moment's silence, I gave the only answer I dared.

"Yes."

"I could do that to you."

"Yes." As nonchalantly as I could, I took the gun from his hands, put the safety on, and walked back into the house, where I returned it to its place in the master bedroom. Then I went back outside to watch the sun set behind White Rock Mountain. When the sky was dark, I fetched my skyrocket and walked out into the yard, keeping well clear of where the dead gopher lay. I pushed the stick end of the skyrocket into the ground and leaned the rocket end away from the doublewide. I pulled a Bic lighter out of my pocket, lit the long fuse, and ran. The firework hissed as it streaked into the air then exploded with a loud *crack*, the explosion etching a faint dandelion against the dark sky. Looking up, I was suddenly overwhelmed by that darkness. I know rationally that, on a cloudless summer night, there must have been stars, but all I remember seeing was the feeble after-image of my skyrocket against a vast, enveloping blackness, not air but thick substance, infernal and suffocating. For the few seconds it lasted, it was unbearable, one of the most terrible sensations I have ever experienced. I stood in the yard until the feeling passed, then I looked around to make sure no sparks from the skyrocket had fallen to earth and went back to the deck where my parents sat in silence.

"I'm leaving," I told them. Then I walked into the house to call Delta Airlines.

An hour later, the house was in an uproar. I was packing for a flight to Boston. I had no business in Boston, but the flight was the first one out of Salt Lake City in the morning, so I would be on it. As I packed, one sister shouted that I couldn't just leave; it was horrible and selfish and unfair. My other siblings had said the same thing on the phone, one after another, until the words began to blur and run together like wet paint in the rain. My mother was crying, not quietly weeping as she had for the last four days but wailing loudly that I mustn't go, I mustn't. She needed me. My father just glowered, occasionally muttering something I couldn't hear.

"He didn't mean it," said my sister for the twentieth time. "He's a bully, but he wouldn't *kill* you. He's a sick old man. He's on crutches. He was just trying to act tough."

"He did mean it. At the moment he said it, he meant it, and he had a loaded shotgun in his hands. It only takes one deranged second to shoot someone."

"We'll take the guns."

"Or stab someone or strangle someone or crack someone's skull with a rock. This is a man who kicks children in the head, remember."

"Not for years."

"Not since I grew up and moved out, you mean. Now I'm back under his roof, and who knows what he'll do? He's acting exactly like he used to, only now he's abusing painkillers, too."

"What about Mom?"

"I can't do a thing for her. She just keeps telling me to go away."

"What about *us*? You say Dad's dangerous; isn't he just as dangerous to us?" She knew the answer to that question as well as I did: no, not really. But I was suddenly too exhausted to remind her that, though he abused all of his children in one way or another, he beat only the eldest.

"Look," I sighed, "you live five minutes away. Just come over a couple times a day and do for them. That's all they need; that's all they *want*. If there's an emergency, they can phone you."

"The hell with you, Donna. You know I can't do that. Well, run away, then. It's what you always do."

I didn't enjoy Boston. I thought the sheer relief of being out of Utah would make me feel better, but it didn't. I had dinner with the parents of a good friend and spent a whole day at the Museum of Fine Arts—activities that would normally bring me great pleasure—but I felt gloomy and alienated from everything I did. The feeling persisted after I returned home. I had a joyful reunion with my son, but I barely felt the joy; it was like a party in an adjoining room with no connecting door. I went hiking in the mountains with my girlfriend—nature has always been my greatest solace—but the beauty all around me seemed distant and inaccessible, even the path right under my feet. The only thing I felt was a heavy fog of hopelessness. It was classic depression, something I had experienced a lot when I was young, but not so much since I excavated and worked through my childhood trauma. I knew the depression was linked to the debacle in Utah, but I couldn't figure out *how* it was linked. Every time I sat down to reflect on the episode, to do what I've been advocating throughout this book, I got stuck on a pair of facts. First, that nothing I did or said or thought or observed or discovered or suspected during my time in Utah seemed worthy of global despair. Second, that I had done such a thorough job of excavating my past that surely there were no new surprises lurking in my history. After a few weeks of grappling with the problem on my own, I phoned Daisy.

"So, you returned to the scene of the crime." she joked, after I told her the story of my visit. That was how we always described visits to our families of origin.

"I did."

"With no boundary support." Boundary support was the term we used for strategies such as staying in a hotel or bringing an ally along.

"Faust is in the middle of nowhere, Daisy, so no hotels. Besides, I had to be right there in the house in case my mom had a problem."

"Tsk, tsk, tsk," said Daisy. "Rent a Winnebago, buy a baby monitor—*voila*, boundary support!"

"I didn't think of that," I admitted.

"Your first mistake."

"Okay," I acknowledged. "But I don't think the problem was boundary failure."

"The problem is always boundary failure," said Daisy. "One way or another. So let's start with the obvious: your father."

"Ugh," I shuddered. "He was as nasty and brutish as ever, but I don't think that was a trigger."

"Killing a small, defenseless creature for fun? Threatening to do the same to you? Not a trigger? Really?"

"I had a natural, reasonable response to what he did and what he said. I recognized a threat, and I got away from it. I feel fine about that. The truth is, Daisy, he was perfectly awful the whole time, just like he used to be, and I genuinely feel that my boundaries with him were strong. I was proud of that. He didn't rile me up or make me doubt myself or feel unworthy, not once! I felt sad that he's so fucked up and disgusted occasionally—okay, more than occasionally—and afraid when fear was appropriate, but no, I don't think what I'm going through now is about my father."

"I hear you. Well, what do you think it is?"

"Guilt maybe? I reneged on a deal, walked out early, left my siblings with a mess."

"Do you think guilt is appropriate in this situation?"

"Some," I said slowly. "A little guilt is natural."

"But that's not what we're dealing with, is it? So pull on that string: what's attached to that guilt?"

"Something my sister said: 'Run away. You always do.' Maybe that hit a nerve, like I sacrifice other people to save myself, not just this time but regularly."

"You mean like going off to college and moving to Phoenix and making a great life for yourself. That's running away and sacrificing other people?"

"When you say it that way . . . ."

"It's a younger sibling thing, Donna, especially in screwed-up families. Trust me, I know. When you watch your older siblings escape from the hell that is your home, you feel conflicted. Part of you is happy for them. You hope that you'll be able to get away, too. At the same time, you feel abandoned. I think what your sister said was all about your sister and not about you. It stung because you love her, but I don't see it connected to much of anything that's an issue for you. Do you?"

"I feel bad for my siblings. I wish I could help them more.

"Would your staying in Tooele all these years have helped them?

"No."

"In fact, your 'abandoning' them is the only reason you're able to help them at all, isn't it?"

"You're right. Okay, then, what about shame? I'm a therapist, a professional. Maybe I'm ashamed because I failed at something I should have been able to handle."

"Being a therapist makes you *bulletproof?* Goodness, who knew a doctorate was so useful! I'll have to start studying for mine right away!" I did laugh at that. One thing I always loved about Daisy: she knew how to make an entertaining point.

"You know what I mean," I said.

"I do. So, okay, let's say that, in protecting yourself, you inconvenienced some people you care about—"

"More than inconvenienced."

"After you left, were your siblings shot? Threatened? Hurt in any way?"

"No."

"I'd say 'inconvenienced' is about right then. Anyway, would a reasonable person think that protecting your life was worth some inconvenience to your siblings?"

"Hmmmm," I murmured. I was silent while I thought about the question. "I'm not sure I was just protecting my life."

"Aha!" said Daisy. "Now we're getting somewhere. What else were you doing?"

"Extricating myself from a horrible situation."

"What was horrible about it?"

"Caregiving is hard, harder than people think who haven't done it."

"But you're an old pro. You took care of your son and what's-her-name, your old girlfriend, for much longer than you nursed your parents. Your son almost died. That must have been a much more horrible experience."

"My mother almost died, too."

"Was that the horrible part?"

"No. I was scared—we all were—but just at the beginning, when she was in the hospital."

"Okay, so think about the day you walked out. Close your eyes and think back."

"I'd rather not," I shuddered, "but okay."

"It's the Fourth of July. You're at the ranch. Is it hot?"

"Not too bad."

"So what's horrible?"

In my imagination, I stood in the living room of the doublewide. My father was to my right, glowering at me from the kitchen. My mother was straight ahead, taking a slow, painful lap across the living room. The answer to Daisy's question was suddenly obvious.

"My mother's pain," I replied. "Nothing makes it any better. It just goes on and on, and she cries and cries, and I can't do anything to help, no matter how hard I try. She just says 'go away' and cries some more. I feel completely helpless and really scared."

"How old do you feel?"

"About six."

"And what happened when you were six? Not with your father but with your mother?"

Suddenly, a new picture came into my mind: a little camp trailer on a faraway Indian reservation, where my family had lived for a year, two adults and (then) four children in a trailer so tiny that the children slept on shelves. For most our time there, my mother cried in bed all morning while I cared for my younger siblings. She was sick, I assumed at the time, because people cry when they are sick. Sometimes, after breakfast, I would line us children up beside her bed, and we would pray for her recovery. Our prayers would bring on more tears, so we would think we had failed and pray harder. It was a miserable time, forgotten because the cure—sending my mother and siblings away—turned out to be worse than the disease. It left me truly alone with my father for the first time.

"Wow," said Daisy after I shared the memory, "I feel so sad for that little girl! I really see the parallel with what just happened, too. Your mom in pain, you trying hard but unable to help, feeling so responsible for your siblings. This revises the picture I have of your mother, though. When you talk about her, she always seemed the busy Mormon enabler: gardening or canning or baking or sewing, making quilts while your dad whacked you with a belt. This crying-on-the-bed mom is new to me. Did that happen often?"

"No," I acknowledged. "And, you know . . . that's actually kind of strange when you think about it."

"Why?" asked Daisy. I could hear real interest in her voice.

"Because . . .." My words halted as I groped for truth. "Because what my mother wanted in life was the exact opposite of what she got." I explained to Daisy that, when young, my mother had worked alongside her father on his large, successful farm. Happiest baling hay or riding out on horseback to search for a missing calf, she longed to be a son who could take over the farm, rather than a daughter. She had no interest in dating boys and shared none of the domestic ambitions of her Mormon girlfriends, so her pregnancy and "shotgun" marriage at seventeen threw her into a deep depression. "I'm told she spent the first three months of my life crying, just as she had on the bed in the camp trailer," I finished.

"So your mother wants to be a boy but instead gets married and has five kids, and the guy she marries turns out to be a violent, abusive bastard, only, being a Mormon, she can't divorce him without spending eternity in hell, which is presumably worse than the hell of spending eternity with the bastard. That about right?"

"Mormons don't really do hell," I replied, but yeah."

"How awful! I'm amazed she didn't spend your entire childhood in bed weeping. I would have."

"You would have been out of that marriage before the last slice of wedding cake was served," I said, and we both laughed heartily. "Seriously," I added, "I never thought of it that way before, not 'Why did she collapse into prolonged tears a few times?' but 'Why didn't she cry a whole lot *more*?'"

"I think we both know the answer to that," said Daisy.

"So my mom manages most of the time to maintain a profound state of denial, but, once in a while, that pain breaks through and she just goes to pieces."

"Like when she has a heart attack," Daisy added. "When it's acceptable to be in pain, then that huge pain you described, the pain that goes on and on, that the doctors can't account for, that narcotics can't touch, that makes her cry and cry and cry: that pain comes out, too, and makes itself felt."

"That's what I ran away from," I acknowledged.

"*Tried* to run away from," Daisy corrected.

"Okay, fair enough," I laughed.

"So whose pain are you carrying right now, Donna? Right this minute? Is that pain yours?" There was silence on the line.

"No, it's not," I said finally. "Mostly not. Some of it is Little Donna's, though."

"And whose pain was *she* carrying?"

Daisy's questions led me back to Legacy's sister program, the Survivors Workshop, where I discharged that carried pain. I'm happy to report that my depression cleared right away and has never returned.

CHAPTER TWELVE: Carried Feelings

We all have carried feelings, emotions that do not originate with us. As babies, we are continuous with our worlds and have to learn what is "me" and what is "not me." Only gradually do we develop the emotional boundaries necessary to navigate adult life and develop meaningful relationships with other people. Before fully developing the capacity to differentiate between our feelings and those of other people, we easily absorb emotions in our environment, mostly from caregivers, but also from siblings, friends, institutions such as school or church, and even media. The excited hope some people feel while shopping, for example, is the logical result of protracted childhood exposure to advertising, which links true happiness to buying things. No matter how many times the new coat or the new power tool or the new sports car disappoints us by not bringing the hoped-for happiness, we shop again and again with the same sense of joyous anticipation because what we feel is carried hope, and carried emotions operate independently of real-world feedback loops.

Most of the emotions uncovered in trauma work are carried. Some have almost no natural basis. For example, little children do not naturally feel sexual shame. If they take pleasure in touching their bodies, which many do, it does not occur to them to feel embarrassed about the fact, as red-faced parents discovers when that pleasure is taken in a supermarket or park. A young child who feels sexual shame is feeling someone else's, someone old enough to understand what the culture deems acceptable sexual behavior and to fear real or imagined violation of that limit. The shame that is transferred may be acknowledged by caregivers, unacknowledged, or something in between. For example, when a four-old, discovered playing "doctor," is punished rather than engaged in a discussion about privacy, that child absorbs the father's sexual shame. The father may not interpret his emotion as shame—he may feel it as righteousness or a duty of care—but he's conscious of the feeling and passes it on in a relatively straightforward manner. At the other extreme is sexual shame that is completely disowned. Adults who rape children, for example, do not feel appropriate shame. Very commonly, they project it onto their victims, who then assimilate the projection. That kind of blame was my father's way of handling his shame. Abusers may also may hide their shame from their conscious minds but "leak" it unconsciously, where it's perceived and absorbed by their victims. Even pure psychopaths, who have no feelings, can pass on a legacy of shame when their victims become aware that they are engaged in activities other people regard as shameful.[64] When their abusers fail to manifest the appropriate shame, victims assume that the responsibility falls completely on them and take on a double burden. All of these examples are carried shame.

Carried feelings also include emotions that young children have naturally. Fear is a good example. Being small and relatively helpless, children are no strangers to fear, even well-adjusted children. The world is full of scary things: loud noises, dentists with pointy tools, and closets with more monsters than clothes. For traumatized children, the world is many times more terrifying. When the people who should protect you harm you instead, the result is a lot of natural fear—not necessarily productive fear, as we saw in the last chapter, but fear that originates in the child's own experience. But there may also be referred fear. In cases of domestic violence, for example, the children may be physically untouched yet damaged by empathic fear for the primary victim, especially if the victim does not respond appropriately—by leaving, say. Again, it matters little whether that victim expresses, denies, or simply doesn't feel the fear, the children carry it anyway. During Legacy, I often repeat the following maxim about abuse in the home: if it happened to *anyone*, it happened to *you*. Finally, like carried shame, carried fear may originate with caregivers unaware of their own fear, especially men taught from birth that they must always be brave.

Sometimes it's important how carried feelings develop. Sometimes it's not. Take the case of a narcissistic father and his emotionally abused daughter. Psychologists generally agree that narcissists despise and disown their true selves, creating instead a grandiose false self that must be maintained at any cost. If the daughter has a persistent feeling of worthlessness, that could be because she absorbed her father's unacknowledged self-loathing or because her father belittled her to aggrandize himself. Or both. It doesn't really matter because the end result is the same. Sometimes, however, it's useful to reflect on the different mechanisms by which carried feelings develop, as was the case with my mother's pain. Emotions that are disowned—whether felt or not—can be powerful influences, strong enough to pull me from a happy, productive adult life into a serious depression. But, because they are not on the surface—or not reliably so—they may have to be excavated or inferred through careful reflection. As I have so often said, collaborators can be invaluable in such investigations, as Daisy was to me.

Before we continue, I want to underscore that carried feelings are not always disowned adult emotions that are picked up by children. They are sometimes feelings that are owned and transmitted quite straightforwardly—modeled or taught, for example. They are sometimes natural emotions that persist beyond their original circumstances, like the fear veterans may feel long after they finish a tour of duty in a combat zone. These feelings are carried in that they're less responsive to the here and now than they are to traumatic events in the past. New circumstances don't extinguish or appreciably alter them, though they may cruelly reinforce them. We say they originate with other people because, in childhood, the kind of emotion that gets carried almost never arises spontaneously and independently. It's conveyed by adults—or much older children—and, fortunately, it can be symbolically returned to its source.

Carried feelings, though often extreme and hyper-visible, can also be largely unconscious. They may have to be inferred from our own words and actions. Take the case of a client raised by a father who despised any form of weakness and punished it severely. When Reggie became a father himself, he vowed to raise his children in an atmosphere of love and acceptance. He worked hard to reject patterns of thought and behavior he had learned in his family of origin and to develop new, healthier patterns. Reggie was particularly careful when his children became involved in sports because athletic prowess was, for his father, the most important indicator of a child's strength or weakness. He was pleased when he was able to cheer with his whole heart for all of his children, whether they excelled in sports, struggled in sports, or avoided sports altogether. By the time Reggie had four children in their teens, he was confident that the chain of abuse was broken. His children were thriving.

He was shocked, therefore, when he overheard his only daughter talking with a friend on the phone.

"My dad thinks I'm disgusting," she confided. "You should see his face when I take seconds of anything at dinner. I asked him to pass the butter last night, and he pretended not to hear me." As soon as he could, he reported the conversation to his wife so that, together, they could figure out why their daughter would say such a terrible thing about him. He got another shock when she answered.

"Well, honey, you are critical of her weight."

"I've mentioned it to *you* a couple of times, never to *her*," he replied. "Anyway, I'm just worried about her health. I'm not *disgusted* with her."

"Why don't you talk to Donna about it?"

Reggie was a wonderful father who had, through hard work, learned to control his emotions and his behavior. But he was "leaking" disgust for his daughter's extra ten pounds, disgust he did not consciously feel. Working together, we discovered that his own father had regarded obesity as a weakness of the will, and had, throughout his childhood, made disparaging comments about overweight people. Reggie had not been overweight himself, so he had forgotten about his father's prejudice, though he was still carrying it unconsciously.

Carried feelings that are unconscious are very hard to discern. Reggie needed feedback from his daughter, his wife, and me to become aware that he still carried some of his father's contempt for what he called "weakness." And he was much more receptive to feedback than most people, so the fact that he needed three sources suggests how resistant most people are to the idea of unconscious carried feelings. It requires great courage and humility to consider feedback that conflicts with our conscious ideas about ourselves. Implicit racial bias, for example (possibly the most common carried feeling in the US), can be as hard to eradicate in people who oppose racism as in professed bigots. Because of their conscious commitment to tolerance, they reject evidence of racial bias in their own thoughts and behavior, so they perpetuate it. Reggie had the courage and the humility to entertain the possibility that other people saw something in him more clearly than he did. He was also fortunate to get feedback that was both honest and respectful. His experience was just about ideal, but it can be replicated within a trusting relationship built around collaborative reflection, like my relationship with Daisy. I will say more about how to do that in the next chapter.

If feedback is one way to gain insight into unconscious carried emotions, what are some other ways? Timothy Wilson believes that we can detect these emotions if we observe ourselves very carefully. He is not talking about introspection here but about watching how we act in the moment. A person who looks inward and honestly finds no ill will toward any minority group may still treat members of that group differently, just as my client treated his beloved daughter differently when she reached for a second dinner roll while her slightly thinner brother was on his fourth. Only by looking through what Wilson calls a "smoke screen of conscious theories about how [we] feel"[65] can we infer unconscious carried feelings and rid ourselves of those last stubborn legacies.

As I mentioned earlier in the chapter, the best way to understand carried feelings is to contrast them with natural feelings.[66] Natural feelings, though they may cause transient discomfort, are ultimately positive and purposeful. With natural guilt, for example, people feel regret or dismay when they hurt another person or fail to live according to their values. Such uncomfortable feelings move them to action: apologizing, making amends, and resolving not to repeat lapses. Carried feelings—persistent, intense, and overwhelming—are purpose*less*. With carried guilt, people feel existentially defective most of the time, regardless of what they actually do. And these terrible feelings do not spur reform; rather, they paralyze and destroy hope. To understand carried feelings more fully, we need to discuss them individually, though they rarely manifest that way.

Anger is powerful when it is natural, rather than carried. In the short term, it allows us to defend ourselves and others. In the long term, it gives us strength and energy. All of us know—or know of—people who transform anger into action. A familiar example is John Walsh, host of the television show "America's Most Wanted," one of the longest-running shows in the history of television. After his son was abducted and murdered in 1981, Walsh became an activist on behalf of missing and exploited children and still testifies before Congress on their behalf. Six years later, he debuted the show that would make him famous and contribute to the apprehension of 1,202 fugitives from justice. Dr. Martin Luther King wrote "Letter from Birmingham Jail," one of the most eloquent documents from the Black Freedom Movement, after being attacked in print by eight Alabama clergymen. It remains a powerful testament to the greatness natural anger can produce. Even the founding of the United States was an example of anger transformed, as colonists angry at British economic policies used that energy to imagine a new system of government and to make it a reality. And most of us know less world-changing examples, people who parlay their anger over rejection into redoubled effort, personal change, or learning.

Carried anger destroys, rather than creates. It's expressed as rage, like the sidewalk explosion I described early in this chapter. It can involve physical violence, destruction of property, a litany of insults, or an icy silence; the point is that it's excessive and only superficially linked to its present-day provocation. Almost every morning, it seems, I read a story about road rage or gun violence exploding out of minor incitements such as a disrespectful glance, a scratched car door, or a spilled drink in a nightclub. The reporter or columnist usually marvels at hair-trigger violence like it's a dangerous new phenomenon, but that's only half right. It's not new; carried anger has been around a long, long time. Carried anger is why we yell at our kids after promising ourselves over and over again that we won't. It's why we throw a vase we love (or a bare-knuckle punch) at a wall. It's why we explode at people who cut in line or Twitter trolls or drivers who won't let us merge into traffic. One criterion for natural anger is appropriateness: most people in the same situation would feel anger. Another is understanding the cause of the anger: when people don't know what they're angry about, the anger may not belong to them. Yet a third criterion is proportion: not reacting explosively to minor, or even moderate, provocation. When anger doesn't meet all those criteria, it's likely carried.

Fear is a necessary response to physical and emotional danger, as long as it is natural. It is the normal "fight or flight" response that I talked about in the last chapter; it prepares us physiologically for action in emergencies. Carried fear, however, tends to be paralyzing, both in the short term and in the long term. It can literally freeze us in our tracks so that we don't have the ability to get ourselves or others out of danger. It may also prevent us from living fully, achieving success, and even getting our basic needs met. Carried fear perceives overwhelming danger where risk is actually minimal—or when we can easily handle potential threats.

I once had a client, Lena, who had great expertise to share but whose success was hemmed in by fear. When I met her, Lena was doing groundbreaking work on Fetal Alcohol Syndrome, work that was becoming widely known and admired. As her international profile rose, she began receiving invitations to lecture at prestigious institutions, but she always declined, panicked by the prospect of speaking in public. Eventually, she did make one terrified try, which only served to amplify her fright. Then she found Legacy and learned the reason for her debilitating fear. Her father was a famous physician who devised a procedure that saved millions of lives. Gone by 5:00 a.m. every morning, he returned home fourteen hours later for a sit-down dinner for two with cocktails and wine. Before his return, the children were banished to their rooms, where they could hear the clinking of glasses and the rising volume of their parents' voices. Later they would hear uglier sounds: their father hurling insults, dishes breaking, bodies colliding with furniture. Though they rarely saw their father, they lived under his shadow, while the rest of the world treated him as a god. Yet when I asked whether her mother wasn't afraid every single day, Lena said "Oh, no!" with absolute certainty. Though her mother was in complete denial of her fear, she nonetheless passed it on to Lena who would be the one to suffer from its ruinous effects. Fortunately, Lena was able to discharge her carried fear and learn how to manage the natural fear that most people feel about speaking in public. Carried fear leads to persistent anxiety, panic attacks, and paranoia, psychic problems that damage our bodies and our lives.

Pain is unavoidable. Natural pain—from failures, problems, or losses— helps people to grow and gain in wisdom. Grief over a loved one's death is natural pain, and it's absolutely essential to psychic wholeness. Natural pain is essential to empathy and the inevitable result of love in a world of impermanence. As with other natural emotions, it is appropriate and commensurate with its source. Though it may never truly end, in the case of a major loss, it can be integrated. Carried pain, by contrast, tends to be diffuse, overwhelming, and interminable, often taking the form of depression or despair. Because it's so amorphous, even psychologically literate people can have trouble spotting it on their own, as I did with my carried pain. It's really important to spot, however. I have known many suicides over the course of my long career, and I cannot think of one that did not involve carried pain.

Shame is a painful feeling that's hard to like in any form. Carl Jung called it a "soul-eating emotion," Shakespeare dismissed it as a "waste," and most other writers treat it as something to be avoided at all costs, even if the alternative is walking into a hail of bullets, arrows, or rocks. Nonetheless natural shame tells us when we have failed to live up to the values of our culture, so, searing as it can be, it protects us socially and psychologically. Natural shame tells us we've been cowardly, unkind, boastful, aggressive, or selfish—and, if we're really mindful, it can signal that we're about to be. Carried shame, in contrast, makes us feel fundamentally bad in comparison to other people, regardless of how we behave. In the grip of carried shame, we *know* that something is profoundly wrong with us, and we carry an existential burden of misery and self-loathing.

If shame is a social emotion, then how can it become a core feature of personality? In dysfunctional families, shame may be so pervasive that children internalize it. For example, two very different caregivers may use shame to shape a child's eating behavior. One, seeing the child snag the last two cookies on a communal plate, might ask the child whether he was sure no one else wanted one of them. In that case, the caregiver is helping to inculcate a sense of natural shame, an awareness that we shouldn't take an excessive portion of shared resources unless no one else wants them. A less functional caregiver might take a different approach.

"Don't be a pig." Here shame is attached, not to the action of taking two cookies, but to the child's essential nature. Moreover, if this kind of shaming is habitual and attached to lots of different eating behavior, the child will internalize that shame. Now every impulse to eat becomes further evidence of piggishness, and a feeling that should have set healthy limits on a child's behavior once in a while instead becomes a crippling burden. When Jung called shame "soul-eating," it was this toxic internalized shame that he most aptly described. It's important to know, however, that caregivers needn't overtly shame children in order for children to internalize shame. Caregivers who are habitually too busy, distracted, or intoxicated can passively shame children by implying that there's something wrong with their need for attention or that they're simply not good enough, interesting enough, or lovable enough to warrant attention.

Carried shame comprises both this internalized toxic shame and shame from other sources. It may originate in the overwhelming self-disgust of perpetrators, whether acknowledged, deflected, or denied, and from the child's own awareness of being implicated in shameful activities. Regardless, abused children develop a core of shame that subjectively defines them and that exacerbates other carried feelings. In forty years of practice, I have never seen a survivor of childhood trauma without this core of shame. A moment ago, I mentioned the steady stream of news stories devoted to gun violence with minimal provocation. It's no accident that these provocations, some as slender as a sideways look, are almost always interpreted as forms of disrespect or social shaming. High levels of carried shame transform a minor slight—or even a clumsy mistake—into an intolerable public humiliation worthy of a double sacrifice, the life of the victim and the life of the shooter, too.

Less dramatic examples of carried shame are everywhere. Years ago, I witnessed a typical episode in a laundromat. A young girl of about nine was helping her mother with the family's laundry, but the clothes were in the dryer, and there was nothing for the child to do. She didn't have a book or a game with her, and the age of smart phones had not yet dawned, so she just sat on one of the folding tables and swung her legs while her mother watched the clothes go around in the dryer. By and by, she began surreptitiously studying the vending machines in the corner of the laundromat. After about ten minutes of stolen glances, I watched her shyly tug on her mother's arm. Pointing to the soft drink machine, she said something I couldn't hear. I heard the reply, though, loud and clear. The mother unleashed a torrent of condemnation, chastising the girl, not just for asking, but for *wanting* a soda. I watched as the child literally folded under the onslaught of criticism, her head dropping, her shoulders collapsing inward, and her arms tightly hugging her chest. Recalling how long it took the child to ask for the soft drink, I knew the harangue was not an isolated loss of control but a common occurrence. My heart ached for the little girl and for the heavy weight of shame she would likely carry into adulthood.

The movie *Radio Flyer* affords a similar example. In that film, two brothers suffer under an abusive, alcoholic stepfather, the younger enduring regular, savage beatings. Though the film ends in fantasy, its depiction of carried shame is very realistic. The stepfather, who makes everyone call him "The King," denies his own shame as he drunkenly hits and berates his eight-year-old stepson. The boy's response mirrors that of the little girl in the laundromat: he folds in on himself, head and shoulders drooping as he covers his face in shame. Carried shame can be harder to see in adults, but its effects are global, and the worst of them may be that it makes sufferers feel unworthy of help.

Guilt, in its natural form, results when people commit an offense. So it also tells us when we've behaved badly and overlaps with shame quite a bit. A vegan who seeks to outlaw fossil fuels might feel both ashamed and guilty after driving 20 miles for a midnight pint of Häagen-Dazs—but only a little. Functional adults feeling their own natural emotions do not excoriate themselves for minor transgressions. In addition, they use their feelings of guilt to make amends, where possible, and to figure out how to do better in the future. The vegan with a late-night sweet tooth might make a point of stocking up on sorbet, for example.

Carried guilt does not inspire amends or amendment. Instead it estranges and immobilizes. With carried guilt, we do not believe we deserve to move forward in our lives. In extreme cases, we may not believe we deserve to live at all. The twentieth century saw a horrific version of this phenomenon in the transgenerational trauma of the Holocaust. Though the descendants of Jewish and other victims have received much more attention, the descendants of

Nazi perpetrators have also suffered terribly, inheriting a legacy of their parents' unacknowledged atrocities that they perceive as a stain on their own souls. With few exceptions, most former Gestapo, SS officers, and Nazi Party leaders remained, at best, unrepentant and, more often, defiantly proud. So it was their offspring whose minds and bodies suffered torturous guilt. A great-niece and -nephew of Hermann Goering, grandchildren to another influential Nazi, even had themselves sterilized to, as the nephew put it "cut the line."[67] As some scholars point out, the more parents and grandparents deny their guilt (the younger Goerings recall their grandmother shouting "Lies!" during a television program on the Holocaust), the more guilty and traumatized the descendants feel. This is carried guilt on a massive scale.

CHAPTER THIRTEEN: Discharging Carried Feelings

So how do we discharge carried feelings? The first step, of course is recognizing them, understanding where they come from, and observing how they influence your thoughts and behavior. Most of this book has been dedicated to helping you do that, both by explaining the causes and effects of childhood trauma and by showing how they influenced a single life. If you have begun working with the material in the book and following some of its suggestions, you already have tools that will help you understand your history and develop resilience. But there are also formal steps you can take to support and expedite those positive changes, your own version of the Legacy or Survivor's Workshop. I wish everyone who needed it could participate in a workshop, but I know many people lack the time, the access, or the resources. So, for this book, I developed a version that you and your collaborator(s) can do independently.

The first step is to set aside time free of duties and distractions and make a formal commitment to use the time for this work. Setting aside special time is very important. You may think it's unnecessary, that your interest and enthusiasm make a formal commitment superfluous or that you'll get more done with a "catch as catch can" approach. But enthusiasms wane, especially when the work gets difficult or other demands encroach upon your time and attention. And there will always be other demands, many that seem more pressing than dealing with your own past. Most importantly, a formal commitment sends a signal, not just to other people, but to yourself: this work matters to me. *I* matter to me. I matter enough to carve out time for a process that will change my life—and the lives of those around me. Remember that your adaptive unconscious "learns" by watching your actions. How and when to set aside the time is up to you and your collaborator(s). Consider making a joint commitment to a regular gathering at someone's home or to an ad hoc retreat, such as a weekend hotel stay or camping trip. Whatever you do, devise a clear plan and stick to it. If the plan needs revision, by all means revise it, but revise deliberately, not via last-minute postponements and cancellations. The commitment itself is part of the healing process, so make it mindfully and keep it.

The first exercise is compiling a trauma inventory. You may already have discussed or written about parts of your history; now it is time to compile a more comprehensive catalogue. Such a task may sound both impossible and woefully misguided. Why inventory trauma? And how? The why is easy: to begin exerting control over it. With trauma, there is chaos, disorder, a lack of limits. An inventory—any kind of a list, really—imposes order. It begins to organize and make sense of experience. It can even give us a little distance on our material. An inventory also promotes insight. It can reveal patterns and relationships or demonstrate that something we dismissed as minor may actually be important. It can lead us to discover new material, as one recollection leads to another and another, and suddenly we're remembering (or half-remembering) an incident we had completely forgotten. These reasons alone would make an inventory useful, but there are more. It gives you and your collaborator(s) an overview of your history that's independent of the narrative goals we talked about in chapter two—or even the narrative ambitions we take on every time we tell a story: to entertain or horrify or impress or make a point. Having raw data makes it easier to see how we are shaping our own stories and how we might do that better. No document is truly objective, of course, but an inventory is as close to raw data as we can come. Finally, an inventory helps to identify carried feelings so that they may be successfully discharged.

The easiest way to compile an inventory of childhood trauma is to use the form at the end of this chapter. Though it's generally self-explanatory, I've included some tips for filling it out. Once you finish, you will have an overview of your history, of the child that you were at various ages, what happened to that child, and what feelings those experiences generated. You may find that the inventory confirms your general sense of the past or you may discover unexpected surprises—that a particular type of abuse was more prevalent than you remembered, for example. Looking at your inventory, you will see patterns and tendencies that will help you understand why you feel and act as you do. Such insights are invaluable. Excited by your discoveries, you may be tempted to share your inventory with your family of origin, whether to confront them with a record of the harm they did, to solicit their support, or any one of a thousand other reasons. Don't do it. Don't even *consider* it. No matter how loving or fair-minded they are, your family members cannot share your perspective. "No two persons read the same book," said Edmund Wilson, meaning that, even when we're looking at exactly the same sequence of words, two people don't ever see the same story unfolding. How much more different, then, are the stories of two people who aren't looking at the same words. In dysfunctional families particularly, people can be very invested in shared illusions and in their own interpretation of events. Intentionally or not, they may challenge, undermine, or dismiss your story to protect their own.

Let me offer an example. My client, Naomi, was a woman in her early forties who had difficulty holding down a job or sticking with any activity beyond a burst of initial enthusiasm. She lived in a house owned by her much-younger brother Ned, who had made a fortune in tech. Their single mother had been a violent drunk who sobered up when Ned was four and Naomi was twelve, stayed sober for ten years, then died in a car crash. Sober, Mom doted on Ned but fought with Naomi, who resented both the chaos of her childhood and the new discipline she now lived under as a teenager. When the mom died, she left a modest insurance policy that allowed twenty-two-year-old Naomi to take custody of fourteen-year-old Ned during high school and send him to college, where he majored in computer science.

As an adult, Ned felt grateful for Naomi's help, which is why he allowed her to live rent-free in one of his houses. And Naomi adored him, as she always had. But their versions of the past were radically different. Ned remembered a loving mother who died tragically young, while Naomi recalled a woman with two faces, neither particularly loving. Moreover, in the present day, Ned saw himself as having succeeded despite enormous difficulties, a view he maintained by comparing himself to the sister who grew up in the same family but failed to thrive as he had. Proud as she was of him, she wished he could be a little more understanding.

When Naomi finished her Legacy inventory, she ignored my warning not to share it with family. She believed that all the specific detail she had recorded would demonstrate, once and for all, how different her and Ned's childhoods had been and would discourage him from using her struggles as a foil for his success. As soon as she finished the inventory, she drove to Ned's house and insisted he read it. Unfortunately, it's not hard to guess what happened. Ned accused Naomi of exaggerating (even fabricating) their mother's alcohol-related offenses, saying, "The person I knew would never do that." Then he reminded her that, as a teenager, she had been rebellious and "would try the patience of a saint." Angered by her negative portrait of the mother he revered, Ned turned the entire inventory back on Naomi, charging her with "playing the victim" to justify her own failures. Not all familial perspectives are as obviously distinct as Ned's and Naomi's, but it's important not to invite any scrutiny that could erode your confidence in your own truth. Sharing your inventory with a family member is nearly always a mistake.

You are the authority on your own past. Period. If your history involves a lot of mental abuse, where caregivers tried to control your thoughts and perceptions, saying "No, Mommy and Daddy weren't fighting" after you heard an altercation late at night or "Grandpa's just affectionate" when the old man slid his hand up your dress, then you may not be comfortable with the notion that you are an expert on anything, even your own history. You are. Yes, memory is a tricky thing at the best of times, apt to distort and revise and fill in gaps—and sometimes to fall down on the job completely. It's unfortunate that the legal system places such faith in eyewitness testimony, given how inaccurate it can be. But we're not in a court of law here. We're trying to gather the best possible information on ourselves, and no one else in the world is better equipped to do that than we are. When we make a good-faith effort to remember the past as fully and accurately as we can, then that recollection must be respected as truth, both by ourselves and by other people. Sometimes, however, we may venture beyond memory, particularly when dealing with trauma that occurred when we were very young. We may have fragmentary recollections or suggestive gaps that gesture toward a particular type of experience. A colleague of mine, for example, remembered what she thought was a very early dream—of sitting on her mother's lap while her mother pulled a long white creature out of her mouth. As an adult, she casually mentioned the dream to her mother, who gasped.

"That actually happened!" My colleague was recalling, not a dream, but the removal of a two-foot tapeworm when she was a baby. I'll spare you the unappetizing details, because the point is that very early memories can appear to be other mental phenomena. They can also, as we saw earlier, disappear completely. So what do we do with this insight? In the absence of corroborating information—and there's rarely corroborating information—what do we do when we suspect the presence of inaccessible memories of trauma?

As I explained earlier, a lot of controversy surrounds this question. We know that a significant percentage of trauma memories will be obscured or distorted, especially memories of violence and sexual abuse, and especially in children. We must remember that sobering fact. We also know that false memories are easily generated and that such fabrications can cause turmoil and pain, including new trauma for the one remembering. When I'm working with clients, I encourage them to trust their own intuition. I sometimes say to them, "If you think it happened, it happened." But I do that because I'm present and can pull them back if they stray from intuition into fantasy. So what I say to you is this: if you suspect inaccessible memories of very early trauma, please find a therapist who can help you sort through this material. There are few places in the world where no professional help is available, even for people with very limited means.[68] In the absence of such help, the best approach is to cautiously credit your intuition, something like, "If you think it happened, it *likely* happened." Include it in your inventory, draw on it during the next steps, but don't make it the basis of accusations, life-changing decisions, or your identity as a survivor.

With your inventory complete, what can you do with it? We've already seen that sharing with family members is a bad idea, but sharing with your collaborator(s) is very helpful. I recommend both making copies and reading the inventory out loud, which has three purposes. First, it extends the control that writing the inventory began. Second, it enables access to carried feelings. Third, it strengthens the collaborative bond, establishing both trust and a sense of shared purpose. With your collaborator(s) following along on their copy, read through your inventory, pausing to explain what's unclear or supply necessary context but not veering too far into narrative or analysis. This is not the time for formal storytelling. As you speak, keep the focus on what happened to you and how you felt about it, rather than universalizing. Say "When my parents left me alone at night, I felt afraid," rather than "When parents leave children alone at night, they feel afraid." or "When your parents leave you alone at night, you feel afraid." Universalizing language keeps trauma at arm's length, makes it more an abstraction than something that happened to the little boy or girl that you once were. Using first-person singular pronouns such as "I" and "me" prevent such distancing. The goal is not to re-experience the trauma but to gain access to the child who experienced it from a position of strength and safety, which lie in the orderliness of your task, the wisdom you bring to it, and the help of your collaborator(s).

When you become the witness, rather than the reader, your focus will change radically. First, be aware that your collaborator's inventory will be very different from yours. It will certainly cover different material, and its language will likely be different, too. It may be a lot longer or a lot shorter. None of these things matter unless they become ways of depersonalizing the inventory: covering up pain with ornate language and masses of detail or rushing by it with too few words to convey the experience. As the witness, you should ask questions when facts aren't clear or when focus strays from the reader's experience and feelings as a child. If the reader says, "Children feel afraid," jump in with, "And how did *you* feel?" If the reader says, "I felt sad for my brother," jump in with "And how did you feel for *you*?" Sometimes you'll have to prompt when feelings are elusive: "What if you saw someone do that to a kid? How would that make you feel?" If you need more information to understand an entry, ask for it: "Did your grandmother live with you?" "Did he say that often?" "Where was your mom all this time?" As is already obvious, most of your input should take the form of questions or prompts, not comments. If comments occur to you, note them briefly on a piece of paper and save them for later. Don't assume that there's an optimal number of questions to ask. When I'm at the equivalent stage of Legacy—we call this stage Debriefing—I may listen to a half-dozen inventories in a row. With one, I might jump in frequently, asking a lot of questions and prompting the reader to speak more simply or personally or candidly. With the next, I might say very little. Don't feel pressured to contribute a certain amount or to match the contributions of your collaborator; it may not be necessary. Sometimes, less really is more. And, above all, don't compare one inventory with another. You created an inventory that was useful for you; your collaborator did the same; one is not "better" than the other. If you got ideas from your collaborator's inventory, great. Anything that helps you think about your own experience is a plus. Hearing about Daisy's experience always helped me to process my own, and I know for certain that she felt the same way about hearing mine.

One kind of comparison is worth special mention. You and your collaborator(s) must not compare the severity of your trauma. Measuring your history against someone else's is not only pointless but also harmful to your recovery. It's pointless because children do not distinguish degrees of suffering. To children, a hurt is a hurt, whether it's a skinned knee or a compound fracture of the leg. And that's who experienced your trauma, not the adult able to distinguish degrees of suffering. But invidious comparisons are more than just a waste of energy; they are also a way to avoid our feelings, which disrupts the work we are trying to do. In thinking "Well, I really didn't have it so bad, compared to him" or "Wow, her parents make my parents look really bad," we focus on what a reasonable adult *should* feel, rather than on what an unhappy child *did* feel. Recovery demands respect for—and access to—that unhappy child's feelings, and few things impede that goal more than the conviction that the feelings are not legitimate or appropriate.

After the inventory is finished, you will have time to make some brief comments. These should be descriptive, rather than evaluative. In other words, tell your collaborator what you heard and what feelings came across in the telling. It can be useful to share images and impressions. "I saw a little girl curled up in the hallway closet waiting for the shouting to stop. She seemed so afraid." "I saw a skinny kid with a crew cut trying to protect his mom from a man twice his size. What a brave, loving kid! Another useful formula is, "When you said _____, I felt _____. Often, you will feel sadness and pain at specific incidences of abuse or neglect and joy at moments of resistance or defiance. Whatever form your comments take, keep the focus on the person who has just read, rather than making connections to your own story. Making connections is a valuable activity, but right now your job is feedback. You're not judging your collaborator(s) or trying to fix them but offering the honest responses of an enlightened witness.

There are many ways to organize the exchange of inventories. You and your collaborator(s) could dedicate one meeting to each of you, or you could take turns over a longer session. In Legacy, it usually takes between an hour and ninety minutes to present (and respond to) a single inventory. It's a good idea to leave time for an important preliminary, the meditation on boundaries at the end of Chapter Ten. It's very important, when doing this work, not to over-empathize or allow yourself to be triggered by another person's history. You need to maintain clear boundaries between other people's feelings and your own. Understanding is wonderful, a precious gift to your fellow human beings, but experiencing their emotions as your own is not healthy for either party. If you have a history of enmeshment or other emotional boundary issues, you should be particularly watchful. Similarly, when you are the one reading, it's important to maintain the boundary between past and present. Valuable as it is to remember the child who suffered, becoming that child again or re-experiencing the trauma is a very bad idea. If that should start to happen, remind yourself who and where you are at the present time, using the reality check I demonstrated earlier. If you see it happening in your collaborator, gently suggest such statements to reinstate your partner's present-moment awareness.

Simply cataloguing our abuse helps us understand and control our feelings. So does sharing our inventories. If that is all you do after reading this chapter, you will experience those benefits. Some people also report a feeling of relief at having faced and communicated their painful histories. Some even notice that they are less reactive, their thoughts and behavior less driven by emotions that feel chaotic and out-of-control. If you're also becoming more mindful through meditation, more self-fashioned through storytelling, and wiser through collaborative reflection, then compiling and sharing your inventory will add focus and energy to your recovery from childhood trauma. But there's a further step you can take, one that may seem odd at first but that accords with new discoveries about the physiology of trauma and resilience. This step enlists the body, the imagination, and the adaptive unconscious to make changes that are hard to effect solely through rational means.

When we talked about meditation, we observed that something as simple as sitting down and watching the breath can transform our minds. So, it turns out, can other simple activities, including movement, rhythm, verbal repetition, and dramatic performance. Ritual, a fundamental element of all human cultures, can help convert understanding into action. That action can help circumvent or overcome habitual ways of thinking that keep us locked into trauma-based patterns of behavior. Because it involves physical, emotional, and mental learning, ritual can establish a firmer foundation for new perceptions than purely cognitive strategies. After all, we experienced the abuse with our bodies, hearts, and minds, so it makes sense to involve all three in our recovery. Even if our trauma was primarily mental, our bodies responded with stress reactions, which is why one of the most important recent books on trauma goes by the title *The Body Keeps the Score*.[69] In addition, ritual is an unsurpassed way to exercise creativity, a vital component of resilience.

In the twenty-first century, ritual has developed something of a public relations problem in the west. Many of us associate ritual with religion and regard it as empty ceremony that we honor out of habit or respect for tradition—or that we reject in favor of more spontaneous or rational behavior. But rituals retain tremendous social and psychological power, as we recently saw when, led by Colin Kaepernick, some football players began kneeling to protest police violence against unarmed African-Americans. Regardless of where we stand on that issue, it's worth thinking about the way he made his point, because it offers useful lessons about how to communicate difficult ideas in an immediate, emotionally powerful way. First of all, he chose his gesture very carefully.[70] He did not turn his back or sit down; he took a knee. Taking a knee is a complex gesture. It's not rude; in fact, it's normally a way to show respect. We kneel to gods and kings and people we want to marry. In football, taking a knee is what a quarterback does to end a play but keep the clock running. It's risky because the kneeling quarterback is vulnerable and could be badly injured by defensive players who get through the line. So, with one simple gesture, Kaepernick respectfully called for an end to racist violence. And we all got the message. We had many different responses to it—from rage to admiration to profound discomfort—but those responses were immediate and visceral. If there were people scratching their heads and wondering "What the heck is that guy doing?" I never encountered any of them.

So what's the relevance of a huge public gesture by a famous football player to anything we can do? Surely such a ritual becomes meaningless without an audience. That's true, it does. But everything we do *has* an audience: ourselves. Remember that the unconscious, in particular, draws inferences from our behavior. These inferences are crude, lacking rationality or fine distinctions, less like balanced assessments and more like "Snake! Run!" or "Mmm, beer." With this crude operating system continuously mining our experience for data, we always have an important witness, one that influences our behavior but doesn't take direction well, as anyone who has ever been on a diet knows. We've talked about the importance of giving this witness new stories and new behavior to learn from. We can also use irrational means of communication, such as music, art, and movement. Often the most effective messages we can send to ourselves combine rational and irrational elements organized around images or symbols with personal meaning. In other words, some of the most effective messages are rituals. Fortunately, recent research has discovered that rituals are effective whether we believe in their efficacy or not.[71] So, if you're still skeptical, you won't have to overcome your skepticism to give this ritual a try. You just have to show up and make a good-faith effort.

A ritual to discharge carried feelings works, in part, by reifying emotions and bringing them into the present moment, rather than talking about them abstractly. When we use a rock to represent a carried feeling, we assume a kind of control over the feeling, just as we did when we listed it in our inventory or wrote about it in one of our stories. When we then exert power over that rock, we exert power over that feeling. The overriding goal of the ritual is to eject carried feelings, which never belonged to us in the first place. We do that by naming the source of those carried feelings, our abusers, and holding them accountable for the trauma they caused, whether or not they meant to cause it. Then, using the combined power of our bodies and our imaginations, we return those carried feelings to their sources. As you will see, the process involves a carefully orchestrated emotional and incantatory build-up that culminates, more often than not, in speech that becomes cathartic and transformative. The effect is achieved, in part, through rhythm and repetition, ritual elements used to alter consciousness in a wide range of human activities, from drum circles to the Super Bowl.

The following is a rough sketch of a feelings reduction ritual. Only your creativity can transform the sketch into a vivid, transformative experience, so feel free to adapt and embellish. To begin, arrange an outing with your collaborator(s). Ideal would be a camping trip or a day hike out in the country, but may other environments would work, too. Bearing in mind your physical capabilities and your resources, choose a location that requires a journey of some kind, because the effort required to get there matters. It's no accident that voyages, quests, and pilgrimages are important ritual elements in many cultures; they help our minds "get to another place" for transformative work. It's not necessary that you and your collaborator(s) travel a particular distance, just that you exert yourselves in some way.

To prepare for the ritual, write letters to two abusers explaining what they did to hurt you. Most recipients will be caregivers, though some survivors may want to address an institution as well. It's not necessary to be comprehensive, which you have already done in your inventory; just hit the major points. Do not try to be fair or reasonable. You are speaking on behalf of the child you once were—anguished, confused, sad, lonely, angry, terrified or lost. Address your abuser as "you" and describe what he, she, or it did and how that abuse affected you, both as a child and as an adult. Be specific about what happened and describe your own feelings, rather than making general statements about caregivers or children. After you finish describing your trauma, announce that you are giving back the feelings your abuser gave you. Name each carried feeling that you are returning to its source, using simple declarative sentences.

"I give you back your anger."
"I give you back your pain."
"I give you back your fear."
"I give you back your shame."

Such simplicity and repetitiveness may seem unnecessary now, but they will contribute enormously to the power of the ritual. Even the grammar of the sentence is important. In philosophy of language, "performative speech" does more than just describe reality; it changes reality. The classic examples are "I apologize," "You are under arrest," and "I now pronounce you man and wife" (yes, performative speech was identified before modern feminism or marriage equality). Using strong present tense verbs aligns your sentences with performative speech, giving the ritual's efficacy a boost before it even begins. When you finish writing, sign your letters, and place each one in an unsealed envelope addressed to the abuser. You may use an actual street address, new or old, or you may fabricate a symbolic address of some kind.

Next, find or make a carrying device that can be safely disposed of—not recycled but destroyed. In other words, the material must be burnable, shreddable, or biodegradable. (The shreds can be recycled, just not the whole device.) A paper grocery sack is a good option because it can be burned or shredded. Another good option is a burlap sack, which is easily biodegradable.[72] Your carrying device can also be just a large square of burlap or very heavy kraft paper (unbleached) that you can gather into a bindle and tie with rope. Or anything else you can come up with, as long as it can be safely destroyed. You should work out the details of your ritual before deciding on your carrying device, but make sure your decision takes heed of symbolic, as well as practical, considerations. Your carrying device represents a difficult burden you seek to unload permanently, so don't find or make something fancy that you'd secretly prefer to keep.

The next article you need is a representation of yourself as a child: a photograph, a figurine, or a stuffed animal will work best. Don't strain to find the *perfect* representation, one that somehow encompasses who you were at different ages and stages of development. Such a representation doesn't exist. You changed profoundly throughout your childhood, and the traces of those changes may be found in the many different ego states that persist within you today. As I mentioned before, we talk of "*the* wounded child" ego state or "*the* adapted adult child" ego state, not because there's only one, but because it's practical to act like there's only one. Let me explain. One of the things this ritual does is to change your relationship with who you were in the past. That's almost impossible to do in the abstract, which is where your mind gets stuck if you have to maintain awareness of all the different "children" whose traces remain with you today. If you pick one, however, you can stop conceptualizing and act in clear, intelligible ways that your unconscious can understand. You can build a relationship with one child that you could not build with the dozens, hundreds, or thousands of children you once were. So choose a representative that feels apt, but don't obsess over whether it's the absolute best you could possibly devise. What's more important, in some ways, is choosing one you can relate to. During the ritual, you will address this representation as "you" and speak to it as though speaking to a precious, beloved child. You will imagine it witnessing your actions and responding to them. Some people can do that with any object; others will fare better with one that is more personal or anthropomorphic. Fuss as much or as little as you want over your representation, as long as you remember how it will be used. For instance, it's great to embellish a photo of yourself and make it really special but counterproductive to create a collage with lots of different photos. Discuss your representation with your collaborator(s) if you're not sure what will work.

Before the day of the ritual, plan your journey: where you will meet your collaborator(s), what route you will take, what supplies you will bring. Planning in advance will help you focus on the journey's true purpose and be mindful along the way, so you don't squander unnecessary attention and energy on logistical details. That said, make plans with some flexibility so that surprises don't upset you. Good plans are the result of good boundaries, knowing what you can control and what you can't control. You may not be able to anticipate the rock slide that blocks your chosen route, but you can certainly foresee the need to carry a trail map and enough water to accommodate a delay. Having made your plans, gathered your supplies, and met your collaborator(s), you are ready to set out on your journey.

As I said before, the journey's length and destination are entirely up to you. Because I have been a dedicated backpacker all my life, my ideal version would be a weekend camping trip in the wilderness. I would hike into the backcountry with my collaborators, set up an isolated campsite, and find a spot nearby that would be good for the feelings reduction ritual. As a facilitator, however, most of my feelings reduction work has been done in cities, including on a popular beach in Seattle, so I know for a fact that the location really doesn't matter, as long as it's not too public. Feelings reduction is intense work that may be hindered by self-consciousness, so find a place where you won't feel too conspicuous. (If outsiders do stumble into your location, however, tell them you're rehearsing a play, which will explain any displays of strong emotion.)

At some point, before you get to your destination, start picking up rocks to put in your sack or your bindle. When you begin collecting will depend on the nature and length of your expedition. For example, if you drive to a trailhead then hike one mile, start picking up rocks when you begin hiking. If you walk from the Empire State Building to the Ramble in New York City, start picking up rocks when you enter Central Park. These rocks represent the carried feelings you're about to return, so you've lugged them around for many years, but you need not lug them all the way from your home to your ritual site—though you certainly can if you wish. As you pick up the rocks, put them into your sack or bindle and carry them in a way that keeps you aware of their weight. Those who are more fit may wish to challenge themselves with larger rocks, but be careful: once you pick up a rock, you should carry it all the way to your destination. With painted rocks something of a vogue these days, some people may wish to paint their rocks to represent specific carried feelings. Though I like the idea symbolically, I don't think it's environmentally responsible to leave painted rocks in the wilderness or a park, if that's where you're going. I also worry about other people who may stumble across the rocks you throw away. I would find it very disconcerting to look down while I'm hiking and see a rock painted with "shame" or "anger" in my path. If you do use paint, make it washable and non-toxic, and consider representing different carried feelings with different colors or shapes, rather than words.

By the time you reach your destination, you should have accumulated a significant burden of rocks to represent your carried feelings. When you're ready to begin the feelings reduction ritual, find a spot from which you can safely throw your rocks: into water or brush, over a fence, down a ravine, wherever you can hurl the rocks without the risk of hitting anyone. You should not be able to see your rocks after they land, which is why throwing into a body of water is ideal. But there are plenty of alternatives for those who don't have a pond handy, including throwing rocks into a rocky field where they will be indistinguishable from other rocks. If logistics limit your options, get creative. Throw clods of dirt, which will break apart. Throw chunks of ice, which will melt.

Choose which of you will act first. The other(s) will witness and assist. When it's your turn to act, get out whatever you're using to represent yourself as a child and hold it in your arms while you close your eyes and form a mental image of yourself as a young child. The image can be based on memory or on a photograph; the important thing is that you form as clear a picture as you can before you begin speaking. When you have that clear picture, begin talking to that child as though he or she were in your arms. Speak from the heart, and stress that he or she is safe and cared for by the adult you are today. You might say:

"You deserve to be loved and appreciated because you are a precious child."

"When you were little, I know you were scared because there was no one to protect you."

"I'm sad about what happened to you, but I'm an adult now, and I can take care of you."

"What your dad did to you was not right, but I'm here today to give you the help you needed but didn't get."

"I love you."

At moments, you may feel foolish speaking such lines. You may go along fine for a while then suddenly realize that you are talking to a stuffed animal or decorated photo. If you like, your witness(es) can listen for hesitation or sarcasm or other indicators of reluctance and help out with encouragement.

"Say that again like you mean it" is good. I use that line a lot in Legacy.

When you are finished speaking, place the "child" with a collaborator, who will take care of him or her while you take care of you both.

Next, retrieve your rocks and pile half of them in front of you. Open your first letter, and read it out loud, as forcefully as possible. You are telling your abuser what he or she did, so speak with authority, whether you feel it or not. If necessary, a collaborator may say "Louder!" or offer other encouragement, but such help may not be necessary. A collaborator's job while you are acting is support, period. It's not to empathize or in any way worry about having an authentic emotional experience; it's to help *you* have one. If that means faking intensity in shouting "Like you mean it!" fine. Collaborators are not responsible for orchestrating your performance, and they're certainly not responsible for its success, but they can and should assist you where they can. It's a good idea to discuss beforehand how much help you expect to need. That being said, both of you must leave room for the unexpected. If you anticipate needing lots of encouragement but start reading your letter like dragon breathing fire, your collaborator(s) should back off and let you rip!

When you finish your letter, drop it and pick up a rock. Throw it as you shout one of your final sentences—for example, "I give you back your anger!" Shout the line again while throwing the next rock. Do the same thing again. When you're ready, move onto another carried feeling from the end of your letter. The point is to throw and shout at the same time, building up a powerful rhythm in which body, voice, and emotions work in concert. Your collaborator(s) can be invaluable here. They can help you ramp up the intensity by shouting "Again!" and "Louder!" If you get stuck on one feeling, they can prompt with another from your letter. They must, however, be mindful of your rhythm. Prompts at this stage should be single words so as not to disrupt your flow. Shouting these sentences while throwing has several important results. First, both simplicity and repetition create what's called the "truth effect," or the impression that what's being said is accurate. You are more inclined to believe you're giving back anger or shame when you repeat these simple sentences. Second, simplicity and repetition punctuated by the act of throwing create rhythmic patterns that affect your brain. Rhythmic motion plus repetition of sound is the very definition of incantation, which literally means "singing [something] into being. Incantation transforms intention into fact, making "I give you back . . ." true performative speech. Third, simple words, simple sentences, and repetition are all characteristic of heightened emotional states in which the mind's self-awareness and analytical tendencies—not to mention defensiveness and denial—all but shut down. In such a state, deep change can take place unimpeded by habitual patterns of thought or resistance. Continue to shout and throw as vigorously as you can without injuring yourself until your rocks are gone. Then stop and take a breath. Repeat with the other letter and the rest of your rocks.

When you are finished with both letters, pick them up and place them in your empty sack or bindle to be taken home and destroyed. Put this material away where you can't see it. Now retrieve the item that represents your younger self from the collaborator who is holding it. Addressing the item again as your younger self, explain that he/she has now seen that you can protect him/her, so he/she can now become the secure, happy child he/she deserves to be. Imagine taking him/her into your heart to live, and designate the representation as a permanent symbol of his/her presence in your life. Then repeat the ritual for the other collaborators. When everyone is finished, destroy the sacks and/or bindles and their contents. In some cases, you will be able to burn or bury your materials right where you are--if those materials are non-toxic and if local regulations permit. In other cases, you will have to take the materials home to destroy them. You can burn them in a fireplace, bury them in the back yard, or feed them into a paper shredder; in fact, you can do all three by shredding them first, then burning them, then burying the ashes. The method doesn't matter; the point is to represent the final relinquishing of your carried feelings. Having returned them to their rightful owners, you now destroy your links to them, once and for all.

When I discharged my carried feelings, just about twenty years ago, my life changed. My depression went away, and it has never returned. I still feel pain, of course, but it is normal, transient pain with clear causes, not the amorphous, persistent despair that used to creep over me—or, as happened on my parent's ranch, bury me suddenly in an avalanche of darkness. Natural pain, when it comes, does its job, which is to register the magnitude of a loss and help me appreciate what I had, as well as what I still have. Without pain, there is no gratitude. In the months after I completed the Survivors Workshop, I noticed that all my emotions felt more natural: cleaner, quieter, and easier to manage. My life seemed to calm down, even as my son hurtled into adolescence and my five-year relationship revealed the fissures that would break it apart. The change was not in my circumstances but in myself.

And there was another, unexpected benefit. It happened, of all places, back in Utah. After I left, my father's hip healed quickly and well. He didn't develop an opioid addiction because he never did get that refill he was hoping for, despite a lot of hollering and his best impersonation of a soldier with an unexploded mortar round in his side. So he was off his crutches and back at his chores within two weeks. My mother was a different story. She remained in agonizing pain, and her doctors could not figure out why. Her incision was healing; the bruises from the rib-spreader were gone; yet still she cried and complained and paced and barely slept or ate. In truth, *she* was the one in danger of an opioid addiction, getting refill after refill just for the tiny bit of relief the medication brought. As I headed for The Meadows to participate in the Survivors Workshop, I wondered if my mother had permanently succumbed to the pain she had so long managed with denial and distraction. I didn't want to carry her pain any longer, but I didn't really want her to carry it either, not if it was so vast and overwhelming—and not now when her health and strength ebbed so low.

After I finished the workshop, I stayed in Wickenburg for a few days to visit Daisy and other old friends. Daisy wanted to hear all about the workshop and was ebullient when I described the powerful experience of returning my mother's carried pain. Her excitement was short-lived, however, vanishing completely when I informed her of my immediate plans.

"You're *what?*" she shrieked. "Returning to the scene of the crime *again?* Are you *nuts?*"

"Just for a few days," I assured her. "It's what I promised. What I owe."

"You damn well better be planning to rent a Winnebago," she muttered darkly.

I did rent a Winnebago, a brand new Adventurer, and I drove it up to Faust so I could have a couple of days to enjoy the drive. I dawdled in spectacular northern Arizona: Sedona, Humphrey's Peak (which I stopped to climb), Marble Canyon and Jacob's Lake on the edge of Grand Canyon National Park. Once I crossed into Utah, I stopped dawdling and drove straight north to Faust, where my sister Julie was finishing her rotation at the ranch.

She was surprised to see me, as were my parents. I told them I wasn't staying long, just long enough to finish my shift. I carried several bags of groceries into the house, including a bottle of Day-Glo orange salad dressing, said goodbye to Julie, and set to work. During the few days I spent at the ranch, I did nothing special. I did very little that I hadn't done a month earlier; I just it differently, and I felt differently about it. When my mother cried and told me to go away, I did. I went out to the Winnebago and read a book or called my son. I felt sorry for her suffering but not anguished about it—either about the suffering or about my helplessness to alleviate it. I did not feel like that little girl in the camp trailer trying to make everything all right and terrified by the overwhelming evidence of her failure. I felt like an adult in a challenging situation, an adult with the skills and the emotional resources to handle that situation.

As I went about my business, cooking and cleaning and caregiving, something amazing happened. My mother suddenly began to get better. She stopped crying and complaining about her pain. She started eating and sleeping—not a lot, but more than she had been. She skipped doses of her painkillers. For the first time since her heart attack, I felt cautiously hopeful: maybe she wanted to come back to us after all. Then, as I was getting ready to return to Seattle, I heard her say something she had never said before in her entire life. My father, seated in the living room, called to her in the kitchen, where she had gone for a glass of water.

"Maurine," he bellowed, "bring me a Doctor Pepper when you come."

"Get it yourself," my mother replied. I couldn't believe my ears and rushed out of the laundry room, where I had been folding sheets and pillowcases. Rounding the corner to the kitchen, I caught a little smile on her face. I smiled back and, in that moment, I suddenly understood what was happening. My getting well, unloading my carried pain, was helping my mother get well. There was nothing mystical about the phenomenon: when you change one part of a social system so dramatically, you change all the parts. But that's a topic for the next section, where we'll talk much more about what happens in families when survivors of abuse reclaim their lives.

Practice: Compiling a Trauma Inventory

A good inventory needs clear organizational principles in order to be useful. For many years, I have used versions of the form below in Legacy and found that it works very well.

TYPE OF ABUSE	WHO DID IT	AGE	WHAT HAPPENED	HOW YOU FELT THEN	HOW YOU FEEL NOW

There's a full-sized downloadable version of the form on my web site.[73] But you can also make your own by drawing lines on pieces of ruled paper, as above. From left to right, the columns should be titled "TYPE OF ABUSE," "WHO DID IT," "AGE," "WHAT HAPPENED," "HOW YOU FELT THEN," and 'HOW YOU FEEL NOW. If you're really ambitious, you can skip the line-drawing and use a spreadsheet program such as Excel. What's important is that you gather specific information in a way that is clear and comprehensible—and that gives a good overview of your history.

On the form, list incidents of abuse that happened to you from birth to age seventeen. In addition, note the following information about each incident: the type of abuse; who did it; how old you were; what happened; how you felt about it at the time; and how you feel about it now. Under "type of abuse," you simply list one or more letters: "P" for physical abuse, "S" for sexual abuse, "E" for emotional abuse, and "M" for mental abuse. If the incident involved all of them, write "PSEM." Under "who did it," list the perpetrator(s), not by name, but by relationship to you (e.g. "babysitter" or "uncle."). Under "age," it is okay to guess or list a range. Under "what happened," sketch a bare outline of the incident. You need not re-name the perpetrator but can start with an action word such as "chased" or "told."

Under "how you felt then" and "how you feel now," focus on simple, direct expressions of feeling, such as "angry," "ashamed," and "afraid," rather than casting about for more nuanced terms. Children's emotions are fairly simple, and, if we're to track ours into the past, it's helpful to keep our terminology clear and straightforward.

As I've observed before, some ongoing childhood trauma doesn't neatly fit the category "abuse." If you underwent a long series of painful medical treatments, for example, or experienced repeated evictions, you may have trouble answering the question "Who did it?" It's perfectly fine to answer with an abstraction, a collective noun, or the name of someone who was only partly responsible. Remember that part of the feelings-reduction process is holding abusers accountable and returning their carried feelings to them. Who or what should get those carried feelings back? In answering this question, pay particular attention to carried shame, which will often point you in a useful direction. All of that said, don't get stuck on this question; there may not be a perfect answer. Note the imperfection with a question mark, and move on.

A few more tips will help you complete the forms. First, list incidents in whatever order you please, and don't worry too much about sequence. Some people proceed in chronological order. Others organize by category of abuse or by perpetrator. I don't recommend forsaking order entirely, as that diminishes some of the value of the exercise, but you should definitely not fuss over it. It's normal to have a bit of anarchy at the end, as there are always incidents that come to mind belatedly. Don't worry about it. Second tip: some of you will be dealing with abuse that was habitual for extended periods. List it as such, but also list some particularly notable examples. In my case, I would mention that my father beat me regularly from age two to seventeen, but I would list separately the beating he gave me after I talked to Mr. Waldo, as well as a few others that were distinctive for their ferocity or their location or some other feature. Don't worry about overlap; a comprehensive picture is more important, and, in order to be comprehensive, an inventory has to include both general tendencies and specific details. What you are really trying to do, overall, is thoroughly catalogue the experiences and the feelings that you had growing up. Finally, some people have problems recalling how they felt when abuse originally happened or perceiving how they feel about it now. If that happens to you, imagine watching a child get the same treatment you did. How would you expect the child to feel? Write the answer under "how you felt then." How would you feel witnessing such treatment? Write that answer under "how you feel now."

Part VI

Moving Forward

CHAPTER FOURTEEN: Like Watching Reality TV

In the dozen years after I discharged my carried pain, my life continued to improve. My son James grew into an exceptional young man: strong, successful, and compassionate. I began a life with Deb, the wonderful woman I wed when our state recognized marriage equality. My practice thrived, and my Legacy workshops helped more than a thousand survivors of childhood trauma. Though subject to ups and downs like anyone else, I suffered no further depression or any other indicator of carried feelings. In fact, as my focus shifted more and more toward other people, I enjoyed a sense of profound emotional freedom. My own history became principally a tool to help other survivors, rather than a driver of my thoughts and behavior. Outside of AA, CoDA, and Legacy, where I sometimes used a recollection to illustrate a concept, I rarely even thought about it. In that spirit, my final story is about saying goodbye to my abuser.

My father's death showed me how far I had come in dealing with my trauma. It is not a moving story of reconciliation—in my experience, most of those stories read more like fiction than fact—but a complex narrative of acceptance, catharsis, and transcendence. The story began right before my father developed the Alzheimer's Disease that would kill him. On a brief visit to their Faust ranch, I was folding laundry alone in my parents' double-wide when my father walked in unexpectedly. Though I no longer feared him, I had a brief visceral reaction to his sudden appearance in the doorway. Partly, it was a startle reflex, as I had thought he was miles away looking for a missing heifer. Partly it was a faint relic of old terror. He took a few steps toward me, his cowboy boots oddly silent on the linoleum floor, but he did not say anything. Neither did I, just kept folding. Still a very tall man, especially in boots, he loomed over me, but I kept my eyes on the plaid shirt I was smoothing and did not look up. After a moment, I was surprised to hear my father sniffling. As a therapist, I'm accustomed to weeping, though not from my father. I waited to see whether he would explain himself, and, after crying softly for a few more minutes, he did.

"I'm so sorry for everything I did to you," he said, his voice hoarse. "I want you to know that I love you, and I'm proud of you. Proud of everything you've achieved." I set the folded shirt aside and picked up a pair of jeans, feeling surprisingly calm. "Is there any way you can forgive me?" I put the shirt back down and looked at him for the first time, considering the question. Then I answered slowly and deliberately.

"I think forgiveness is between you and your higher power," I said, looking him straight in the eye. "I *can* tell you that I'm not angry with you. For a long time I was, but I'm not any more. I don't resent you. I don't resent you because holding onto resentments is bad for me. So, if you worry about that, you should know that I don't resent you." Now I paused to look down for a moment then met his gaze again. "You're my father, and I love you." No sooner had I said the words when my mother returned from shopping. The conversation turned to lunch, after which I drove to the airport, boarded a plane, and returned to my home in Seattle. We never did discuss his apology or my response to it; nor did I think very hard about it, though there were questions to think about. Were my father's words sincere? Did he feel true remorse for his unspeakable abuse all those years? Was he genuinely begging for my forgiveness in humility and love? Or was he just an aging man worried about divine judgment and hoping I could issue him a get-out-of-hell-free card?[74] I have my suspicions, but I can never know for sure. The real value of the apology, to me, was in demonstrating its insignificance. Where once I would have given most anything to hear my father admit guilt—even just a little, even as a cynical hedge against divine retribution—now I truly did not care. I had done the work necessary to neutralize his influence. Yes, I had some atavistic responses to him, responses too ancient and unconscious to eradicate completely. The gut-twinge when he surprised me in the kitchen was such a response. But, in every way that mattered, his once-dark shadow had faded nearly away.

The last time I saw my father, his Alzheimer's had grown severe enough to require a nursing home. I was not surprised by his diagnosis or the rapid decline that followed; at some level I had always expected he'd suffer dementia. As I explained in the first chapter, he had been a rodeo cowboy competing in one of the most dangerous sports in the world: bronc riding. Every ride on a bronc, a horse bred for bucking, is an invitation to brain damage, not just at the end of the ride when the bronc throws the cowboy off, but during the ride, when bucking whips the cowboy's head back and forth with such force that his brain collides repeatedly with his skull. Like so many bronc riders, my father had suffered too many serious head injuries to count and a host of minor concussions besides. Alzheimers, while not inevitable, was always likely.

Still, his appearance shocked me. In honor of James's and my arrival, he had left the nursing home for the day and waited in the double-wide with my mother, his brother, and his sister-in-law. He wore his best western clothes—knife-creased blue jeans, a red-and-grey plaid western shirt with pearl snaps, and ornately tooled cowboy boots—but the finery hung on his emaciated body when he stood to greet us. He was so thin that his championship buckle—a brass bronco on an etched nickel oval—looked huge by comparison. As I greeted him, his face remained blank, though he accepted my stiff hug and James's more affectionate embrace. We sat on opposite sides of the room, the older folks in chairs, James and me on the sofa together. Conversation focused on how everybody was, the likelihood of rain, and James's studies. My son, just starting his senior year in college, planned a thesis on rural and urban gangs, so my mother, uncle, and aunt peppered him with questions. All the while, my father stared mutely at the floor. I saw no glimmer of recognition until he suddenly began to weep. My mother ignored him, so I did the same; Alzheimer's can produce dramatic mood swings. Soon, however, he surprised us all by speaking.

"Donna," he cried. "My daughter. You're here." His frail shoulders shook with his sobs. My mother's mouth literally dropped open.

"That's right, Clel," said my uncle with a broad smile. Donna came from Seattle to see you. And Ja—"

"James!" my father said smiled. "I know James!" Leaning forward, he launched into a familiar story. "Remember bringing the herd down from the hill that day, you remember, James? You always helped with that. We couldn't find the gimpy calf, so I told you to re-ride the DNR fence, and you said 'You mean re-re-ride, Grandpa, 'cause you'd already done it once, and I said, 'Don't you stutter now, boy!" He laughed softly. James laughed too, delighted by the memory.

My mother, aunt, and uncle looked shocked. My father's Alzheimer's was so advanced that he barely functioned, yet there he was, lucid in his cowboy best, regaling us with an anecdote! But a moment later his laughter stopped, and he resumed staring at the floor.

"I guess he's done now," I said. The six of us chatted for a few minutes more until my father's head began to droop.

"We'd better take him back to Aspen Valley," said my uncle, at which everyone stood to leave. Outside the double-wide, my big-hearted son folded his grandfather in a bear hug.

"Bye, Grandpa," he murmured. "We'll see you real soon. You take care." My own farewell was more restrained. I put my arms lightly around my father's thin shoulders but kept a large gap between our bodies.

"I'll probably never see you again, Dad," I murmured into his ear. "I love you. Goodbye." He made no reply.

Three months later, he passed away, though we would have one last, peculiar moment of contact. As he lay dying in the nursing home, nearly fifty people came and went, crying as he drew his last breath, then another breath, then another. After two days of watching my father "breathe his last," my mother wondered why he would not let go. He needed my consent to die, she decided, so she phoned me to get it while I was in session. Having left a client to take the call, which I do only for the direst emergency, I was exasperated to hear why she was calling. My mother sounded even more exasperated as she described the interminable deathbed scene.

"I'm going to put the phone up to his ear," she snapped. "Will you *please* give him permission to die so he'll be dead?"

"Whatever you say, Mom," I sighed and waited while she carried the phone to my father.

"I'm going to put the phone on his pillow," said my mother after a brief silence. "Go ahead."

"Dad, this is Donna," I began before suddenly realizing I had no idea what to say. I plunged on anyway. "Mom thinks you need my permission to die, so I want you to know that it's okay for you to die now." I stopped for a moment, listening. I heard what I thought was my father's breathing, though I couldn't be sure. Looking out my office window, I studied the scabbed bark of a Sitka Spruce and thought for a minute. Then I spoke again one last time. "Dad, I forgive you. You can let go." Then I hung up the phone and returned to my client. My father stopped breathing within the hour.

Deb, James, and I flew to Utah for the funeral, spending a week at my brother's house. From the first moments of our reunion, my family of origin was split, one faction acknowledging that my father had been a domestic tyrant and serial abuser, the other faction upholding my father's public image: a fine and decent man who occasionally got a little rambunctious but was otherwise an exemplary Mormon patriarch. The first faction outnumbered the second, which consisted of my mother and one sister. I don't know whether the two women were actually grieving inside, but they seemed to feel that we all should be—or, at the very least, should *appear* to grieve. They soon grew visibly annoyed by the irreverence of my other siblings and me.

Our first stop in Tooele was the funeral parlor to pick out a casket. The irreverent faction laughed and joked throughout the process, while the solemn faction spoke in soft murmurs.

"What about this one over here?" cried one sister gaily, pointing to a white casket lined with rose-pink satin. The half-open lid appeared lavishly padded, and a giant pink pillow nearly filled the space. The pillow had a two-inch ruffle around the edge, also pink.

"Nah, that's a casket for . . ." Leaving the sentence unfinished, I pointed at my siblings.

"Sissies!" they chimed. The idea of our father in a frilly pink-and-white coffin was too hilarious for words, and the irreverent faction laughed so hard we could barely breathe.

Across the room, the solemn faction sighed, shook their heads, and frowned, yet we never reigned ourselves in, even a little bit. We knew our behavior appeared outrageous, but something in us needed the release. We weren't just avoiding the hypocrisy of feigned grief, which would have been intolerable; we were celebrating our liberation. No matter how old, sick, and pitiable our father eventually became, he had once exercised terrifying power over our lives, power he did not control but brutally unleashed. Worse, institutions that should have checked his power—the community, the school, the church—instead buttressed it, making it absolute. The abused sometimes experience a kind of wild elation at the death of their abusers, no matter how fallen the abuser or belated the death. This is especially true when victims suffer permanent consequences, as I do spinal damage sustained during childhood beatings. Though my mortified mother and sister condemned our loud joking about caskets, I'd bet any amount of money that the employees of the funeral home had seen such cathartic laughter before, perhaps many times.

Over the week, we spent a lot of time in the funeral parlor, where my father was laid out for private viewing before the funeral service. Mormon men are buried in temple clothing, so my father's corpse was dressed in a manner just as offensive to his cowboy style as the pink-lined coffin would have been. Like many Christians, Mormons believe in a literal, physical resurrection, where the spirit reunites with the earthly body, "perfected" to remove all infirmities. So Mormons want that body dressed properly for the big day. My father wore a white shirt with vertical ruffles and a small green apron across his crotch. The apron was supposed to represent the fig leaves worn by Adam and Eve after their heroic "fall" in the Garden of Eden,[75] but the color was all wrong, not the emerald green of a fig leaf but the shiny parakeet green of a Sprite can. Between the ruffles and the apron, my father's outfit was definitely "for sissies," and we laughed to imagine him cringing in embarrassment after his resurrection.

"Is he at least wearing cowboy boots under there?" asked my brother. The bottom half of the casket was shut, so we couldn't see our father's footwear.

"If Mom wants an invitation to the Celestial Kingdom,[76] she'd better make sure he has 'em on," I replied.

"We should remind her," said my brother. "And maybe suggest she tuck in a pair of jeans, a hat, and a championship belt to replace that green apron."

"And a shirt without ruffles," said a sister.

"And spurs."

"And a bandana," I added, "but only if there's dust in the Celestial Kingdom." We proposed some more additions to the casket and laughed some more, enjoying each other and our giddy irreverence and, underneath it all, our freedom. It was the day's final burst of hilarity because visitation, a Mormon funeral rite, was about to begin. Irreverent as we had been among ourselves, with only the funeral-home staff as witnesses, visitation was a somber social ritual, and none of us wanted to embarrass our mother in front of the whole community.

Thinking about the community put me in a somber mood. Though I had returned to Tooele County many times since leaving home at seventeen, I had minimized my exposure to the community by limiting my attendance at large public events, especially church-related events. Over the years, I had attended a few weddings, but always as a guest, not a hostess. And the weddings weren't the sort to draw in the whole town. Now I was center stage at an event likely to involve a good percentage of the local population, not just the folks who had lived and worked with my father all his life, but every Mormon in the county. My father, when he wasn't disfellowshipped for brawling, was a popular man, charming and gregarious, the type who turns strangers into lifelong friends with a single conversation. He also had considerable standing in the community, mostly because of the family he had married into. His funeral would be a big deal, so, taking my place in line, I prepared for an onslaught. That it would be an onslaught, rather than merely a tedious chore, I was quite certain, for my story—a version of it, anyway—was very well-known among the Mormons of Tooele. It was not the story I have told you in this book, a story of challenges met and suffering redeemed. It was a very different story, based on the Mormon version of the Fall of Lucifer.

In Mormon theology, Jesus Christ and Lucifer were spirit-brothers and the two oldest sons of God. Back when everybody was a spirit, including all the human beings who would ever live, Lucifer rebelled against his father and persuaded one-third of the other spirits to join his rebellion. The other two-thirds followed Jesus Christ, who remained faithful to his father. God then threw Lucifer and his followers out of heaven, whence they fell a vast distance into the outer darkness. Lucifer became Satan, the father of lies, and his followers became demons, devils, evil spirits, and other supernatural mischief-makers. The spirits loyal to Jesus were rewarded with human bodies, which set them on the path to salvation and eternal life in the Celestial Kingdom.

The story of Lucifer's fall is not unique to Mormonism. From medieval Catholic drama to the powerful lines of Milton's *Paradise Lost*, the story of the magnificent angel who succumbed to pride, defied his creator, and plunged from heaven into hell is a perennial favorite. For Mormons, though, Lucifer's fall is more than just an explanation of why evil exists. Mormon Lucifer and Mormon Jesus Christ were once like us, children of God in a disembodied "premortal" state. Having once been our spirit-brothers, they are much more like us than their mainstream Christian counterparts. Their feelings, motives, and actions are not so different from ours, so they serve as models for human behavior in a way they could never be for most Christians.[77] Mormons believe that every day we have the choice to be like Lucifer or Christ. We can daily choose to follow God's plan or try to revise it for our own glory. We can be cast out of heaven or remain among the saints. We can spread lies and lead people astray or to speak truth and bring people to the Celestial Kingdom. I had made the wrong choice, and I was notorious for it.

I wasn't just bad, said my detractors; my history bore an uncanny resemblance to Lucifer's. I too had been thrown from a great height because I thought I knew better than God.[78] I had been born into the Mormon aristocracy, descended from pioneers who had followed Brigham Young to Utah. My great-great-great grandfather was John D. Lee, who took the fall for Mountain Meadows Massacre when the great leader's vision turned paranoid and inspired his zealous followers to slaughter a wagon train bound for California. Some think Lee was a great martyr in the tradition of Joseph Smith. My grandfather was mayor of Tooele and a member of the high priesthood. Ancestry matters to Mormons, and mine could scarcely have been more illustrious.

Nor did I fail to live up to my inheritance, at first. As a child, I excelled in school and in church activities. Public speaking was my forte from the time I clambered onto a podium at age three to deliver my first speech, "Utah, the Beehive State." Difficult as my home life often was, in public I seemed an ideal Mormon girl: chaste, popular, accomplished, and widely regarded as a future leader. In college, I attracted the attention of Spencer W. Kimball, president and prophet of the Mormon Church, who gave me a series of long private interviews and kept track of my progress for the rest of his life with regular telephone calls to my mother. Like Lucifer, I occupied a favored position close to the seat of power then rebelled against that power out of sheer pride and perversity.

My rebellion was simply living my life, though it was nonetheless perceived as open defiance of the church. My first offense was being an alcoholic and drug addict. I hadn't careened drunkenly around Tooele or sold amphetamines to schoolchildren, just identified myself as an addict after the fact, but that was enough. As everyone knows, Mormons are a famously clean-living bunch, avoiding alcohol, tobacco, and hot drinks. When even one glass of wine breaks a commandment, there is no room for a disease concept of alcoholism, no "grey area" in which acceptable use can develop into abuse. In fact, addiction of any kind is considered the personal province of Lucifer, who envies human bodies and encourages their defilement with alcohol and drugs.

Much more importantly, I defied the law of chastity, which holds that sex is the sole privilege of two heterosexuals married to one another. The church has always been adamant that homosexuality is a sin, no matter the participants or their circumstances. Same-sex marriage isn't just sinful; it further offends by mocking "God-sanctioned marriage," whose purpose is child-rearing. The church has been consistent on this point, leaving no room for dissent or individual interpretation. Some gay and lesbian Mormons have begun to hope that the church will abandon its anti-gay policy the way it did polygamy and white supremacy, but that change is a long way off, if it's possible at all. On the day of my father's funeral, I would have said that a visit from the angel Moroni was more likely. Finally, I want to stress that breaking the law of chastity is no minor infraction to Mormons; it is the "most abominable above all sins save . . . the shedding of innocent blood."[79] In other words, to some mourners at my father's funeral, being a lesbian was nearly as bad as being a murderer. Because I acted on my desires and persisted in my "abominable sin," I had been disfellowshipped and would have been excommunicated had I not already left the church.

Leaving the church was my last and worst defiance. Already considered an apostate for disobeying the law of chastity, I went further and abandoned the teachings of the Mormon Church. To Mormons, that's defying God, worse than unchastity and *equivalent* to murder. Under such opprobrium, charges of apostasy should be rare, you'd think, yet few people fling them more readily than Mormons, who call the entire period between the death of Jesus Christ and the divine vision of Joseph Smith (that's 1,787 years or 88.5 percent of Christian history) "the great apostasy." So I had joined a pretty big club—though its Tooele chapter was vanishingly small. At any rate, the large number of apostates does not induce the church to relax its vigilance, which it exercises in a variety of ways. Though Mormons do not officially practice the extreme form of shunning seen in groups such as the Jehovah's Witnesses, there's still a lot of semi-official pressure on church members to ostracize apostates, even close family members, for their own good. (Yes, Mormons perfected "tough love" long before the recovery movement.) Church elders repeatedly advised my mother to sever all ties with me, which she, to her credit, simply refused to do. Other family members were not so generous; nor were many in the community, including people I had grown up with. Having minimized my exposure to such people over the years, I had no idea how many there were in Tooele or whether respect for my father would mitigate their "loving" censure.

Readers with no experience of living in an insular religious community may not readily understand just how profound an experience it was to go from idealized insider to disfellowshipped outsider, how my formal ostracism complicated every social interaction in Tooele, no matter how small. At home in Seattle, my sexuality, my religious beliefs, and my history of addiction were sources of affinity, not sources of alienation. To my west-coast liberal friends, the situation I faced in Tooele was so alien I had difficulty explaining it. Even gays and lesbians raised in homophobic evangelical families were unfamiliar with disfellowshipment and excommunication because most Protestant denominations simply don't practice any form of church discipline—not since the 19th century, anyway. These days, there's just too much competition, too much pressure to fill pews. Even Catholics have to work hard to get themselves excommunicated—and work harder to merit anathema, which is formal shunning. All I had to do was be me.

Waiting in the receiving line during the last moments before the doors opened, I turned around to glance at my wife and my son, who sat behind me against the wall. Deb, looking casually elegant in a black pantsuit, gave me a thumbs-up and a big smile. James jumped to his feet and asked me if I wanted his chair. Just seven weeks past hip surgery, I was unsure how long I'd be able to stand, but I shook my head "no." I would stand as long as I could. I wasn't just being tough—though that was certainly among my motives. I wanted to stand primarily because I wanted optimal control of my physical boundaries. Seated, I would be easy to encroach upon and easy to strand. Standing, even with a cane, I could more easily adjust my position in relation to others. As I waited for the doors to open and the visitation to begin, I knew that boundary control—physical, mental, and emotional—would be the task of the day.

"Boundary up," I reminded myself, as I had reminded so many Legacy clients over the years.

When the doors opened, I was shocked to see the huge number of people waiting. The funeral parlor's vestibule was full, and I could glimpse a line spilling out the front door and into the parking lot. Dress was not the somber black of mainstream Christian funerals but church wear: suits and dresses in various hues, perhaps a little more muted in color than usual but not classic mourning. My father was supposed to be enjoying spirit paradise with his deceased loved ones—not the Celestial Kingdom that would be his ultimate reward after the resurrection, but pretty nice nonetheless. To a true believer, there was no cause to mourn him.

I watched the first visitors come down the line: a couple I did not recognize, middle aged and nondescript in matching navy blazers. They knew me, though; I could see them glancing my way while they were greeting my mother and my sisters. Between glances, they looked at one another with raised eyebrows, and I could almost read their thoughts: "What should we say to her? Should we say anything? Should we shake her hand?" I had considered positioning myself last in line to make it easier for guests to peel off without greeting me, but my brother planted himself in that spot and refused to budge. For his own reasons, he didn't want to give the judgmental side of Mormonism any assistance.

"Hello, I'm Donna. Thank you for coming," I said to the first navy blazer, extending my hand. After a half-second's hesitation, her hand appeared, cupped as though she were holding an invisible orange. It shot forward and back so quickly that my own hand clasped only air as she mumbled something and moved toward my brother. Her husband, when it was his turn, nodded in my direction but did not offer his hand.

"Your father was a fine man," he said, studying the air between my brother and me.

"Thank you for coming," I repeated before turning to the next visitor.

"Hello, I'm Donna. Thank you for coming." I repeated the phrases over and over, smiling and offering my right hand. Some visitors reciprocated politely, but I often found myself shaking just the ends of people's fingers. A few visitors wheeled out of the line after greeting the last of my sisters, and I was amused to see that they all put on a little performance, suddenly noticing the time, for example, or waving at someone across the room. One man ignored my hand and my greeting but stood in front of me waiting for my brother, who made him wait an extra minute, just for being a jerk.

Most snubs were subtle, however, especially those orchestrated by uncles and male cousins who had risen to positions of power within the church.

"So sorry for your loss, son." said a well-padded man in a three-piece suit. It took me a moment to recognize the skinny cousin I had played Monopoly with, now an elder, but I recognized his insult right away. I decided to ignore it and turned to the next visitor in line. "I thought she was one of Clel's grandsons," my cousin explained to no one in particular.

"And I thought you were a grown-up," said my brother. "Looks like we were both wrong."

"I'm so glad you came," said another cousin, this one a high priest. "So glad." As he expanded on the theme of his gladness, he stood almost three feet away with his arms folded, backing into another guest when I took a small step toward him. He was not just a relative and a childhood friend but a cousin I had lived with as a child, someone with whom I had once been very close. In another community, our reunion would have been a joyful embrace, rather than an awkward dance of personal space.

A little later, an uncle, his grey hair dyed shoe-polish black, made a beeline for me after glaring from across the room for a while. He had already been through the line shaking everyone's hand, including mine, and offering condolences. This man was not as prominent in the church as my cousins, despite a lifetime of trying. He had briefly advised a bishop once, but so had my father, who came late to his Mormon faith and was repeatedly disfellowshipped. Nonetheless, he thought his brief stint in the bishopric elevated him above ordinary folk, and he was glaring at me over my father's corpse with the wrath of an Old Testament prophet. When I looked back at him, he strode over and stood in front of me, hands on his hips. For a full minute, he said nothing.

"Is there something I can do for you, Uncle Earl?" I asked finally. He replied by shaking his head in a wide, slow arc and striding off. The message was clear: I deserved a good telling-off, but he was too virtuous to give it to me.

"Must have forgotten his outline," murmured my brother. Uncle Earl was notorious for rambling testimonies based on elaborate notes.

"Maybe the aroma of brimstone got to him," I whispered back, and we both laughed.

Occasionally, my being a lesbian came up in a roundabout way. Late in the afternoon, I turned to see a woman I had coached when she was a girl and I was her high school sports director. Thrilled that she had come to the visitation, I called out to her as she turned toward me.

"How wonderful to see you, Gay!"

"I changed my name!" she barked, jumping back away from me even farther than my cousin had. Suddenly, I felt very sad for her. This middle-aged woman, whatever her own desires, was so terrified of mine that she could not touch me or acknowledge our shared past. She had even disowned her name, a fundamental part of her identity. Along with that sadness, I had other responses, a complex mix of thoughts and feelings. I was mildly disgusted, of course, as I always am by expressions of homophobia. No matter how many I encounter, I never get used to the idea that sexual orientation supplies a warrant for fear and hatred, and I think less of people who believe it does. I was also, I'll admit, a little disdainful. Not-Gay's backward jump and name change seemed extreme, almost parodic. At the same time, I felt sympathy. Perhaps her childish overreaction sprang from desires she dared not acknowledge. As she walked away from the reception line, her purse clasped to her chest, her shoulders tight and high, I felt an almost-physical sensation of her confinement in a world that was narrow, dark, and cramped. On its heels came an equally physical sense of my own freedom. Ironically, given that I was fresh from hip surgery and walking with a cane, I had the sudden feeling that I could move infinitely far in any direction, and with that feeling came a sudden surge of gratitude. I could have become Not-Gay, but I had escaped!

I did not act on any of these feelings. With a neutral expression, I thanked not-Gay for coming and turned to the man after her in line. As she walked stiffly away, I felt no urge to run after her, to invoke our shared history or explain my choices or argue for tolerance. I would remember our encounter because it was a great illustration of how some Mormons express community norms, but I had already let go of the feelings it had roused. In other words, my boundaries were functioning very well.

I needed them. In addition to my odd experiences in the receiving line, I heard murmurs from people standing nearby: "What is *she* doing here? What, in Heavenly Father's name, is *she* doing here?" For the six hours I stood in the receiving line that afternoon, people gathered in clusters watching me, and from many clusters I heard the word "she" like a hiss of steam from a locomotive. *She.* The lesbian, the liar, the ungrateful child who dishonored her parents. *She*, the schismatic, the apostate, the troublemaker. *She* is an alcoholic, you know, and a druggie. *She* killed her father—or as good as killed him—and will probably kill her mother, too. *She* has some nerve coming here! Had I still been seventeen or twenty-eight, it would have been excruciating. Had I been older but not dealt with my trauma, it would have been worse.

Fortunately, some of the mourners were wonderful. My father's favorite cousin wrapped me in a huge bear hug, murmuring into my ear how glad she was that I had come back to Utah. And her welcome wasn't the only surprise, as I suddenly realized that she was a lesbian, too.

"Donna, you didn't tell me about *her*," whispered Deb, who had just brought me a cup of coffee. My father's cousin was adorable in a pixie haircut and cowboy regalia, her slim jeans tucked into finely-tooled cowboy boots.

"How did I miss that?" I replied with a grin. And the rest of her family were lovely to me, too, more than compensating for the censure of some others.

At the end of the day, the funeral director shut down the visitation so he could close the facility. The next morning, we returned at ten o'clock and shook more hands until two o'clock. People had come from all over the United States, from Mexico and Europe. I had always known my father made friends easily, but I had no idea he knew so many people—people who thought enough of him to attend his funeral, some traveling considerable distances.

"Who *are* all these people?" I asked more than once. Still, most were locals, the social harvest of a gregarious man, a natural storyteller who was also interested in other people's stories and considered every human encounter the basis for a friendship. Like many troubled people, my father was kinder and more comfortable with strangers than with intimates. He could show his best side—his cowboy charisma, his sense of humor, his musical talent—then move on before his rage or his dark desires became visible.

Finally, the visitation was over. It was time to shut the casket and proceed to the funeral proper. With only first- and second-degree family remaining in the room, we folded our arms and bowed our heads for the special prayer that accompanies the closing of the casket. As we said the words, an employee of the funeral home reached into the casket to slip a hairnet over my father's hair. Hearing a choking sound to my right, I knew that my brother had seen the hairnet too. Tears ran down my face as I tried to suppress my laughter. I dared not look at my brother. All I could think of was my father spending eternity in a hairnet to match his ruffled shirt and his little green apron. If the Celestial Kingdom sorted "sissies" from real men the way he did, my father was in trouble! By the end of the prayer, my brother and I had regained control of ourselves and, as we rejoined the crowd outside the funeral parlor, no one realized that the tears drying on our cheeks were tears of laughter.

For the funeral proper, we drove to the Tooele stake house, where I had been baptized so long ago. Though the service had been planned for the chapel, the huge number of mourners required us to open the accordion doors at the back to expose the gymnasium. The front half of the venue was solemn, dignified, and hushed, with beige carpeting and dark oak pews, while the rear half was bright and full of echoes. Flowers filled the chapel area, some whisked over from the funeral parlor and some newly arrived, making the air heavy with the scent of roses and carnations. Following the casket, I didn't see that the accordion doors were open until I turned to enter the front pew with my family. I had thought there were a lot of people at the visitation; now I saw hundreds of new faces as well.

Looking at the people filling the chapel and the gymnasium beyond, some visibly weeping, I felt a rare moment of sorrow for my father's death. He truly did have a good side, and it was more than just protective coloration or a way to improve his odds of making the Celestial Kingdom. He had authentically generous impulses, and he followed through on them with a minimum of fuss. I remembered many winters in which he rose in the dark to chop and stack wood for elderly neighbors. When snow fell, as it often does in Utah, he plowed everyone's driveway for blocks around. He didn't expect thanks; as a strong man in good health, he was glad he could do such chores. He also had a lot of charm and the "gift of gab." He genuinely liked people. He listened to them, which is rare enough these days, and he could talk with them about whatever they cared about because he had a magpie brain that absorbed information on huge range of subjects, rather than concentrating on a few that particularly interested him. The man my father was to most of the people at his funeral: that man I could mourn.

But he was another man to the people sitting at the front of the church. Looking down my row, I counted two women he had raped for sure and three more that he had probably raped. None was an isolated assault; he raped me for years and likely did the same to all of his victims. Turning to the row behind me, I saw two more rape survivors, both of whom had reported my father's assaults to police only to find the cases transferred to a Mormon disciplinary council, where my father was exonerated on his own assurance that the victims were mistaken. At the time of their rape, all of my father's victims were underage, some young children. All the rapes but one were incest. Sitting in my pew, I suddenly remembered one more victim, also a child but not related, though she lived with my parents on and off. She was not sitting somewhere behind me because she could not attend the funeral, having killed herself a few years earlier—after another Mormon disciplinary council gave my father another pass.

Sitting in the front row, I faced the rostrum, an elevated platform on which sat the dignitaries of the church, including the stake president and the two cousins who had greeted me equivocally the day before. Except for the organist sitting stage left with her back to us, everyone on the high platform was male. Though they varied in age and build, all wore dark suits, somber ties, and identical haircuts: short and side-parted. Sitting among them were some of the officials who had failed to hold my father accountable at his last disciplinary council hearing. These elders had heard shattered young women describe years of sexual abuse. They had heard testimony that was credible from witnesses whose accounts corroborated one another. The only testimony that wasn't credible came from my father, who asserted that victims had mistaken innocent affection for rape, yet his was the testimony they believed. Then, as though clearing my father weren't bad enough, they publicly rebuked his victims.

"Shame on you for making these terrible accusations!" the stake president had said to each of the two women sitting behind me. One had meekly left the room, redoubling her efforts to become a perfect Mormon wife and mother; the other had become a bitter near-recluse. Behind me, they sat at opposite ends of their pew with downcast eyes. I had barely seen them at the visitation but resolved to check in with them later in the day. From my own experience, I knew the anguish they must be feeling. The stake president who had cried "Shame!" was seated on the rostrum, along with several of the elders who had heard the case. As I had with Mr. Waldo so many years ago, I glared at the stake president and was pleased when he frowned and shifted position several times. Childish, I know, but it made me feel better to see him squirm a little. And I was sending a message: I see you. You had the opportunity—and the responsibility—to render justice, and you not only failed but added your own portion of cruelty. I see you.

The service was long and dull, though I enjoyed singing the hymns. Speeches, starting with the bishop's introduction, featured the usual panegyrics and supernatural assurances, including a description of the vast rewards my father's virtue had earned him. I coughed a time or two at the mention of his lifelong chastity, expressed as devotion to the woman he had married for eternity and with whom he had fathered five children.

"They counted us," whispered my brother, also an apostate. "I'm shocked."

"They had to," I whispered back. "If you subtract the apostates, Dad's not much of a patriarch."

The speakers made much of that role: patriarch of a large Mormon family, now into its fourth generation. Over and over, they referred to "the family he created," as though my father had single-handedly dug up a mound of clay, shaped us with his own hands, and breathed life into us, just as he would someday when he became a god with his own planet to populate.

"His biggest adventure and his largest legacy was the family he created," thundered the last speaker at the close of the service.

"Created and broken," I murmured to my brother. As we sang the last hymn, "Each Life That Touches Ours for Good," I reflected on the lives touched for ill by my father's life and wondered, not for the first time, how far down the generations that touch might be felt. In the midst of sorrow for that legacy, I felt a rush of gratitude that it had not reached the son who was sitting beside me.

After the service, about a hundred mourners crossed the street to the cemetery, where still more flowers waited. Idly I wondered if there were any

roses or carnations left in the flower shops of northern Utah. We said a few
more prayers as the casket sat above the grave that would receive it, then we
dispersed; Mormons don't watch as the casket is lowered into the ground. As
everyone headed for their cars, two of my church-official cousins discussed
my presence at the funeral service.

"She shouldn't have come to the stake house," said the high priest. "It's
disrespectful."

"Abominable," said the portly elder. "But then what else do you expect
from an abomination?"

"Why was she allowed in? An apostate in the stake house!" They went on
in the same vein, not bothering to lower their voices or check to see who
might be nearby. James and I were right behind them, and, though I was
unfazed, James took the criticism hard. He stopped walking and, putting his
head in his hands, began to cry.

"I'm so sad our family is like this," he said. As I put my arms around my
son, I suddenly experienced a moment of clarity: I saw, all at once, how the
Mormon Church had infected and divided my family. It wasn't responsible
for all of our problems, but it had a large role in most of them. With the stake
house visible over James's shoulder, the church suddenly seemed to be
everywhere in Tooele, its values shaping the lives of everyone I knew,
whether Mormon or apostate. Some values are admirable: the emphasis on
family, for example. Some are truly pernicious, and the worst of these are
values the church disavows but reveals through its actions. No official church
doctrine proclaims the superiority of men, yet nearly every man holds the
sacred function of priesthood, and all church leaders are male. No official
church doctrine supports sexual abuse, yet the church takes an active role in
promoting it. Yes, I said promoting it. Let me be clear: I don't mean just
failing to curb it, though the church does that, too. But the church also
promotes sexual abuse by diverting the prosecution of offenders from the
criminal justice system, where it belongs, to itself. My father's victims came to
the police with *crimes*, yet their complaint ended up in a church council with
no legal safeguards for victims, no procedures to ensure fairness, no
community oversight, and no accountability. In Mormon Utah, church and
state remain so fused that church leaders without secular authority regularly
pressure police and prosecutors to "let us handle it." Once they take over,
their principal aim is to promote, not truth, justice or compassion, but the
power of the church and the men in it.

I knew those things before my father's funeral, but somehow they
seemed clearer now, more distinct. I saw how the church led my mother to
turn against her children when they were abused, something I cannot imagine
doing to James or any child. For my mother to enter the highest part of
heaven after she dies, my father has to call her secret name when she is
resurrected. That's not negotiable, so, to secure her eternal happiness, my

devout, uneducated, unworldly mother needs my father to be virtuous and loving—virtuous enough to reach the Celestial Kingdom himself and loving enough to invite her in. Hearing about abuse, she doesn't weigh competing stories and ask which teller has more credibility or which tale better explains the noises she heard through the paper-thin walls of the double-wide trailer all those years. She asks which one gives her eternity in the Celestial Kingdom. And if abused children have to be ignored make that work, then so be it. All of this I realized as I embraced my big-hearted son, hurt by the family fissures this faith had wrought.

When James finished crying, we rejoined the rest of the family in the stake house parking lot. As half of us climbed into David's car, I facetiously sang a few lines of the old gospel song "Amen." Getting the joke, my brother joined in, then one of my sisters. Surprised and delighted by our unaccustomed show of piety, my mother joined in, and the whole family sang "Amen" all the way to the reception, the women an octave higher than the men, my youngest sister soaring further still, improvising high harmonies. Our singing sounded good. My family always sang a lot, even for Mormons, who have been singing up a storm ever since God told Joseph Smith that "the song of the righteous is a prayer unto me." My father had been a fine singer, and some of our best times together involved singing country classics while he played guitar. Beyond sounding good, though, our singing turned into a powerful experience for all of us, even though our reasons for singing were very different. When sung in the closing moments of a basketball game by the team headed for victory, "Amen" is a taunt to the losing team. "We won," it proclaims. "You're finished." When sung in the spirit of the original, it's a prayer. Mormons also say "amen" after rituals and testimonies, even recorded testimonies, to indicate acceptance and agreement. So, for my mother and one sister, the song was an "amen" to the message of the funeral, which affirmed the truth of Mormon theology and my father's life as an expression of that truth. Some of us were passionately singing "good riddance, Dad" while others were passionately affirming their faith, yet these contrasting motives produced a single song and a moment of shared joy.

It was a strange and wonderful moment, and I wish I could end my story with it, but there was one challenge yet to come, one that's important to the theme of this chapter. After many choruses of "Amen," we arrived at a potluck reception, and, yes, it featured plenty of Mormon Funeral Potatoes, a decadent, cheesy potato-and-onion casserole with butter-soaked cornflakes on top. If you haven't tried this famous dish, you should, even though your arteries will curse you for it. We had six or seven batches, each from a different cook with a different family recipe. One batch lacked the cornflakes, which, in my book, made it just a regular casserole and hardly worth eating when there were real funeral potatoes on the table. The others were delicious, and I was very hungry, having not eaten for many hours. While James looked for cousins his age, Deb and I searched out my father's charming cousin, and the three of us loaded up plates and looked for a place to talk. We nabbed a relatively quiet corner and were about to tuck in when I remembered I wanted to take some Tylenol with my food. Standing in the receiving line for so long had not been good for my hip, which hurt. Leaving my plate, I went in search of a medicine cabinet or a well-stocked handbag. On a landing at the top of a flight of stairs, I heard my name from the left, so I headed that way. The next sentence stopped me in my tracks.

"Honey, you can't believe a thing Donna says. She's a liar." The voice was my mother's. I heard a woman respond too softly to hear. "Her whole life she's been angry at her father for being strict with her, so she makes up stories. Terrible stories." Another too-soft response followed. "No, honey, that didn't happen. It just didn't happen. The words you're saying are Donna's words, not your words; she put those terrible ideas in your head. That's her job, what she does to earn a living. So you can listen to Donna's words, or you can listen to Heavenly Father's words; it's your choice." I walked softly back down the stairs, my hip pain forgotten. When I rejoined Deb and my father's cousin, they immediately asked what was wrong, so I must have looked a bit off. Had the question come from Deb alone, I would have answered frankly, but I could not involve another person in the matter, so I went with a half-truth.

"I'm just tired," I replied, "It's been a challenging day."

CHAPTER FIFTEEN: Family, Functionality, and Forgiveness

The whole point of doing this difficult inner work is to free ourselves from the maladaptive patterns laid down by childhood trauma. It's not to get stuck in the trauma or even in the process of healing from it. We want, ultimately, to move beyond it, to grow strong in the injured places, to develop the wisdom and compassion that arises from deep self-knowledge. Many challenges will test us as we grow stronger and more mindful, though none more consistently than dealing with our families of origin. To illustrate, let me tell you about a conversation I had with a client the other day. I've had the same conversation hundreds of times—and, to be honest, I've been on both ends of it. I'm going to call my client Ellie and tell you that she's a talented woman, a fledgling interior designer with a master's in art history who sits on the board of a major museum. She's married with two sons in college, and her modernist home was recently featured in *Dwell*. Ellie has participated in one Legacy workshop and seen me individually for about four months. Here's the conversation.

Ellie: It happened again, Donna. I was doing great, feeling really strong. I landed an important commission; Ricky got into med school; Bob and I are staring to really talk to each other. I feel like things are finally on track, then Mom calls. It's almost like she knows when I'm flying high and calls to shoot me down.

Me: Doesn't she also call when you're feeling low?

Ellie: Well, yes.

Me: Don't give her more power than she has, Ellie. We've talked about this. Who thinks Mommy knows everything?

Ellie: I get it. That's my wounded child.

Me: So what happened?

Ellie: She wanted to tell me about an article she had read, about orcas imitating human speech.

Me: Are whales a particular interest of hers?

Ellie: No, nor of mine. It was just an excuse.

Me: What did she really want to talk about?

Ellie: Nothing, that's why the conversation was so weird. She didn't hint that she had something important to say, like she usually does, so I'll drag it out of her. We discussed talking whales for a few minutes, then she asked me how Bob and the boys were, and that was it. No agenda, as far as I could tell.

Me: So what's the problem? You said "It happened again"; what happened?

Ellie: By the end of the conversation, I felt like absolute crap. She didn't say anything terrible, just shared an article she liked and asked about the family. The perfect mother, right? Meanwhile, I ended up in a filthy mood, whereas five minutes earlier I had been on top of the world, and I tell you, Donna, I felt like a crazy person. Bob asked me what was wrong, and what was I supposed to say, "I'm upset because my mother likes whales?" For Pete's sake, what's the matter with me?

If you read the last chapter carefully, you can probably guess the answer to Ellie's question. She and I had talked a lot about her overbearing, narcissistic mother and the trauma she had inflicted, but we hadn't yet discussed the pain her mother might be suffering. I probed a little, and, sure enough, Ellie's mother showed signs of depression. Ellie was likely carrying around some of her mother's pain and would have to deal with it.

I mention this phone call now because it illustrates a major challenge we face as we recover: dealing with the people who perpetrated, enabled, and witnessed our trauma. No matter how robust our recovery, such interactions are always challenging. What's exciting is that they can also provide a way to measure our progress, to see how far we've come. First the challenge: why did Ellie feel, as she said, "like absolute crap" after speaking with her mother about whales for a few minutes? There was nothing passive-aggressive or disingenuous about the conversation. Ellie's mother did not hint that the talking orca was a better communicator than her daughter or sigh theatrically that she would *so* enjoy a trip to Sea World if only she had the resources Ellie took for granted! The conversation was neutral. The problem was that the boundaries between Ellie and her mother, which had been non-existent while Ellie was growing up, were still extremely weak, so everything her mother was feeling flooded over Ellie. She was working hard to establish boundaries with her clients and her husband—maintaining her perspective when challenged, for example, rather than reflexively adopting the challenger's—but with her mother she remained wide open, unable to resist any influence or withhold any part of herself. Ellie couldn't, for example, tell her mother a polite social lie, such as "I have to hang up now, Mom, my phone's almost dead," even though Mom lived two thousand miles away. It wasn't a principled refusal; Ellie could tell the same lie to a friend. Rather, she believed that her mother could see into her mind and would spot the lie instantly. In addition, without always being aware of it, she felt a deep sense of obligation whenever her mother expressed a desire. Even if she dared risk the lie, she would feel so bad about it that she'd rather just stay on the phone.

Most trauma survivors come from families with extremely dysfunctional boundaries. There are exceptions, of course, as in cases of medical trauma, where loving caregivers have to hurt children physically in order to help them, but, in general, abuse involves boundary violations, as we have seen. As we begin to repair our damaged boundaries—or create them from scratch—we seek the company of people who respect them and who have good boundaries themselves. We become less drawn to partners and friends who impose on us or who programmatically withhold themselves in ways that make us feel unworthy. We spend time with people we can trust, people who are trying to live as functional adults, and these social bonds over time create a community that is safe for us, one that supports our recovery and our growth, as we support the recovery and growth of others in the community. We become part of a healthy new social system.

When we return to the people who raised us, we often pull ourselves out of this new healthier system, particularly if our original families live at a distance. Moreover, we reinsert ourselves into an unhealthy system, the system responsible for many of our worst problems. It's important to think of our families as systems, even if they are very small and even if we are largely estranged from them, because the word "system" captures the interdependence and contingency of family life, whether we are aware of it or not. In the system we were raised in, we had an assigned role that we played for a long time, often for decades. When I say "assigned," I don't mean to suggest that we had no input whatsoever. Assigned roles emerge from a combination of factors, including temperament and individual choice; the point is that once all of these factors have generated a role, we're expected to play it. The family system, to function as usual, requires that all members behave in their accustomed ways. When one member changes, the system can't function as usual. Even in a large family, it's extremely disruptive for one member to make a significant change, far more disruptive than most people would guess. That's because family systems are dynamic, with lots of moving parts, so a small change can produce large consequences. Think of it this way: if a family were a parking lot, and one member decided to park sideways, rather than nose-in, then maybe the parking lot would look a little different over on one side, but the other cars wouldn't be affected. But if the cars were all moving around, and one member decided to drive sideways, then things would get chaotic. There might be collisions, not just with the sideways-driving car, but between some of the other cars as they adjusted their accustomed paths to accommodate the sideways car. That's the difference between change to a system and change to a static group.

Analogies aside, there is always pressure to resume our assigned roles, especially in the early years of our recovery. We have to expect it, and we have to prepare for it. Sometimes this pressure is conscious and hostile, but often it is neither, just people instinctively nudging us back toward more familiar behavior so the whole system can return to normal, however suboptimal "normal" is. The point is not necessarily to call out the nudging but, rather, to be mindful of it—especially when it it's also coming from inside us. Ultimately, the real challenge is our own minds, which can relay social pressure so that it seems to be arising from within. Let me give you an example from the story I just told.

One old role that I dealt with during my father's funeral was the scapegoat, the role I described in the first chapter and one of the most difficult for me to abandon. As a child, I had so thoroughly absorbed the notion of my fundamental wrongness that I needed many years' hard work to unlearn the idea that, no matter how hard I tried to be otherwise, no matter how many good deeds I piled up, I was simply a "bad seed." Returning to Tooele, I once again received the message that I was evil, and the message was louder and stronger than ever. Where once it had come from my parents with the support of the church, now it came straight from the church, amplified by the many people who regarded church decisions as binding and infallible. It may seem ridiculous that I felt any pressure to resume the scapegoat role; after all, I did not believe for one second that I was evil for being a lesbian or an alcoholic or a lapsed Mormon. But it wasn't the *reasoning* behind the community's contempt that pressured me; it was the *feeling* of it, that ancient, familiar sense of wrongness that my disfellowshipped status brought back. It matched up too well with how I had felt as a little girl terrified that baptism could not expunge her evil. At the funeral I felt that pressure relayed internally when I began to suspect that I had been unfair to my father, that I had not adequately valued his strengths while overemphasizing his weaknesses, that my doing so was wrong and all the hundreds of people who had loved and admired him were better people than I was for seeing the good in him. That suspicion, brief as it was, surprised me. Fortunately, I recognized it as an old role from an old script, and I dealt with it quickly.

I dealt with it by rehearsing facts: the rapes I suffered, the rapes I witnessed, the rapes I knew about, the rapes I suspected, the beatings I suffered, the beatings I witnessed, the beatings I knew about, the beating I suspected, the emotional cruelty I suffered and witnessed and knew about and suspected, on and on, one after the other. Lists are great therapeutic tools. A list enables a kind of double vision, the ability to see the forest and the trees (or the whole and the parts) at the same time. A list demonstrates a claim, rather than just stating it, so it offers a more powerful way to convey a truth, which is why lists are prominent in epic poetry. When Homer wanted to convey the magnitude of the army that descended on Troy, he didn't say, "The Greeks assembled a really, really *huge* army," using elaborate metaphors of size. Instead, he listed the contingents one by one. We used the same principle when we compiled our trauma inventories. Once we laid out our histories, item by item, and looked over the whole list, we gained a clearer picture of the experiences that shaped us, along with confidence in that picture. We can do the same thing on the fly, as I did when I noticed myself starting to worry about being unfair to my father. In addition to listing his offenses, I reminded myself that I had publicly praised his virtues many times, that I consistently recognized and acknowledged his strengths. In other words, I short-circuited the temptation toward self-blame, the unearned guilt of the scapegoat, by focusing on facts. Just as rehearsing the facts of our lives can bring us out of an emotional tailspin, rehearsing the facts of a situation can keep toxic patterns from making us doubt our own truths.

What allowed me to do that was mindfulness. I paid attention to everything that happened as it happened, and I paid attention to my responses. As I've said before, this kind of moment-to-moment awareness is not a gift that we either have or don't have; it's a skill we develop through practice. We should maintain that practice during stressful times, especially when dealing with family. If we meditate, we should plan how to keep at it. In some circumstances, we may not find much support for meditation, so it's important to work out in advance how we will make the opportunity. If we expect disruption, it may make sense not to advertise what we are doing but just quietly do it, sitting in a chair and listening through headphones to one of the guided meditations in this book. Another option is micro-meditation, taking a free moment here and there to focus on the breath or on a nearby object with gentle awareness. Even thirty seconds helps. For those with a regular practice, micro-meditation is surprisingly effective at returning our attention to the present moment. We can also flash back to some of the images we've created while meditating. Before a stressful event such as a family reunion, it's a great idea to log some time practicing the mountain meditation and the boundary meditation we learned. At high-stress moments, simply recalling our mountain or our moated castle can provide access to some of the qualities we associated with them during our practice.

Mindfulness's twin is non-attachment. Paying attention to our moment-to-moment experience—our environment, the people around us, our behavior, our thoughts and feelings—we see more clearly how little of what we perceive is truly about us. That my cousin thinks I'm a spiritual danger to his community reveals nothing about *my* spirituality; instead it shines a spotlight on *his*. That Not-Gay recoils in horror from my greeting reveals nothing about *my* sexuality but speaks volumes about *hers*. With healthy boundaries in place, such facts are immediately apparent. What other people do and say and think about me has far more to do with who they are than with who I am. Does that mean I dismiss all feedback as "not about me"? Of course not. As a functional adult, I evaluate the content and the source, consider the occasion, reflect on the message, and, if warranted, take it on board. What I don't do is conclude, "If so many people think I'm dangerous, then I must be dangerous."

My experience at my father's funeral showed me that my boundaries were healthy. Often throughout the week, especially in the receiving line, I felt like I was watching reality television, a series of performances that had little to do with me. Hour after hour, I saw and heard ugly behavior but felt mainly disinterested curiosity about it. Had there been a microphone in my brain, it would have recorded "Well now, that's odd!" and "How interesting!" There were some moments of pain with people I cared about—or had once cared about. But those feelings were appropriate and proportional. I've already described the quick cascade of feelings I had about Not-Gay's overreaction: pain, then sympathy, then gratitude for my own life. Though I have dwelled on the episode at length to illustrate a point, at the time I experienced a quick sequence of mild emotions that was over in a matter of seconds. I remember it mainly because there's a certain poignancy in the contrast between Gay the carefree girl I knew long ago and Not-Gay the frightened woman I met at the funeral, rather than because the incident was particularly painful. In addition to keeping feelings commensurate, mindfulness and healthy boundaries give us the choice of whether to express what we are feeling. We don't have to react, but we can choose to respond if that seems useful. At my father's funeral, I mostly chose not to.

Setting boundaries works. For people who grew up with healthy boundaries, it may be largely unconscious, like security software that runs in the background while you use your computer, but survivors of trauma have to make a conscious effort to establish and maintain boundaries. As you saw, I still remind myself to "boundary up," which is my personal shorthand for a way of perceiving, thinking, and acting that seeks to regulate everything from which people I touch to what statements I believe. I expect to be telling myself to mind my boundaries for the rest of my life, just as I will always remind myself to pay attention to where I parked my car or left my keys. The reminder saves time, energy, and angst; it's good mental hygiene that improves my life and the lives of people around me. Boundary-setting is not a chore or an imposition because healthy boundaries liberate people: from intrusion, from enmeshment, from manipulation, from second-guessing, from a host of minor breaches and a few major ones. As importantly, by emphasizing choice over compulsion, healthy boundaries liberate people *to* connect.

There are many practical things we can do to set boundaries. In the last chapter, Daisy urged me to visit my parents in a Winnebago, rather than staying in their trailer, to impose a solid physical boundary between me and my family of origin. That was a great idea, not just because it created physical separation, but because physical separation reinforces other kinds of separation. As my story illustrates, I pay attention to what happens in physical space, which always has an important symbolic dimension. Human beings express power relations spatially, from the king elevated on a dais to the bully getting "in your face." I didn't want to sit down in the reception line, even though my recent hip surgery made standing painful, because sitting reduces mobility and makes physical boundary control more difficult. Such practical considerations may seem small, yet they can have potent effects. I had a friend who, the week before her Ph.D. orals, spent an hour the room where the exam would be given, which featured a long table with eight chairs, one on each end and three on each side. She wanted to sit in every chair and find the "power position." Not surprisingly, it was at the end farthest from the door, where no one could easily encroach on her physical space. She got to the exam early, grabbed that seat, and believes to this day that it helped her feel more in control. At any rate, I pay attention to physical boundaries, and I protect mine with everything from an extra hotel room to saying, "No, thanks," when an overeager stranger swoops in for an unwelcome embrace. That's hard, I know, but it's necessary to remind myself that someone else's desires don't automatically override mine. I decide who touches me, and, though there are moments in which I let someone else's desire prevail, the choice to do so is always mine. With my boundaries in place, I don't feel the sense of obligation that I used to.

Technology can complicate boundary control. It's important to realize that, as with conventional advertising, companies such as Facebook and Google have put a lot of money and research into engineering boundary failure. Mechanisms to capture our attention are ubiquitous and clever, aimed to penetrate our mental boundaries so that we behave in ways that generate profits for them, ways that may not be good for us. Tech companies queue sequences and time notifications to keep us mentally tethered to their sites and available to advertisers. This boundary-crushing engineering is so successful at creating a kind of internet addiction that many of its inventors—the man who devised the Facebook "like," for instance—have taken dramatic steps to cut themselves and their families off. When a boundary-crushing designer builds walls around the people he loves, it's time for the rest of us to consider similar protection.

In addition, as one-to-one communication becomes faster and easier, we feel increasingly tethered to that as well. I know people who would leave the house without their pants before they would leave the house without their smart phones; as a result we face the growing expectation that we will be available by phone, text, and email most of the time. As availability increases, expected response time decreases, and, in some professions, the impact has been dramatic. College professors, who used to meet students in weekly or semi-weekly office hours, must now answer emails right away or risk negative student evaluations. In some circles, people expect text messages to be answered immediately unless the recipient is busy doing something that would make texting impossible, which unfortunately doesn't include driving. The most recent revision of the notorious dating guide *The Rules*, which advocates playing hard-to-get for life, suggests waiting a leisurely fifteen minutes to return a text. That fifteen minutes seems a long time to anyone is evidence of a sea change, not just since the days of letter-writing but since the invention of the smart phone. Today's electronic communication creates a persistent threat of boundary collapse in which someone else's desire to connect can take precedence—or, at the very least, intrude upon—whatever our desire happens to be at the moment. Survivors of abuse have to be especially aware of this potential problem and take steps to mitigate it.

For us, technology has to be the front line of boundary control. We must use it to manage access to us, rather than letting it (and its users) manage us. We must make careful, conscious choices about how to use all electronic media, which may mean switching off automatic notifications or even switching off our smart phones some of the time. What each of us does will depend, to some degree, on our temperament, our history, and our circumstances. Parents, for obvious reasons, will have difficulty unplugging completely when their young child isn't with them, but they certainly don't need to know every time someone "likes" the child's latest photo. Fortunately, because people are becoming concerned about the amount of time we spend with digital media and about their constant hijacking of our attention, there's no shortage of ideas, from blogs to Ted Talks, about how to use our devices more wisely. My concern is less with suggesting a specific regimen than with getting across the idea that we don't owe anyone our attention *right now* just because they want it *right now*. If we feel we do, our boundaries need more work.

One of the boundaries most essential to our peace of mind is the boundary between what lies within our power and what does not. We must understand what we can and cannot control. As we found out when we began to meditate, we have limited control over our thoughts. If I suggest you think about a pink orangutan for ten seconds then not think about a pink orangutan for ten seconds, you will likely find the latter difficult. I've always found the advice to "put it out of your mind" exasperating, probably coined by someone who hadn't paid very close attention to how minds work, certainly not someone who had ever tried to meditate. For the same reason, I have trouble with religious doctrine that condemns thoughts as equivalent to actions, not that we shouldn't try to think better thoughts, because we should. But they're not necessarily under our control. We do control our words and our actions, however. When functioning as adults, we decide what to say and not say, do and not do. When we relinquish control and start running on impulse, we are in boundary failure. Too much lies outside the boundary between what we can control and what we can't. But our boundaries can also fail in the other direction when we seek to extend our control beyond its proper reach. Outcomes will always be beyond our control, even when cause and effect are tightly circumscribed—say, when baking a cake from a familiar recipe. A breaker could trip causing the oven to cool and the cake to fall. A dog with a sweet tooth could lick off the frosting. Because much of life is more complex than baking a cake, the variables that can influence outcomes are dizzying. Functional adults minimize risk by taking sensible precautions but recognize the limits of their power. They learn to put their energy into what they can control, their words and actions, then let go. Not surprisingly, mindfulness helps develop this capacity.

Other people, adults at least, lie beyond our control, and failing to recognize this limit is a source of great misery, both for ourselves and for others. Many of us, as we have seen, suffered at the hands of caregivers who failed to recognize where they ended and we began. So it may take a little time and effort to feel comfortable with a new way of thinking. In the meantime we remind ourselves that we don't control—or seek to control—other human beings. We don't control their thoughts. We don't control their feelings. We don't control their behavior. Influence, yes; we can, once in a while, inspire or persuade or create conditions that enhance a possibility. But the minute we start thinking, "Okay, I'll do this, then he'll do that, then I'll come back at him this other way, and he'll have to do what I want," we're in boundary failure. Moreover, if our manipulation works, the other person is in boundary failure too, and the result is a classic codependent relationship—one version, anyway.

With children, the issue can feel more complicated. Parents' boundaries must be semi-permeable membranes, allowing our children free passage through but keeping our own stuff contained. Moreover, parents must respect children's boundaries so that they grow up to be functional adults. This principle is critically important, especially for survivors who were enmeshed with their own parents. In general, except when a child is in danger, parents should focus on controlling what we ourselves say and do, rather than trying to control our children. Yes, there will be times when we must exert some control, but it should be limited. We want to control what's on their dinner plates and where they play and whether they get their vaccinations, but not whether they like asparagus or whether they play with a carboard box instead of an educational toy or whether they holler at the prick of a needle.

When we sense a problem, we should always look first to our own actions. For example, if our children don't want to spend time with us, we should examine our own behavior to discover how it might contribute to the children's aversion. We should not try to bribe, guilt-trip, or otherwise manipulate children into spending time with us. That is just another way of trying to control outcomes, another failed boundary. Much more effective than control is allowing children to experience the natural consequences of their actions. Then, if we parents also teach logical thinking and problem-solving, children will gradually learn how to work out natural consequences themselves and will be well-prepared for functional adulthood.

Another way people in recovery sometimes ignore the boundary between what they can and cannot control is worry. Worry is often a paradoxical attempt to mentally control other people and outcomes. The backward logic of worry-as-control goes like this: when bad things happen, they are always unexpected. It follows, therefore, that, if I expect a bad thing to happen, it will *not* happen, giving my worry the power to prevent catastrophe. It is thus my duty to worry about every possible calamity that could befall me and the people I love, even though constant low-grade anxiety causes stress-related illnesses, which *should* concern me but don't because I'm too busy worrying about terrorists, serial killers, and product tampering. This "preventive" worry rests on a logical fallacy: that what comes before (not expecting a bad thing) causes what comes after (the bad thing). But trauma survivors, particularly those of us subjected to intellectual abuse, may be unused to reasoning about existential cause and effect, even though dazzlingly logical when cross-examining witnesses or writing code. The reason is easy to see: causality is often missing or skewed in abusive households. In my family, remember, the logic of punishment was backward: because I was punished so harshly, I must be very bad. To become functional adults, we must learn to think through formerly automatic responses, such as worry. When we do, we find another paradox: that acknowledging the limits of our power actually gives us *more* power by repurposing wasted energy for real growth and accomplishment!

We must also acknowledge the limits of our control in regard to large systemic problems, such as global warming, income inequality, and war. Here, too, functional adults learn to distinguish between what they can and cannot do then let the latter go. In most cases, there is a lot we *can* do, educating ourselves and others, becoming activists for the changes we believe in, and making strong choices, whether in the voting booth or in the grocery store. We can recycle, blog, use public transit, circulate petitions, retweet worthy opinions, demonstrate, organize at work, volunteer, write to our representatives, run for public office, and support people who are doing all of those things. What we absolutely cannot do is change anything by worrying about it. Such anxious worry, sometimes called "future-tripping," is the principal fear that remains, once survivors offload carried fear. The antidote to worry lies both in clear-eyed assessment of what we can and cannot control and in conscious attention to the present moment. A good technique to disrupt future-tripping is to stop and ask:

What am I doing right now?

What can I do right now?

How am I feeling right now?
Why am I feeling that way?
What am I thinking right now?

This is another situation in which micro meditation can be extremely helpful. Stop. Focus on the breath or an object in your environment, and settle your attention there. When a worry intrudes, observe it, rather than getting caught up in it. Do the same with the next one. Feel yourself as an embodied creature inhabiting this particular moment, or, in the famous words of Ram Dass, be here now. Another option, for theists, is to submit whatever problem is causing anxiety to a higher power. What all three of these techniques have in common is that they restore the boundary between what we can control and what we can't control, freeing us to act effectively. In other words, when we worry less about systemic problems, we become more effective at fighting them.

When we get our boundaries under control and consistently behave like functional adults, change begins to happen in our families of origin. I talked earlier about how the systemic nature of the family pressures members to resume old roles, and that pressure is considerable, whether perceived and acknowledged or not. But, if we maintain our boundaries and don't revert to old patterns, then the system has to change. That's how systems work. We don't control that change, and we certainly don't control individual family members, but we do exert influence.

Change may be predictable or surprising. In some cases, family members simply find ways to function around us. Siblings who were once drinking buddies stop inviting us to play poker in the basement after our sobriety helps us clean them out a few times. Spousifying parents shift their focus to another child. My family passed the scapegoat role to my brother, which is one reason the two of us joke around so much today. (If we're supposed to feel evil, we might as well *be* evil, right? A little evil, anyway.) There's not always a substitute available, so avoidance strategies can take the form of withdrawal. Sometimes this and other avoidance strategies sting a bit; usually they are transparent enough not to hurt.

After a time, family members may make healthier adjustments. Noticing that we seem stronger, happier, and more self-assured, they may begin to investigate whether what has worked for us will work for them. Some may imitate our words and actions, "trying them on" to see how they feel. Some may strike out in their own healthy directions. Some may make a dramatic gesture to indicate that they are changing as radically as we are changing. I sometimes think about my father's apology that way: not as sincere remorse *or* as fear of divine judgment, but as a "Hey, look at me changing!" that revealed just how momentous the change in me seemed to him. Quite a compliment, actually.

Overall, the effect of my recovery on the rest of my family has not been immense. I have no miracles of transformation to share. But there has been positive change. As I told you at the end of the last chapter, my mother regained her health when I restored the boundaries between us and stopped carrying her pain. Since then—and fairly steadily—she has become more frank and independent, and she admits to following my example. When her religious anxieties aren't being stoked, she has exhibited real growth in recent decades, and some of it is surely linked to my recovery. That this conservative Mormon octogenarian attended a lesbian wedding may be attributed to the simple fact of our relationship; that she danced at the wedding and spoke warmly to my many gay and lesbian friends betrays a more complex influence. I think I have helped to show her that change, even previously unimaginable change, can be a good thing.

In some ways, my recovery has exerted more influence on the family *system* than on individual members. Because I'm a functional adult, I have relationships with everyone in the family. Though I live nine hundred miles away, I work hard to maintain those relationships. Two people can have a good relationship if only one of them is a functional adult; parents and children do it all the time. Over the years, I've been able to bring my siblings and my mother together by modeling how to develop strong bonds and by offering encouragement. So, where they were once quarrelsome, thin-skinned, and often estranged from one another, my siblings have begun to establish relationships among themselves, which means that I no longer have to serve as everybody's intermediary, the hub of the family wheel. In the past, I've described this general concord as a miracle, and, given our collective history, I'm not entirely sure that's an exaggeration. Miracle or not, I'll take it.

Unfortunately, not all families of origin can change for the better. Some are simply too damaged—and damaging. On rare occasions, a family can be so toxic that conventional boundary-setting does not work. If contact means renewed abuse or if it causes dramatic reversion to destructive thoughts and behaviors, then we have to consider the possibility that contact should be suspended. If there is simply no way to establish and maintain functional boundaries with our families, then we have to rely on the crudest and most absolute physical boundary: distance. It can be temporary or partial—and I have used limited estrangement when my family's dysfunction threatened my recovery—but it may also have to be permanent. Complete estrangement should never be a choice made in the grip of strong emotion but soberly, deliberately, and with the advice of trusted counselors. Detaching completely from the system in which we were formed, no matter how dysfunctional that system, is a kind of psychic amputation and should be a last resort. At the same time, it cannot be unthinkable if self-protection demands it.

The last family issue I want to talk about is forgiveness. I have offered several reasons why my father might have asked for mine, and I'm sure alert readers can come up with many more. I have also said that, in the end, I am less concerned with his motives for wanting my forgiveness than with the way my forgiveness could affect my recovery—and, to a lesser extent, the potential recovery of others in my family. The first thing to consider is what forgiveness is. Psychologists tend to see it as an emotional change in which a victim relinquishes negative feelings about an offense and its perpetrator. But, because it's so central to many world religions, many people have a larger understanding, one that understands forgiveness as potentially affecting other people as well, starting with the perpetrator. In other words, forgiveness is social, as well as psychological.

All we have to do is turn on the television to witness the lofty place forgiveness holds in the repertoire of human interactions. It's not commonplace; it's rare, highly prized, and always dramatic. Oprah Winfrey is a huge fan, and she touts the value of forgiveness in multiple media. So why is forgiveness so important? And what is it, exactly? First of all, Oprah's definition is purely psychological. She claims that she had a "transcendent moment" when she heard a guest say, "Forgiveness is giving up the hope that the past could be any different." Yes, forgiveness is a kind of radical acceptance of the past, but survivors of trauma need to mentally separate that piece from the rest of what forgiveness is.

To arrive at a broader definition of forgiveness, we have to consider its role in Christianity, which has shaped the modern understanding of the term, even for people who profess other faiths—or no faith at all. Though I often experience awe in the mountains or desert, I am not a religious person; at the same time, I recognize that even modern secular culture bears the imprint of religious ideas. Forgiveness can't be fully understood without this perspective. Fundamental to mainstream Christianity (though not to Mormonism)[80] is the prayer Jesus Christ taught his followers, instructing them to, "Forgive us our trespasses, as we forgive those who trespass against us." This line is part of a series of requests: give us our daily bread, forgive us; don't lead us into temptation; and deliver us from evil. Of those four, forgiveness is the only thing we also have to do, and it's clearly stated as a mirror image of what God does. In other words, forgiveness is not just giving up the hope that the past will be different; it's much more.

Mainstream Christianity holds that we human beings are born sinful due to the original sin of Adam and Eve. Then we go out and commit a lot of new sins because we are weak and fallible mortals and because Satan has a big bag of tricks to lead us astray. Mormonism holds that human beings are *not* inherently sinful, but we generally get to work sinning right away because we are weak and fallible mortals and because Satan has a big bag of tricks to lead us astray. So in both religions, the biggest problem human beings have is sin. We do bad things, lots of them. We can't help it. As our sins mount, individually and collectively, we rack up a giant ethical debt. So our biggest need is a way to pay or cancel that debt. The blood sacrifice of Jesus Christ was one way, but it's far beyond the scope of this book. The other way is forgiveness: God wiping out our debt and restoring us to a state of grace or operational innocence. In other words, divine forgiveness is profound.

The human version is a mirror of the divine version. We ask for God's forgiveness "as we forgive," not "as we try to forgive" or "as we accept the past and move on." We're supposed to imitate divine forgiveness and wipe the ethical slate clean, not just come to terms with the fact of the sin. That doesn't mean pretending that the sin never happened, but it does mean excusing it, removing the blame. Forgiveness implies the willingness, even the wish, to see the sinner freed from the psychic burden of the sin and to play a part in that freeing. One reason why it's so powerful to see the family of a murder victim forgive the murderer is that they are actively trying to ease the suffering of someone who caused them greater suffering. Most people won't—or can't—do that.

Christians and non-Christians understand that true forgiveness of a major offense is an emotionally complex process. Like cutting ourselves off from our family of origin, it's not something to undertake without careful reflection. In Chapter Thirteen, I mentioned performative speech, a kind of speaking in which simply saying some words ("I do," for example) makes them true. "I forgive you" is performative speech. Saying it changes our world, so it must not be said lightly.

Taking care with forgiveness is especially important for trauma survivors. Some of us want to forgive abusive caregivers right away, especially those who "did their best" to be good parents or guardians or mentors. Wanting to be fair, wanting to be loving, wanting to feel better ourselves, we may excuse abuse even before we have formed a clear picture of its scope or its effects on our lives. Often the crux of the matter is an abuser's intentions. In our legal system, intent is a crucial determinant of how serious an offense is. Killing someone by accident is a lesser crime than killing someone on purpose, and killing on a whim a lesser crime than planned killing. For the last nine hundred years or so, intention has also been an important religious concern, so, even when we're very young, we learn to reduce blame for an offense by saying, "I didn't *mean* to do it." In our culture, we can feel a lot of internal pressure to forgive abusers who meant no harm or who didn't know any better or who were victims of abuse themselves or who were mentally ill or acted from a number of other mitigating pressures. And, at some point, forgiveness may well be something we should offer—profoundly healing for both our abusers and for ourselves. But we probably should not do it right away, at least not until we have undertaken the work described in this book.

The reason for waiting is that we must be able to hold our abusers accountable for what they did to us. To develop a clear picture of what happened when we were children, we must excavate the facts of our lives from a child's perspective. If we superimpose our adult understanding of motivations and mitigating circumstances, we will be less able to retrieve and process our youthful experience. I talked about this difficulty in the last chapter; now I want to say more generally that grappling prematurely with whether—and how—to forgive our abusers can interfere, not just with making our abuse lists and offloading our carried feelings, but with the whole process described in this book. To do this work, we must bracket the issue of whether our caregivers meant to do harm and focus on what harm they did, not to assign them perpetual blame or to become perpetual victims, but to make it possible for everyone to grow and change and transcend past suffering.

That said, some readers may believe they can forgive their caregivers and hold them accountable at the same time. As F. Scott Fitzgerald wrote, "the test of a first-rate intelligence is the ability to hold two opposed ideas in the mind at the same time, and still retain the ability to function." Unfortunately, this oft-quoted line is from an essay called "The Crack-Up" and describes a naive youthful optimism destroyed by experience. What I take from the quotation is a warning against over-confidence or thinking that, because something is conceptually possible, it's emotionally possible. We can split hairs and say that forgiveness erases blame but not accountability, an intellectual distinction that is hard to maintain at the level of feeling. But I think it's much better simply to table the question of forgiveness until we have some real recovery under our belts. Then, if we do decide it's what we want, we can forgive with our whole heart.

I arrived at forgiveness in stages, the way many survivors do. The earliest was the Oprah stage, the giving up of hope that the past could be different. Of course we all know intellectually that we can't rewrite the past—beyond a certain point, anyway—but trauma work can provoke quite a bit of "what if" thinking. What if I had been born into a loving, stable family; what would I be like? What if x hadn't happened and y had never come into our lives and z had figured out what was going on a little earlier? The questions proliferate endlessly, even if we don't actively pursue them. Thinking about what *did* happen generates speculation about what *could have* happened, about all the contingencies that produced our experience and all the ways it could have been different, mostly better. In a sense, this is the historical counterpart of future-tripping, a pointless waste of time that, just like worry, expends emotional energy while changing nothing—changing *less*, actually, because at least worry about the future sometimes prods us into productive action. So giving up the hope of rewriting the past is a very good thing to do and does not hamper our ability to hold our abusers accountable.

The next stage of forgiveness, for me, was giving up resentment. Long after I discharged my carried anger, I maintained a low-grade acrimony toward my father, a persistent sense that he deserved blame for everything he had done to me. The fact that he continued to abuse young women renewed my acrimony fairly regularly, so I can't say I made much progress beyond the Oprah stage for quite a while. Finally, I became aware that my resentment was like a slow IV drip of poison. I had heard that idea in twelve-step meetings for years, but I finally *got it*, by which I mean that I had a visceral sense of how the poison affected me, not just when I was thinking about my father, but all the time. So I let the resentment go. I let it go in the same way I let go of distraction during meditation. If resentment came up, I didn't feed it, and I didn't try to push it away; I just noticed it and let it pass. As I did, it arose less and less end eventually stopped arising. By the time my father asked for my forgiveness, my resentment was gone, so I told him so. But I did not say, "I forgive you" because I hadn't.

True forgiveness, as I've said, is difficult. It's also sublime. Near the end of *King Lear*, when the king's wronged daughter, Cordelia, forgives him for banishing her, it's a moment of grace in the midst of catastrophe. For an instant, the relentless suffering we have witnessed is redeemed, and we have a fleeting glimpse of humanity at its finest. In just a few words, the king admits his wrong, and Cordelia erases it, leaving just the love between them. It's a beautiful scene. Real life, of course, tends to be a lot messier, yet Shakespeare's scene points to elements important in everyday examples of forgiveness. One element is an offender's remorse. Forgiveness is easier—and more meaningful for both parties—if the person who has done harm acknowledges it. In many religious traditions, there can be no forgiveness without the offender's remorse and a sincere desire not to reoffend. In my experience, however, few abusers express genuine remorse. I'm not sure to this day that my father ever did, though I'm also not sure that he didn't.

In the absence of remorse, forgiveness is sometimes enabled by the offender's suffering. Someone who has caused us to suffer and who is now suffering becomes easier to forgive. Most of us, whether consciously or unconsciously, have a strongly developed sense of fairness, a sense that people should get what they deserve, whether for good or for ill. If an abuser does not demonstrate remorse but suffers some unrelated affliction—a serious accident, disease, or loss—we can still feel that the scales are starting to balance, which makes it easier to offer forgiveness. King Lear not only acknowledged his offenses toward his daughter, but also endured a painful series of betrayals and the loss of everything he had, including his mind. Alzheimer's Disease took my father's mind before it took his life, and, though there's no such thing as "evening the score," I did feel differently about forgiving him once he had suffered the ravages of that cruel illness.

In the end, however, what's really important about the offender's remorse or suffering is that it awakens our compassion. In fact, I don't think there's true forgiveness without compassion. There's moving on, and there's letting go, but there's not the sympathetic sorrow for another human being that moves true forgiveness. Offenders need not be present or aware of our feeling; it can come years after they die. Mine welled up suddenly while my father was lingering in his last moments of life and almost certainly could not hear my words of forgiveness. I, however, reaped enormous benefits. I've talked a lot about cultivating self-compassion in previous chapters. I've stressed self-compassion because, as survivors of childhood trauma, we need it so badly. It helps us to do the work of recovery and to feel better and more grounded while we're doing it. But self-compassion and compassion for other people are not different phenomena; they are manifestations of the same lovingkindness. At some point, if we practice compassion, it will reach into places we don't expect, and the result will be growth we can barely begin to imagine.

APPENDIX

Codependent and Healthy Ego States

Wounded Child (trauma < age 6)	Adapted Adult Child trauma (6-17)	Functional Adult
Lost/Abandoned Needy Hopeless Helpless Worthless	Lacking Needs Lacking Desire Over-Controlling Over-Controlled Punishing Judgmental Performance-Oriented Perfectionistic	Self-Loving Self-Contained Self-Aware Self-Nurturing Balanced

Psychological Effects of Childhood Trauma in Adults

Issue	Expression
Inflated or inadequate SELF-ESTEEM. Thinking you are worth more or less than other people. Source: Claims of worthlessness or superiority from caregivers.	Being a people-pleaser vs. looking down on others. Suffering shame attacks. Not reacting to abuse suffered vs. becoming an offender yourself. Insufficient or excessive attention to external indicators of value: appearance, status, money, degrees, children's accomplishments.
Inaccessible or unexpressed REALITY. Not knowing or being able to communicate what you perceive, feel, think, or do. Source: Discounting of—or punishment for—perceptions in childhood.	Looking to others for what you perceive, think, feel, and want vs. imposing your perceptions &c. upon others. Resenting them if they balk. Existing without passion vs. living vicariously. Experiencing denied feelings as depression, emotional eruptions, and illnesses such as cancer, arthritis, heart disease, & hypertension.

Inability to practice MODERATION. Not understanding what normal is & operating at one extreme or another, sometimes both. Source: Extreme behavior in caregivers.	Guessing wildly at normal vs. staking out a position and rigidly adhering to it. Making decisions based on what other people think is normal. Alienating loved ones & friends by seeming unstable & unpredictable. Replicating the chaos of childhood vs. imposing a stifling order. Tolerating abuse vs. becoming an abuser. Chemical & behavioral addiction.
Problems with ADULT DEPENDENCY. Difficulty perceiving, acknowledging, expressing, or fulfilling your own needs & desires. Source: Caregivers' failure to meet childhood needs. Punishment & shaming for needs & desires.	Getting needs met passively vs. expecting others to know what you need & give it to you. Blaming those who don't for your unhappiness. Ignoring needs and desires vs. not being aware of them. Hypochondria vs. neglecting urgent medical needs & suffering unnecessary illnesses. Confusing needs with desires; buying a new smart phone when you really need a friend.
Weak or impenetrable BOUNDARIES. Damage to the system that protects you from others and others from you. Source: Early boundary violation, especially direct abuse, & caregiver modeling.	Being abused or abusing others. Failing to notice when people intrude upon you physically or psychically & failing to notice when you do it to them. Blaming others for your reality & yourself for theirs. Erecting barriers to keep others from approaching or sticking around. Alternating between isolation & toxic vulnerability.

Natural *versus* Carried Feelings

Feeling	Natural (Your Own)	Carried
ANGER	Power, energy.	Rage.
FEAR	Vigilance, self-defense.	Panic attacks, social phobia, paranoia.
PAIN	Stimulus for growth.	Depression, despair.
SHAME	Fallibility, humility.	Worthlessness, inferiority, inadequacy, self-loathing.
GUILT	Responsibility, lapsed values.	Immobility.

Boundary Violations

PHYSICAL	SEXUAL	INTERNAL
Hitting, slapping, kicking, head-butting, shoving, restraining, or attacking with a weapon.	Forcing any sexual activity, even with a committed partner.	Gaslighting.
Touching in any way without permission.	Demanding unsafe sex.

Engaging in exhibi-tionism or public displays of sexuality without the consent of witnesses. | Discounting another's reality.

Shaming, humiliating, belittling.

Raging, yelling, name-calling. |
| Encroaching on someone's domain, from a private home to a table at a restaurant. | Staring or looking lustfully when it is unwelcome; making lascivious sounds or gestures. | Interrupting or finishing someone's sentences.

Deceiving or betraying. |
| Interfering with another person's belongings or work product. | Making sexual jokes, comments, or innuendoes outside well-defined limits. | Using cutting sarcasm.

Joking or laughing at another's expense. |
| Standing or sitting too close. | Treating innocent comments as sexual innuendo. | Patronizing.

Violating a confidence. |
| Violating privacy in the bedroom or bath. | Leaving print or online pornography visible. | Giving unsolicited advice. |

Snooping on someone else's cell phone, tablet, or computer, either electronically or in person. Reading mail and private journals. Smoking where others are breathing. Exposing others to communicable illnesses. Eavesdropping. Cutting someone off in traffic, tailgating.	Commenting on another person's body or sexual appeal. Sending sexually explicit emails and texts to people who do not solicit them.	Interrogating or asking personal questions. Blaming, criticizing, or judging. Triggering others deliberately Manipulating others with threats or "emotional blackmail."

Kinds of Abuse

This list is selective, not comprehensive, meant to help you think about your own history. Use it as a starting-point.

PHYSICAL
- Hitting.
- Spanking.
- Striking with an implement: belt, strap, hairbrush, flyswatter, paddle, wooden spoon, tool, horse whip, rubber hose, toy sword, tennis racquet, hanger, shoes, switch.
- Striking with a projectile.
- Paddlewheel or birthday spanking.
- Face-slapping.
- Feigned or attempted drowning.
- Suffocating or choking.
- Crushing.
- Hair-pulling.
- Towel-snapping.
- Kicking.
- Head-banging.
- Yanking arms or legs.
- Inflicting wedgies, noogies, and dead arms.
- Throwing.
- Shaking.
- Pushing or shoving.
- Roping.
- Restraining, pinning, or otherwise immobilizing.
- Confining, imprisoning.
- Tickling.
- Tripping.
- Playing physical practical jokes.
- Forcing soap or hot sauce into a child's mouth.
- Poisoning or deliberately infecting.
- Withholding treatment for illness or injury.
- Withholding meals (sending a child to bed without dinner).

- Force-feeding.
- Forcing exercise or exertion beyond a child's endurance.
- Forcing a child to work (beyond age-appropriate chores).
- Deliberately endangering or causing fear.
- Injuring or endangering while drunk or high.
- Giving drugs that sedate or intoxicate, including alcohol.
- Performing unnecessary medical procedures.
- Abusing another family member in a child's presence.
- Failing to meet physical needs.

SEXUAL
- Sexually abusing a child: intercourse, oral sex, anal sex, masturbation (of either party)
- Sexual hugging, groping, kissing, fondling--overt or covert.
- Watching a child voyeuristically.
- Exposing a child to pornography.
- Using a child in pornography.
- Using non-pornographic images of a child for adult sexual gratification.
- Raping, molesting, or seducing a child's peers.
- Making sexual comments or jokes.
- Calling a child "whore," "slut," "horn-dog" or other sexual terms.
- Approaching a child with lascivious looks or behavior.
- Treating a child like a romantic partner ("spousification").
- Sharing sexual or romantic confidences with a child ("over-sharing").
- Competing for sexual attention with a child.
- Misinforming--or not informing--a child about sex.
- Condemning or mocking curiosity about sex or natural exploration, including masturbation.
- Impugning a child's sexual or romantic worth--or potential.

EMOTIONAL
- Screaming, shouting, or swearing.
- Insulting, either directly or indirectly.

- Mocking or mimicking.
- Refusing to speak or barely speaking.
- Verbally abusing another family member within earshot.
- Demanding perfection.
- Ignoring or belittling a child's achievements.
- Neglecting dependency needs.
- Abandoning a child, either physically or emotionally.
- Disrupting or sabotaging a child's relationships with peers.
- Manipulating with fear, pity, shame, guilt, or even love.
- Using a severe, disparaging, or mocking tone of voice or facial expression.
- Using an infantilizing nickname.
- Being emotionally dishonest.
- Threatening violence or other harm.
- Threatening abandonment.
- Discrediting a child's perceptions or sense of reality.
- Gaslighting.
- One-upping or competing with a child.
- Making a child work for affection or attention.
- Blaming a child for family problems.
- Assigning adult responsibilities to a child or requiring adult responses from a child.
- Spying on an older child, either electronically or physically.

NOTES

[1] Jonathan Shay, *Achilles in Vietnam* (New York: Atheneum, 1994).

[2] Herbert W. Page, *Injuries of the Spine and Spinal Cord without Apparent Mechanical Lesion, and Nervous Shock in their Surgical and Medical-legal Aspects* (London: Churchill, 1883), 151-57.

[3] Just to be clear, "gross stress reaction" appeared in DSM-I but was removed from DSM-II when commanders discovered a "cure" for persistent trauma symptoms: send sufferers right back to the battlefield.

[4] In the late 20th century, Ferenczi's reputation was rehabilitated, and he's now enjoying a vogue in academic circles.

[5] Classic Barnum statements include "You have a great deal of unused capacity which you have not turned to your advantage," and "At times you are extroverted, affable, sociable, while at other times you are introverted, wary, reserved."

[6] Keynote address to the 1991 national conference of the American Association for Marriage and Family Therapy by psychiatrist Steven J. Wolin. Cited by Michael J. Lemanski on Addiction Info.

[7] Jane Ellen Stevens, "The Adverse Childhood Experiences Study: The Largest Public Health Study You Never Heard of," *Huffington Post*, October 8, 2012. My debt to this article goes far beyond two quotations, and I highly recommend it to anyone interested in the history and influence of the ACE Study. Stevens also edits a news site called ACES Too High that reports on ACE-related research.

[8] Dr. Felitti focused on the categories mentioned most frequently in his initial obesity study. Other researchers supplemented the original, adding questions about ACEs such as racism and neglect..

[9] Comprehensive, up-to-date information, articles, raw data, and other resources may be found on the CDC web site dedicated to the study.

[10] Dr. Casey Hanson, "The Neurobiology of Trauma," lecture, April 12, 2017.

[11] R. Gilbert, C.S. Widom, K. Browne, D. Fergusson, E. Webb, and S. Janson, "The burden and consequences of child maltreatment in high-income countries," *Lancet*, 2009, 373(9657): 68-81.

[12] Michelle Farivar, *The Play's the Thing: A Qualitative Analysis of Participation in Theatrical Experience for Individuals with a History of Traumatic Stress*, Los Angeles, CA, Alliant International University, 2017.

[13] Ellis, C., Adams, T., & Bochner, A. (2010). Autoethnography: An Overview. Forum Qualitative Sozialforschung / Forum: Qualitative Social Research, 12(1). doi:http://dx.doi.org/10.17169/fqs-12.1.1589.

[14] Gina Smith, *Up, Down, Out: An Autoethnography of Parental Alcoholism and Resilience*, Saybrook University, Oakland, CA, 2017.

---

[15] The word "roughly" acknowledges that no two people experience exactly the same event, just as no two siblings grow up in exactly the same family.

[16] Adapted from Smith (2017), who cites Metzl (2009), Flasch (1988), Taylor (1983), and Almeida, (2004).

[17] Brené Brown, *Rising Strong: How the Ability to Reset Transforms the Way We Live, Love, Parent, and Lead* (New York: Random House, 2017).

[18] Jen Cross, *Writing Ourselves Whole: Using the Power of Your Own Creativity to Recover and Heal from Sexual Trauma* (Coral Gables, FL: Mango Publishing Group, 2017) 295. Note: page number from the e-book, which is off.

[19] Richards, R. (2009). *Dreams of perfection: A tribute to Del Morrison.* Paper presented at the annual meeting of the American Psychological Association, Toronto, Canada. Cited in Smith (2017).

[20] It may seem hypocritical that a sect of erstwhile polygamists would object to anyone's sexual orientation, but Mormon leadership is quite firm on the point, claiming their objections are theological. For me, it underscores that the church exists to protect and extend the social power of elite men. This power is based on—and expressed through—unrestricted sexual access to women and girls, no matter how young or how closely related. Even a century after officially renouncing polygamy, many in the church believe that "plural marriage" will resume eventually and that it remains a requirement for exaltation in the Celestial Kingdom.

[21] An exception to this statement would be the policy I mentioned earlier: that baptism must be denied to the children of gay and lesbian couples until they are eighteen and have furnished "proof" that they accept the church's compulsory heterosexuality. That could be traumatic for the children excluded.

[22] I recognize that scholars of religion discourage the term "cult" because of its negative connotations and because the decision about what to call a cult is so subjective. They prefer "New Religious Movement" or NRM, which has the date of foundation as its sole criterion. I use "cult" to indicate particular features in a religion: authoritarianism, outsider status, a reliance on charismatic leadership, and intolerance of dissent. Lots of religions have one or two of those features; cults have all four. By my definition, Mormonism was originally a cult but has lost most of its outsider status and some of its reliance on charismatic leadership.

[23] Find the sound file "Lovingkindness Meditation" at my web site under "Guided Meditations." For those who need to type in the URL, my web site is www.donnabevanlee.com.

[24] I have changed most of the names in this book to protect innocent people who might be hurt by my revelations. While "Mr. Waldo" was not such a person, he has living relatives who are, and I prefer to tell my story without embarrassing them.

---

25 Mormon underwear, formally called temple garments, remind believers of their covenant with God and protect them against evil. They are modest two-piece garments marked with sacred symbols and meant to be worn under clothing at all times. Made of light-weight fabric, they consist of undershorts that reach the knee and scoop-necked undershirts that are short-sleeved for men and cap-sleeved for women. The design is deliberately anaphrodisiac to protect against the evil of sexual temptation. Only veterans of a sacrament called endowment may wear the garments, which some people believe offer physical, as well as spiritual, protection.

26 The *Book of Mormon* explains that God put Adam and Eve in a terrible bind, commanding them to be fruitful and multiply then commanding them not to eat the fruit that would allow them to be fruitful and multiply (to Mormons, you have to be able to die to reproduce). So they had to break the second commandment to fulfill the first; they were actually heroes. Moreover, to sin you have to know you're sinning, which Adam and Eve didn't, being innocent in the Garden of Eden. Ergo no sin to pass down, so no need for infant baptism, as children come into the world sinless.

27 The description adds that this amnesia can be general or it can be "localized or selective for a specific event or events." See the fifth edition of the *Diagnostic and Statistical Manual* (2013) page 298.

28 In recent years, the term "alcohol use disorder" has begun to replace "alcoholism" and related words. While less pejorative, "alcohol use disorder" makes for awkward sentences--and isn't familiar to many readers. So I use both terms.

29 Timothy D. Wilson, *Strangers to Ourselves: Discovering the Adaptive Unconscious* (Cambridge, MA: The Belknap Press of Harvard University Press, 2002) 177 *passim*.

30 Anna Graybeal, Janel D. Sexton, and James W. Pennebaker, (2002), "The Role of Story-Making in Disclosure Writing: The Psychometrics of Narrative" *Psychology and Health*, vol. 17(5) 572 passim.

31 J. Frattaroli, (2006), "Experimental Disclosure and Its Moderators: A Meta-Analysis, *Psychological Bulletin*, vol. 132, 823-865 and Jorden A. Cummings, Adele M. Hayes, D. Sebastian Saint, and Jeff Park, (2014), "Expressive Writing in Psychotherapy: A Tool to Promote and Track Therapeutic Change," *Professional Psychology: Research and Practice*, vol. 45(5), 378-386.

32 Carey S. Pulverman, Tierney A. Lorenz, and Cindy M. Meston, (2015), "Linguistic Changes in Expressive Writing Predict Psychological Outcomes in Women with History of Childhood Sexual Abuse and Adult Sexual Dysfunction," *Psychological Trauma: Theory, Research, Practice, and Policy*, vol. 7(1), 50-57.

33 Alvin Poon and Sharon Danoff-Burg, (2011), "Mindfulness as a Moderator in Expressive Writing." *Journal of Clinical Psychology*, vol. 67(9), 881-895.

34 Wilson 177-78.

[35] Natasha Dow Schull, *Addiction by Design: Machine Gambling in Las Vegas* (Princeton and Oxford: Princeton UP, 2012) 41. This book, though written for specialists, is fascinating reading, both for gambling addicts and for anyone interested in the role of physical and social environments in addiction.

[36] In 2010 Harvard University researchers published the stunning conclusion that people spent 46.9 percent of their waking time focused on something other than their present experience. Based on 2,200 subjects surveyed in real time, the authors found a positive correlation between wandering thoughts and unhappiness, regardless of whether those wandering thoughts were positive or negative. See Matthew A. Killingsworth and Daniel T. Gilbert, "A Wandering Mind Is an Unhappy Mind," *Science* vol. 330 (2010), 932.

[37] Anonymous letter in the series "Private Lives." *The Guardian*, Friday, October 28, 2016.

[38] Studies, including review articles, have found a positive correlation between childhood trauma and eating disorders. See Seongsook Kong and Kunsook Bernstein, "Childhood trauma as a predictor of eating psychopathology and it mediating variables in patients with eating disorders," *Journal of Clinical Nursing* 8(13), 2009, 1897-1907. For sexual abuse specifically, where the correlation is slightly smaller, see Linda Smolak and Sarah K. Murnen, "A meta-analytic examination of the relationship between childhood sexual abuse and eating disorders," *International Journal of Eating Disorders* 31(6), 2002, 136-150.

[39] Representative studies include Linda R. Goglia, Gregory J. Jurkovic, Afton M. Burt, and Katherine G. Burge-Callaway, "Generational boundary distortions by adult children of alcoholics: Child-as-parent and child-as-mate," *American Journal of Family Therapy* 20(4), 1994, 291-99 and Genie Burnett, Rebecca A. Jones, Nancy G. Bliwise, and Lisa Thomson Ross, "Family unpredictability, parental alcoholism, and the development of parentification," *American Journal of Family Therapy* 34(3), 2006, 181-189.

[40] G. E. Kawika Allen and Kenneth T. Wang, "Examining legalism, scrupulosity, family perfectionism, and psychological adjustment among LDS individuals," *Mental Health, Religion, and Culture* 18(4), 2015, 246-258.

[41] David H. Jernigan, "The global alcohol industry: an overview," *Addiction* 104(suppl. 1), 2009, 6-12. See especially page 9, which describes joint brewing by Guinness and Heineken and by Guinness and Carlsberg.

[42] R. A. Sansone, J. Chang, B. Jewell, and R. Rock, "Childhood trauma and compulsive buying, " *International Journal of Psychiatry and Clinical Practice* 17(1), 2012, 73-76.

[43] A clear, comprehensive summary of recent (and ongoing) research appears in Matthieu Ricard, Antoine Lutz, and Richard J. Davidson, "Neuroscience Reveals the Secrets of Meditation's Benefits," *Scientific American* 311(5), 2014, 39-45. My whole discussion of meditation reflects my debt to this excellent article, which is well worth reading in its entirety. Readers can order paper or pdf reprints from *Scientific American*.

44 Rachael Goodman and Angela Calderon, "The Use of Mindfulness in Trauma Counseling," *Journal of Mental Health Counseling* 34(3), 2012, 254-268.

45 Kirsty Banks, Emily Newman, and Jannat Saleem, "An Overview of the Research on Mindfulness Interventions for Treating Symptoms of Post Traumatic Stress Disorder: A Systematic Review," *Journal of Clinical Psychology* 71(10), 2015, 935-963.

46 Ariel J. Lang, "Mindfulness in PTSD Treatment," *Current Opinion in Psychology* 14, 2017, 40-43.

47 Robin Shapiro, *The Trauma Treatment Handbook* (New York: W. W. Norton, 2010) 64.

48 Alexandra L. Laifer, Kristie A. Wirth, Ariel J. Lang, "Mindfulness and acceptance and commitment therapy in the treatment of trauma," *American Psychological Association Handbook of Trauma Psychology*, ed. Steven N. Gold (Washington, DC: APA, 2017) vol. 2, p. 253-273. The bibliography on this topic is growing, the references I have cited purely representative, supplied to give the reader a hint of where scholarship stands, not a thorough overview.

49 People suffering chronic asthma or other lung diseases may have a great many ideas and feelings about the breath, as may people whose early trauma involved oxygen deprivation. As always, if focusing on the breath feels uncomfortable, choose another object.

50 This practice, like all practices, may be done standing or lying down if sitting is difficult. When lying down, resist the temptation to close your eyes, as this practice involves being aware of your surroundings.

51 Several Tibetan Buddhist traditions offer excellent instruction in mindfulness meditation, but it can be one item on a fairly full menu of spiritual practices. Perhaps the most accessible to those seeking just meditation instruction would be a Shambhala Center. There are many around the world, though they are concentrated in the United States and western Europe.

52 Certification (TCTSY) is through the Trauma Center in Brookline Massachusetts where Trauma Sensitive Yoga was developed and tested. As of 2018, teachers and therapists with TCTSY certification may be found in the US, western Europe, and Australia.

53 Jean-Paul Glaser, Jim van Os, Piet J. M. Portegijs, and Inez Myin-Germeys, "Childhood trauma and emotional reactivity to daily life stress in adult frequent attenders of general practitioners," *Journal of Psychosomatic Research* 61(2), 2006, 229-236.

54 Matthias Michal, Manfred Beutel, Jochen Jordan, Michael Zimmerman, Susanne Wolters, and Thomas Heidenreich, "Depersonalization, Mindfulness, and Childhood Trauma," *Journal of Nervous and Mental Disease* 195(8), 2007, 693-696.

55 The subjective experience of slowed time is well-attested in the literature on mindfulness, though scientific study of the process has just begun. See Marc Wittman and Stefan Schmidt, "Mindfulness Meditation and the Experience of Time," chapter 2 of *Meditation: Neuroscientific Approaches and Philosophical Implications*, ed. S. Schmidt and H. Walach (n.p.: Springer, 2014) 199-210. The authors cite Jon Kabat-Zinn, *Coming to our Senses: Healing Ourselves and the World through Mindfulness* (New York: Hyperion, 2005).

56 Elizabeth Kimbrough, Trish Magyari, Patricia Langenberg, Margaret Chesney, and Brian Berman, "Mindfulness Intervention for Child Abuse Survivors," *Journal of Clinical Psychology* 66(1), 2010, 17-33.

57 Michael D. Earley, Margaret A. Chesney, Joyce Frye, Preston A. Greene, Brian Berman, and Elizabeth Kimbrough, "Mindfulness Intervention for Child Abuse Survivors: A 2.5-Year Follow-Up," *Journal of Clinical Psychology* 70(10), 2014, 933-941.

58 You can find the sound file, "Breath-Counting Meditation" at www.donnabevanlee.com under "Guided Meditations."

59 Over the years, high-volume alcoholics have questioned my claim to have suffered withdrawal from my three-drink-a-day habit, but that is only because they do not understand kindling, a neurological phenomenon in which a weak stimulus produces greater and greater effects as it is repeated. Kindling is why, in someone with a seizure disorder, every seizure lowers the stimulus threshold for the next one. It's why successive detoxes from alcohol can produce more violent withdrawal than simply continuing to drink. Someone like me, who drinks to blackout every night, goes through a mini-withdrawal the next day, whereas someone who starts the day with a beer and maintains a "slow glow" will not suffer the same kindling. Alcohol's effects on the human body are complicated and, let's face it, not well understood even by professionals. For more information, see Howard C. Becker, "Kindling in Alcohol Withdrawal," a publication of the National Institutes of Health.

60 Confirmation would begin with the groundbreaking research of Vincent Felitti, whom I mentioned in the introduction. His research on trauma and addiction was originally published in German, but there is an English translation titled, "The Origins of Addiction: Evidence from the Adverse Childhood Experiences Study" (2003) available online.

61 "Boundary Meditation" is available under "Guided Meditations" at www.donnabevanlee.com.

62 You will find a guided version of this "Mountain Meditation" under "Resources" at www.donnabevanlee.com.

63 Yes, I also have the gene, which causes a disorder called familial hypercholesterolaemia (FH). Hypercholesterolaemia is Greek for "elevated cholesterol blood condition." Sufferers, roughly one in 500 Americans, have a single mutation that produces extremely high cholesterol levels, especially of LDL, the so-called "bad" cholesterol. Even now, the condition is rarely diagnosed; about 85 percent of sufferers don't know they have it. Though asymptomatic for years, they develop coronary artery disease at much younger ages than the general population, commonly in their thirties and forties. Two branches of my family tree are heavy with Mormon farmers who ate well, never smoked or drank, and kept fit with hard work but who nonetheless suffered early heart attacks: 30 in the past three generations. All but two died immediately.

64 This awareness can be dim and partial, consisting of little more than the nagging, question of why no one can know about a "special" activity.

65 Wilson 133.

66 See the chart of comparisons in the appendix.

67 Roc Morin, "An Interview With Nazi Leader Hermann Goering's Great-Niece," *The Atlantic*, October 17, 2013.

68 Low-cost help is available through community mental health centers, which generally assess fees based on clients' ability to pay. Local health departments also make referrals for psychological services, and some universities that train psychologists and psychiatrists operate mental health clinics that are open to the public.

69 Bessel A. van der Kolk, *The Body Keeps the Score: Brain, Mind, and Body in the Healing of Trauma* (New York: Viking, 2014).

70 Kaepernick started his protest by sitting down during the anthem but shifted to kneeling after a conversation with fellow player Nate Boyer, who was a veteran.

71 Francesca Gino and Michael I. Norton, "Why Rituals Work," *Scientific American*, May 14, 2013.

72 You can make or buy burlap sacks (sometimes sold as "potato sacks"); just make sure that what you buy is made of 100 percent natural jute and not treated with chemicals. Stores specializing in garden supplies and natural fabrics are most likely to carry biodegradable burlap.

73 The "Trauma Inventory" may be found under "Materials" at www.donnabevanlee.com.

74 True Mormon hell is known as the outer darkness and is reserved for Satan and others who deny God. Mormons also speak of "spirit prison" as a hell, though it is actually much more like traditional purgatory, a place sinners go after death to expiate their sin while awaiting resurrection and final judgment. That's the hell my father may have worried about—much less terrifying than standard Christian hell but unpleasant nonetheless.

⁷⁵ Mormons believe that Adam and Eve made the right choice by eating the apple, sacrificing an easy life in the Garden of Eden for child-bearing, death, and fulfillment of God's plan. So, to Mormons, the fig leave is a badge of honor, not of shame.

⁷⁶ On their own, Mormon women cannot enter the highest realm of heaven, the Celestial Kingdom. Their husbands must summon them by calling a secret name given to them by the church. Men need not be summoned by their wives.

⁷⁷ There is a tradition of imitating Christ in mainstream Christianity, but it's very specifically focused on imitating Christ's suffering, humility, and care for the dispossessed. Trinitarian theology, which holds that Christ and God are indivisible, makes it problematic for a human being to imitate the triumphant or miraculous features of Christ's life, and the fact that Catholic saints did it now and then was yet another reason that the Protestant Reformation got rid of most saints. Mormons, however, are anti-Trinitarians. They believe that Jesus Christ is an apt model for all of us, which is yet another reason for Mormon perfectionism.

⁷⁸ Mormons make no distinction between God and the Mormon Church; any challenge to church teaching is a direct affront to God.

⁷⁹ "The Law of Chastity," chapter 39 of *Gospel Principles*, an LDS manual, online.

⁸⁰ The Mormon Church regards the Lord's Prayer as a template for individual prayer. In other words, Mormons don't recite the prayer as it appears in the Bible, as other Christians do. They use it to get the gist of what a decent prayer looks like and then make up their own.

INDEX

A

A Bushel and a Peck (song), 26
abandonment, 31, 34, 48, 106, 171, 175, 176, 251
abjection, 49, 50, 116, 117, 244
abuse
    emotional, 34–36, 50–51, 226, 250
    intellectual, 37–38
    physical, 27, 31–32, 32, 33, 34, 249
    sexual, 32–34
    social, 35
    spiritual, 36–37
    types, 31
    verbal, 34, 251
abusers, 79
    accountability, 196, 205, 220, 238, 239
    intentions, 28, 31, 32, 38, 80, 155, 238
    narcissists, 81
abusive families, 41, 44, 75, 227–28
active listening, 153
adaptive unconscious, 78, 81, 82, 83, 86, 88, 188, 194
    and ritual, 195
addiction, 8, 41, 43, 81, 142, 143, 144, 145, 148, 149, 214, 245, 255
    and childhood traua, 257
    and childhood trauma, 148, 149
    internet, 231
    recovery, 83
    sex and love, 33, 108, 152
    shopping, 10, 107
    stigma, 142
    treatment, 150
Adult Children of Alcoholics, 6, 154
Adverse Childhood Experience (ACE) Study, 7–9, 9, 252
Adverse Childhood Experiences (ACEs), 8, 252
advertising, 45, 109, 117, 179, 231
aggression, 34, 41, 103, 108, 117
alcohol use disorder
    family history, 31
    withdrawal, 142, 257

Alcoholics Anonymous (AA), 83, 141, 142, 143, 144, 145, 146, 147, 150, 151, 162, 208
alcoholism, 141, 255
Amen (song), 223
America's Most Wanted, 183
Amish
    Out of Order (tv show), 37
amygdala, 40
Anda, Robert, 8
anorexia nervosa, 115
anxiety, 6, 32, 41, 43, 47, 126, 184, 234
Arizona Republic, 132
Armatrading, Joan, 99, 126
astrology, 11
autoethnography, 9, 10
autopilot, 82, 104, 107, 126

B

Barnum statements, 7, 252
Beattie, Melody, 6, 10
Bevan family
    history, 18, 76, 214
Bevan, James, 162
Bevan-Lee, James, 85, 145, 148, 162, 164, 176, 201, 202, 208, 209, 210, 211, 215, 216, 221, 222, 223, 254
Bible, 77
Black, Claudia, 6, 151
Blake, William, 48
Book of Mormon, 76, 77, 254
boundaries, 33, 45, 102, 108, 109, 111, 115, 116, 175, 179, 198, 227, 232, 235, 236
    alternating, 46
    and technology, 231
    damaged, 45
    emotional, 109–14, 247
    fortified, 46
    healing, 227
    healthy, 218, 229, 230
    intermittent, 111
    mental, 114–16, 117, 247
    non-existent, 45, 226
    physical, 102–3, 104, 230, 236, 247
    sexual, 108, 247
    with dependent children, 233

Y

Z

Made in the USA
Middletown, DE
19 February 2019